Cornell International Industrial and Labor Relations Report
Number 11

WOMEN WORKERS IN FIFTEEN COUNTRIES

Essays in Honor of Alice Hanson Cook

Jennie Farley, editor

ILR Press
New York State School of
Industrial and Labor Relations
Cornell University

861005

Library of Congress Catalog Card Number: 85-2375
International Standard Book Number: 0-87546-113-1 (cloth);
   0-87546-114-X (paper)

Library of Congress Cataloging in Publication Data
Main entry under title:

Women workers in fifteen countries.

   (Cornell international industrial and labor relations report ; no. 11)
   Based on the conference held October 1983 at Cornell University to celebrate the eightieth birth-
day of Alice Hanson Cook.
   "Publications by Alice Hanson Cook": p.
   Includes index.
   1. Women—Employment—Congresses. 2. Women in trade-unions—Congresses. 3. Wom-
en's rights—Congresses. 4. Cook, Alice Hanson—Congresses. I. Farley, Jennie. II. Cook,
Alice Hanson. III. Series.
HD6052.W57 1985   331.4   85-2375
ISBN 0-87546-113-1 (alk. paper)
ISBN 0-87546-114-X (pbk. : alk. paper)

Copies may be ordered from
ILR Press
New York State School of
   Industrial and Labor Relations
Cornell University
Ithaca, NY 14853

Cover design by Kathleen Dalton

Printed on acid-free paper in the United States of America
by Braun-Brumfield, Inc.
5   4   3   2   1

Contents

Contributors   vii

Preface   xi
  Jennie Farley

Tribute to Alice Hanson Cook   xvii
  Lois S. Gray

1. Women's Work in Industrial Countries:
   An Overview from the Perspective
   of the International Labour Organization   1
   Marion Janjic

2. The Soviet Union   13
   Gail W. Lapidus

3. The People's Republic of China   33
   Margery Wolf

4. Yugoslavia   49
   Olivera Burić

5. Japan   57
   Hiroko Hayashi

6. Israel   68
   Rivka W. Bar-Yosef

7. Low-Income Countries   81
   Hanna Papanek

8. Great Britain   90
   Emma MacLennan and Nickie Fonda

9. France   112
   Andrée Michel

10. Federal Republic of Germany   124
    Hanna Beate Schöpp-Schilling

11. Sweden   138
    Ylva Ericsson

12. Switzerland   147
    Ilda Simona

13. Italy   154
      Bianca Beccalli

14. The United States of America   170
      Barbara Bergmann

Afterword   177
      Alice Hanson Cook

Appendix A: Books and Articles by Alice Hanson Cook   180

Appendix B: Conference Participants   184

Index   191

Contributors

Rivka W. Bar-Yosef is professor of sociology at Hebrew University, Jerusalem. She earned the Master's degree and the Ph.D. at Hebrew University and held a graduate fellowship at Harvard University. Her research interests include the status of women in Israel, public policy and its effect on equality for women, and related questions such as the effect of war on women's roles in society and women in the military.

Bianca Beccalli is professor of the sociology of work at the University of Milan. A longtime student of women's labor force participation, the development of feminism, and the activities of trade unions, she is the author of the chapter on Italy in *Women and Trade Unions in Eleven Industrialized Countries* edited by Alice H. Cook, Val R. Lorwin, and Arlene Kaplan Daniels. A member of Italy's Equal Employment Opportunities Commission, she has held a grant from the German Marshall Fund of the United States.

Barbara Bergmann is professor of economics at the University of Maryland. She earned the B.A. in mathematics and economics at Cornell University and the Ph.D. in economics at Harvard University. Author of some forty-five articles in professional journals and monographs, Bergmann has worked at the Bureau of Labor Statistics, the Council of Economic Advisors, and the U.S. Agency for International Development.

Olivera Burić is professor emeritus at the Institute of Social Policy in Belgrade. She has done research on the impact of maternal employment on the family, the position of woman in society and the family, woman's position in the system of social power, family planning, migrant families, types of family organization, and the linkages between the family and the sociopolitical system. Her work has been translated into English, Russian, and French.

Alice Hanson Cook is professor emerita of industrial and labor relations at Cornell University. Educated at Northwestern University and the University of Frankfurt-am-Main (Wolfgang Goethe Universitaet), Germany, with visiting semesters at the University of Leipsig and the Hochschule fuer Politik, Berlin, she joined the Cornell faculty in 1952 and retired twenty years later. Since that time she has traveled to more than twenty countries to conduct research on labor unions, women workers, and, most recently, on the issue of comparable worth. She is author of some fifty articles in professional journals and books.

Ylva Ericsson is political adviser in Sweden's Ministry of Labor, where she reports to the cabinet minister responsible for equality between women and men. She was formerly on the staff of the Federation of Social Democratic Women and has been a teacher at LO, the Swedish trade union confederation.

Jennie Farley is associate professor of industrial and labor relations at Cornell University, where she was cofounder and first director of the Women's Studies Program. She is author of *Affirmative Action and the Woman Worker* and *Academic Women and Employment Discrimination* and editor of *Sex Discrimination in Higher Education* and *The Woman in Management*.

Nickie Fonda is joint director of the Management Programme at Brunel University, Uxbridge, and an associate fellow of the Institute of Manpower Studies, University of Sussex. Her publications include *Mothers in Employment, Work and the Family,* and *Practical Approaches to Women's Career Development.* She has spoken widely on issues related to working women, including presentation of a paper at the 1980 NATO conference in Lisbon.

Lois S. Gray is professor and associate dean of the New York State School of Industrial and Labor Relations at Cornell University. She is also director of the school's Division of Extension and Public Service. She holds the Ph.D. in economics from Columbia University. Her research and writing deals with labor education, labor relations, union-management cooperation, and the effectiveness of training programs for Puerto Rican migrants and other American workers.

Hiroko Hayashi is professor of law and former director of the Institute of Foreign Affairs at the Kumamoto University of Commerce, Japan. She has studied at the law schools of Tulane University and Yale University as a Fulbright Exchange Scholar and is a graduate of the Law School of Kyushu University. In fall 1982, she served as a visiting faculty member at Cornell's New York State School of Industrial and Labor Relations and is coauthor with Alice H. Cook of *Working Women in Japan: Discrimination, Resistance, and Reform.*

Marion Janjic, an attorney, began her career as a typist at the International Labour Office in Geneva, Switzerland, and worked her way up to her current post as the senior official in the Office for Women Workers' Questions. She is well known internationally for her analyses of women's situation and of the national and international policies which affect it.

Gail W. Lapidus is associate professor of political science and chair of the Center for Slavic and East European Studies at the University of California at Berkeley. Her Ph.D. is from Harvard University. She edited *Women, Work and Family in the USSR,* coedited *Women in Russia* with Dorothy Atkinson and Alexander Dallin, and is author of *Women in Soviet Society,* as well as of numerous articles on Soviet society and politics.

Emma MacLennan is deputy director of the Low Pay Unit in London, an independent research and campaigning organization. She has written and spoken extensively on issues related to women's employment in Britain. Her publications include *Minimum Wages for Women, Insuring Poverty at Work, Working Children,* a chapter on women and labor market policy in four countries (with R. Weitzel) in Schmid and Weitzel, eds., *Sex Discrimination and Equalization in the Labor Market,* and *Women's Employment in Small Firms.*

Andrée Michel, research director at the National Center for Scientific Research in Paris, is a sociologist of international repute. Her work has appeared in such professional journals as the *International Labour Review, Revue Internationale des Sciences Sociales, Journal of Marriage and the Family,* and *Current Sociology.* Among her books are works on the sociology of the family, the sociology of feminism, the Algerian worker in France, the professional and home life of the French woman, the sociology of economics, and the impact of multinational corporations on women of the third world. She is editor of *Family Issues of Employed Women in Europe and America.*

Hanna Papanek is senior research associate at the Center for Asian Development Studies, Boston University, and Codirector of the "Comparative Study of Women's Work and Family Strategies in South and Southeast Asia" under the auspices of the United Nations University. She has written extensively about women in South and Southeast Asia on a variety of topics including purdah (female seclusion) in South Asia, women and development, women's education and employment in South Asia and Egypt, and also the "two-person career" in the United States. She is also associate director of Women's Studies International at the Feminist Press.

Hanna Beate Schöpp-Schilling is assistant director of the Aspen Institute in Berlin, where she plans and conducts conferences on economic, social, and cultural topics, including themes having to do with women workers. She holds a Ph.D. in American literature. She has written and spoken on labor market topics from a feminist perspective since the late 1970s. A current research interest is the effect of the advent of high technology on sex roles in the workplace and the family.

Ilda Simona is head of the departments for women workers, youth, vocational training, nonmanual workers, and foreign workers of the International Metalworkers' Federation, Geneva. She joined the federation in 1952 as an interpreter and translator and, in 1963, became head of the newly founded department for women and youth. She is a contributor to a recent book, *Twenty Years' Activity of the IMF Women Workers Committee, 1963–1983*, which details the progress of women workers in the metal industry in Finland, Germany, Zimbabwe, Austria, Japan, Denmark, Great Britain, Switzerland, Kenya, Australia, Sweden, and Belgium.

Margery Wolf is research scholar at the Center for Research on Women, Stanford University. She also serves as associate editor of *Signs: Journal of Women in Culture and Society.* She is the author of *The House of Lim, Women and the Family in Rural Taiwan,* and *Revolution Postponed: A Study of Women in the People's Republic of China.*

Preface
Jennie Farley

IN OCTOBER 1983, one hundred eighty scholars and activists from some twenty countries were invited to the Cornell University campus in Ithaca, New York, to celebrate the eightieth birthday of a pioneer in the comparative study of women workers: Alice Hanson Cook. The conference was sponsored by the Extension and Public Service Division of Cornell's New York State School of Industrial and Labor Relations where Cook served on the faculty for twenty years. The conferees gathered to discuss themes central to Cook's work: the status of women workers; the extent to which their interests are reflected in national labor market policy; and the role of trade unions and women's organizations—both national and international—in initiating policies to improve the situation of women workers.

The conference was generously supported by the German Marshall Fund of the United States and the Ford Foundation. Additional support was provided by the International Labour Office (ILO) in Geneva, Switzerland, and by Cornell University's Women's Studies Program; the Tompkins County National Organization for Women (NOW); and the Ithaca branch of the American Association of University Women (AAUW).

This volume, based on the conference, begins with an overview of the situation of women workers in advanced industrial countries in the 1980s by ILO officer Marion Janjic, who believes that women are at a crossroads. On the one hand, there are sufficient laws and enforcement mechanisms in most of these countries to extend and strengthen women's rights to equality, but, on the other hand, there are now economic constraints that work against equality and evoke misogyny. Janjic holds that labor market policy should be fashioned to fight on three fronts: against unemployment and sex discrimination in access to employment; against the ubiquitous male/female earnings differentials; and for adequate social mechanisms to enable women and men workers to cope with their family responsibilities. She analyzes how such changes can be brought about and notes that some barriers go down more easily than others. She concludes with a review of the issues relating to protectionism versus equality.

In chapter 2, political scientist Gail W. Lapidus analyzes the current policies in the Soviet Union affecting women, who constitute more than half of its labor force. According to Lapidus, Soviet leaders have begun to attach high priority to demographic and family policy. She suggests that future measures are likely to take a pronatalist direction, in part because of the urgent need for labor in the USSR and its diverse ethnic structure.

Anthropologist Margery Wolf takes a close look at recent developments in China in chapter 3. This vast and ancient country is now in the midst of an economic upheaval. The slogan "Equal pay for equal work" has been heard in China since liberation in 1949, Wolf says, but there is still a pay gap between the average wage earned by men and that earned by women. There, it is expressed in work points with men earning 10 to 12 and women, 5.5 to a high of 8, on average. Wolf focuses on the effects of the recent economic changes on women in cities and on farms.

In chapter 4, family sociologist Olivera Burić presents data from Yugoslavia where, she says, it was believed that equality between the sexes had been achieved by 1960. It was not until International Women's Year in 1975 that it was widely recognized that women were disadvantaged in that socialist society. Discrimination against women in hiring can take place, she remarks, without an employer having to say, "No women." All one need do is include in the employment advertisement the phrase, "Candidate must have completed military service." An important goal in Yugoslavia is fuller participation of women at all levels of decision making in a self-managed society, Burić emphasizes.

Legal scholar Hiroko Hayashi analyzes the status of working women in Japan in chapter 5. She points out that law and practice diverge there, as elsewhere, noting that "without workable enforcement mechanisms, the legal guarantee of equality is like a pot of gold at the end of the rainbow: a dream, not a reality." Hayashi reviews the hard-fought legal cases brought by working women against their employers and concludes that there is still much to be done, especially in the private sector.

In chapter 6, sociologist Rivka W. Bar-Yosef describes the dual system of secular and religious law in Israel. Women are put in a double bind, she points out, being expected to be simultaneously modern and traditional. The modernization of the traditional image of women in Israel mainly affects Moslem women and Jewish women from Moslem countries. In the future, Bar-Yosef predicts, society there, despite its legal and cultural diversity, may move toward general acceptance of a "dissimilar but equal" model of the relationship between the sexes.

Asian expert Hanna Papanek considers the situation of women in Bangladesh, Egypt, and India in chapter 7, noting that a full analysis of women and labor market policy should include a review of the status of women in low-income countries in light of the political and economic ties between those nations and more highly industrialized ones. Papanek believes that work has been defined too narrowly, excluding as it does the status producing activities that women engage in all over the world to benefit their families.

In chapter 8, Emma MacLennan and Nickie Fonda, experts in low-pay occupations and in management, respectively, analyze the situation of women in the British labor market. They trace the effect of anti-sex-discrimination legislation and focus on the period since 1979 as one of "deregulation, casualization, and free market philosophy." These trends bode ill for women's employment in a policy climate in which "a distaste for employment protection has been combined with ministerial statements that women would be better off at home" than in the labor force.

Sociologist Andrée Michel describes recent changes in France in chapter 9, where females constitute a higher proportion of the students in post-secondary education than in almost any other European country. Michel notes, however, that despite rising educational levels, women are still concentrated in a narrow range of jobs. In July 1983, thanks to the efforts of the new minister for women's rights, Mme Yvette Roudy, Parliament passed a law to reinforce the principle of equal treatment of men and women at work.

Organizational expert Hanna Beate Schöpp-Schilling traces and weighs the influence of trade unions, women's organizations, and organized feminists on the creation, implementation, and monitoring of antidiscrimination legislation in West Germany in chapter 10. While there is a heightened consciousness of discrimination among all West German women, she says, they have not been able to "overcome their differences and to translate their new knowledge into effective political pressure."

In chapter 11, policy analyst Ylva Ericsson leads off with a discussion of the progress made by and the problems still encountered by women workers in Sweden. Women's labor force participation rate is probably the highest in the Western world and the pay gap between women's wages and men's is relatively narrow. Still, women are underrepresented in positions of power and bear the major burden for home care and child care. This, despite the availability of parental leave and other reforms.

Trade union expert Ilda Simona describes the situation of women in Switzerland in chapter 12. Women were not granted the right to vote in national elections there until 1971. Despite new legislation, there are still formidable barriers to equality, Simona notes, among them the "deeply rooted traditional belief that women and men have different roles" in society and should continue to do so. The legal reforms in recent years, Simona holds, can be traced in part to the efforts of trade unions, women's associations, and especially to the Swiss Federal Commission for Women's Issues.

In chapter 13, sociologist Bianca Beccalli outlines the history of women's work in Italy, showing that, despite constitutional guarantees of equality in place since World War II, inequality prevails. Some Italian feminists, she reports, reject protective legislation as reactionary and find equality positions equally distasteful, based as they are said to be on men's values. In the battle to bring about equality in the workplace, Beccalli observes, the state is in fact an unreliable partner.

Economist Barbara Bergmann considers the extent to which antibias laws have helped improve the status of American women workers in chapter 14. She concludes that while there has been progress, the laws have not proven to be a panacea. Bergmann presents an analysis of the practicality of comparable worth—equal pay for work of comparable value—and details alternative ways in which this concept could be implemented. She concludes with a feminist legislative agenda for the 1980s in the United States of America.

After each paper, excerpts from the discussion it elicited are presented. Only discussion which supplements or illuminates the situation of women in that specific country is included. The general discussion, which was conducted with intensity and good will across disciplinary boundaries and from a variety of political perspectives, identified common threads in the reports.

In every country, there is a substantial gap between women's average earnings and men's, with the widest gap to be found in the United States. Women are everywhere found in a narrow band of occupations, due in part to the education they choose (or are permitted) to pursue. Virtually every country has instituted legal measures to outlaw sex discrimination but the problems persist, in part because of the rigid job segregation by sex found everywhere.

Women's changing perception of their roles and the extraordinary increase in their participation in the paid labor force is well documented here. The agonizing delays in their acceptance as workers is a theme that surfaces again and again. The major difficulty on the home front appears to be the problem of getting men to share the home care and child care traditionally believed to be women's responsibility.

The short-term and long-term effects of various workplace reforms (increase in opportunities for part-time work, provision of maternity protection and parental leave, and the like) were discussed with verve and lively disagreement as were the more radical possibilities of refusing to participate in a man's labor market on men's terms and instituting comparable worth across occupations to bring women's wages for the important work they do up to parity.

Omitted from these papers are the sincere tributes the presenters paid to the scholar-activist who brought these international experts together. Speaker after speaker mentioned the effect on their own work of Alice Cook's broad vision and sharp sensitivity to the everyday problems of working women. It is fitting that the last word should be Alice's. As her afterword shows, she sees what needs to be done and shows us, by her example, how to do it.

A Tribute to
Alice Hanson Cook

Lois S. Gray

ALICE COOK has always been in advance of her times. She got an early start. With her mother, a leading suffragist, she marched in demonstrations for the woman's right to vote. She graduated from Northwestern University where she studied speech, which she turned into a considerable asset over her lifetime.

In the 1920s, she joined a group of remarkable women who established the Industrial Department of the YWCA, a unique institution that provided social and educational support for factory women and encouragement for social activism. But, early on, she also developed an interest in international and cross-cultural studies and went to Germany for graduate study.

In the 1930s, she applied her talents to building the labor movement, working as education director of the Textile Workers Rayon Division and later with the Amalgamated Clothing Workers Joint Board. During this period, she married a labor leader, took time out of the labor market to give birth to a son, Philip, and then became a working mother—a subject she has since written about with insight and sensitivity.

Following World War II, she was enlisted by the American military government to help rebuild democratic institutions in Austria and Germany, where she worked on labor and adult education. Each of these moves, from social work to labor leadership to adult education, involved embarking on a new career, but each had roots in past experience.

In 1952 she went to Cornell University to direct an experimental and innovative adult education project that was designed to interest labor leaders and involve them in community action, another idea before its time. As her expertise as a teacher became known to the resident faculty, she became involved in teaching undergraduate and graduate students, enriching the curriculum with her background and experience in the labor field. Her contributions to excellence in teaching and research were recognized by her colleagues and she was quickly promoted through the ranks to full professor.

While heavily involved as a scholar, Alice Cook never lost sight of her lifelong commitment to social action. For example, when she arrived at Cornell, the university had an admissions quota for women—approximately five to one, five men to one woman—set by the presumed availability of housing and dormitory space for women. Alice Cook never accepted this rationalization and fought hard to permit the admission of students on the basis of merit, without regard to sex. Among other drives, she led the campaign to open the facilities of the faculty club on an equal basis to women faculty and she was a co-founder of the university's Women's Studies Program, one of the first at any American university.

At Cornell, research and writing occupied an increasing proportion of her time. Her writings include articles, books, monographs, and testimony before congressional hearings. These reflect the interests that she has developed throughout her career. Early writings dealt with labor unions, labor and politics, the governance of labor unions, and labor-management relations in the United States. On a sabbatical leave, she went to Japan and wrote one of the early pieces on industrial relations in Japan, a topic very much in vogue today. Over the years, the status and problems of working women have been a major focus, one that showed up early in her work. In 1968, she published "Women in American Trade Unions," an often-quoted and reprinted piece. Later publications dealt with equal opportunity, the working mother, social support systems for women workers, and comparable worth.

Never confined to the ivory tower, Alice Cook has always been in the thick of the action. For example, in the late 1960s, a time of student upheaval, Cornell University established the office of ombudsman and recruited Alice Cook to resolve student grievances. She played an unusual, probably unique, role as ombudsman and as an activist in the women's movement. She served both as an advocate and as a mediator. While pursuing equal opportunity for women faculty, for which she was the leading advocate, she also served by appointment of the university administration as a lifetime member of the Provost's Advisory Committee on the Status of Women at Cornell.

Upon retirement, Alice—now professor emerita—took on still another career combining her talents as a scholar and her interests in women, labor unions, and international exchange, when, with a grant from the Ford Foundation, she undertook a series of around-the-world studies, which have culminated in the volume, *Women and Trade Unions in Eleven Countries.*

In her eighty years, Alice Cook has entered and achieved distinction in several careers—social worker, labor leader, adult educator, college professor, author, and mediator—any of which would require a lifetime of dedication for most of the rest of us. Along the way, she served as a teacher and role model to many who aspired to follow in her footsteps. I am one of those influenced by Alice Cook, early and continuously, throughout my career at Cornell. Perhaps what we admire most about Alice Cook is that she is a fiercely independent thinker, a person who is steady and serene in her support of the causes to which she is committed, a joyful battler who relishes the challenge.

1.
Women's Work in Industrialized Countries

An Overview from the Perspective of the International Labour Organization

Marion Janjic

THE INTERNATIONAL LABOUR ORGANIZATION (ILO) now has 150 member states and must keep a balance in its activities between the concerns of women in the most advanced industrialized countries and those in the developing world where women's daily struggle for survival often takes precedence over their desire for more equality with men. In recent years, the bulk of the research activities of the ILO has been devoted to the needs of women in the developing world whose problems are very different from those of women in the industrialized world, although they have some common features. This report, however, is focused on women in industrialized market economy countries and on ways in which their situation can be improved.

The economic and social situation of the market economy countries of the industrialized world is undergoing a three-pronged evolution that has profound implications for women's employment. First, the economic slowdown and recession following the oil crises brought about rising unemployment for both men and women. Then, the rapid increase in the use of advanced technologies, such as micro-processors, began to change the occupational structure and to bring about a noticeable shrinkage in labor demand, especially in sectors that used to employ many women, such as the service sector. Finally, the shift of labor-intensive industries with low skill requirements, such as textiles, clothing, and electronics, to developing countries adversely affected women workers in industrialized nations where their employment in these industries used to be high. In the textile industry alone, the countries of the European Economic Community (EEC) lost some 900,000 jobs between 1960 and 1977, about a third of all EEC employment in the industry.[1]

These three trends in the economies of the industrialized world came at a time when the participation of women in the labor market increased at a particularly rapid pace. While in the 1950s and 1960s women's contribution to the increase in the labor force in the Organization for Economic Cooperation and Development (OECD) countries was slightly more than half (51.7 percent in the 1950s and 52.9 percent in the 1960s), in the 1970s their contribution amounted to 62.6 percent.[2]

Parallel to the trend towards increased female participation in the labor market, there has been increased concern in OECD countries to provide women workers with equal opportunity and equal treatment. Early emphasis was placed on encoding relatively narrow prohibitions against sex discrimination, first in matters of pay, along the lines of ILO Convention No. 100, and later in matters of employment in general, in line with ILO Convention No. 111.[3] Later, prohibiting discrimination on the basis of sex became only one among many legislative means for bringing about equal opportunity, a goal also pursued by a number of nonlegislative methods like affirmative action.

We are now at a point where a rather sophisticated set of legislative instruments and monitoring bodies has been created and adopted

---

1. Annette Robert, "The Effects of the International Division of Labour on Female Workers in the Textile and Clothing Industries," *Development and Change*, vol. 14 (London: Sage, 1983), pp. 19–37.

2. A large proportion of the new entrants work on a part-time basis.

3. International Labour Office, Convention (No. 100) concerning Equal Remuneration for Men and Women Workers for Work of Equal Value (Geneva: ILO, 1951) and Convention (No. 111) concerning Discrimination in Respect of Employment and Occupation (Geneva: ILO, 1958).

in most countries to extend and strengthen women's right to equality at the same time that very severe economic and technical constraints make the competition for jobs sharper, evoking misogynist reactions. Given this gloomy reality, how should labor market policy be oriented to avoid a deterioration of women's employment situation, to preserve the gains made during the years of prosperity and equal employment, and, if possible, to progress further on the long road to equality and equity? Labor market policy should be fashioned to fight three battles: (1) against unemployment and sex discrimination in access to employment, (2) against male/female earnings differentials, and (3) for an adequate social infrastructure to enable women and men workers to cope with their family responsibilities.

Unemployment and Discrimination in Access to Employment

By the end of July 1983, the number of people registered as unemployed in EEC countries was 11.6 million, of whom 4.84 million were women; the average unemployment rate was 10 percent—11 percent for women and 9.5 percent for men; and the duration of unemployment was longer for women than for men.

In analyzing women's situation, a clear distinction must be made between the quantitative and qualitative consequences of economic and social change. In light of the unprecedented increase in the number of women who entered the labor market after 1970, an increase in the female unemployment rate in OECD countries from 2.8 percent in 1960 to 6.6 percent in 1980 does not seem so bad, particularly in comparison with an increase in the male unemployment rate from 2.8 percent to 5.2 percent during the same period. This is the conclusion reached by an OECD study:

> On the whole, it appears that in the majority of countries female labor participation rates were not affected in the final outcome by the last decade's unemployment changes in one way or another. To some extent, the "discouraged" and "additional worker" effects were likely to cancel each other out. However, the long-term growth trend of female labor force participation had a strong enough autonomous impetus not to be patently influenced by the cyclical fluctuations of the last decade, at least in most countries. It was determined primarily by factors entirely independent of the labor market, mainly demographic factors and factors related to economic growth and social change.[1]

----

4. Liba Paukert, "Trends in the Employment and Unemployment of Women in

It would be an error, however, to rely on quantitative effects alone. Indeed, in most countries the increased participation of women in working life has not broadened their range of employment opportunities to any significant extent. There continues to be a dual labor market—entirely distinct occupational sectors for women and men—even within industries. Women workers predominate in the services and in the low-paid blue-collar jobs in textile manufacturing, food processing, and electronics that require "traditional" female skills—accuracy, dexterity, speed, and endurance. Even in a country like Finland, where the proportion of women workers is among the highest of any capitalist country, the percentage of women workers in manufacturing has remained virtually unchanged since the 1960s: women constitute 48 percent of the total work force but only 25 percent of the work force in manufacturing.

It is not surprising that women, lacking appropriate technical background, are more vulnerable than men to the impact of new technology, especially since the jobs women customarily fill are those which the new information technology is beginning to transform. Even if it is true that the factors that influenced women to enter the labor force—new patterns of parenthood, growing availability of goods and services that reduce the amount of household work, and the rise in female educational levels—will continue to do so, it may nevertheless become more and more difficult for women to satisfy the changing labor demand.

The first studies of the impact of new technologies on women's employment show that, even if widespread unemployment does not result, many women may be displaced from their jobs and have a more difficult time than men in finding new ones because of women's occupational concentration, low skills, and relative lack of mobility.

> The skills made redundant by new technology are by and large not appropriate for the new opportunities that are emerging. The clerical jobs such as typing, stenography, filing, and book-keeping that the new technology will affect will require skills which are often low-level, task specific, and relevant often [only] to a particular firm's activities.[5]

OECD Countries" (Paris: Organization for Economic Cooperation and Development, 1984).

5. Diane Werneke, "Microelectronics and Office Jobs: The Impact of the Chip on Women's Employment" (Geneva: International Labour Office, 1983).

This means that women should understand the necessity of acquiring new skills to broaden their occupational base and that governments and employers should launch training programs to enable women to adapt themselves to increased job specialization. It has already been observed that where new technology is used to increase the specialization of the work, jobs change gender.

Various policies have been developed to broaden the range of employment open to women and, at the same time, to limit the impact of unemployment on them.[6] The country that seems to have achieved the best results in keeping unemployment rates under control is Sweden, which implemented a labor policy preventing layoff and dismissals and providing education, training, and work for two groups of women—young, first-time entrants into the labor market, and older women looking for employment after spending an extended period of time at home.

Earnings Differentials

It took some time to realize that earnings differentials between men and women were not only embedded in discriminatory practices which could be eliminated by legislative measures, but also had deeper roots which were more difficult to attack. The failure to remove these differentials by legislative measures alone is now obvious. In 1951, the ILO adopted Convention No. 100, which calls for equal pay for work of equal value. To date, it has been ratified by no fewer than 105 countries. In addition, Article 119 of the Treaty of Rome established the principle of equality of remuneration for men and women workers. There also have been two EEC Directives, one on equal pay for men and women (February 10, 1975) and one on equal treatment for men and women in terms of access to employment, vocational training, promotion, and working conditions (February 9, 1976). Yet despite numerous pieces of legislation adopted in various countries, there are still significant differences between the average earnings of men and women performing equal or similar jobs. It is well known that women doing different work from that of men are paid less than men. What has now been clearly demonstrated is that

6. Marion Janjic, "The Diversification of Women's Employment: A Fallacy or a Real Step Forward?" ILO W.2/1980 (Geneva: International Labour Office, 1980).

the more an occupation is dominated by women, the less it pays to both women and men.

According to the results of a 1984 study of earnings differentials in OECD countries, average earnings of year-round full-time women workers ranged from 58.6 percent of men's earnings in the United States to 80.7 percent in Sweden. In the Netherlands, women earn 76.8 percent of men's wages; in Australia, 76.5 percent; in Austria, 74.3 percent; in France, 73.5 percent; in Canada, 66 percent; and in the United Kingdom, 65.7 percent. The differential in the United States has changed little since 1970 when women, on the average, earned 57.2 percent of men's wages; in the remaining OECD countries for which statistics are available, the gap between men's and women's wages has narrowed since 1970 and continues to do so.[7]

Pay inequities due to openly discriminatory practices are comparatively scarce now because they are prohibited by legislation. What is more difficult to eliminate is the hidden discrimination based on social attitudes. These prejudices result in systematic undervaluation of jobs performed mostly by women and of skills attributed to women, such as speed, accuracy, adaptability to monotonous work, and the like. It has been noted that "instead of getting equal pay for equal work, women get different pay for different work."[8]

Two types of measures can be taken to eliminate these wage differentials. The first set of measures should help to resolve the problems women encounter in the workplace and in finding work since the two phenomena have common roots: women are prepared for a limited range of occupations; there are interruptions in women's careers; women lack technical skills; and the like. Since 1970 most industrialized countries have adopted policies to lessen the horizontal and vertical segregation of women and generally to eliminate discrimination in employment.[9]

There have been other efforts including research, information, and recruitment campaigns. In the United Kingdom, the Equal Op-

---

7. Liba Paukert, "Male and Female Earnings Differentials in OECD Countries," in *OECD Working Party on the Role of Women in the Economy* (Paris: Organization for Economic Cooperation and Development, 1984).

8. UN Economic Commission for Europe, "The Economic Role of Women in the ECE Region," E/ECE/1013 (New York, 1981).

9. International Labour Office, "Equality of Treatment between Men and Women in Employment: Changes in the Legislation in Selected Western European Countries,"

portunities Commission and the Engineering Council are joining forces to launch a campaign to persuade more women to become engineers; at present, 94 percent of all women employed in engineering are operators, clericals, or in unskilled jobs. In the Federal Republic of Germany, there are programs to recruit girls and women for apprenticeships, vocational training, and work in nontraditional areas. There are also programs to recruit young women into occupations where they have been underrepresented, to provide training opportunities for labor market reentrants, and to implement affirmative action. Public bodies have been established in most countries of the EEC to monitor the implementation of laws against sex discrimination.

Even before the post-1970 evolution, equality provisions were to be found in diverse sources, which varied from country to country. They were in the Constitution of the Federal Republic of Germany; in collective bargaining agreements in the Scandinavian countries; in case law in England; and in the *Code du Travail* (labor code) in France. Legislation since 1970 has signaled a shift of focus from equal pay alone to equal treatment and equal opportunity in general.

The role that workers' organizations and other nongovernmental groups play in the implementation of the new laws is of interest. In some cases, their support is explicit. For example, legislation adopted in France in 1983 authorizes trade unions to bring a sex discrimination case before a tribunal unless the injured party is opposed to such action. In other countries, such as Norway and Sweden, legislation is complemented by collective agreements on equality and by an active labor market policy. Trade unions are also often represented in bodies set up to monitor the implementation of equal opportunity laws.

The second set of measures to remove earnings inequalities relate to job evaluation. ILO Convention No. 100 provides that measures should be taken to promote objective appraisal of jobs on the basis of the work to be performed. According to a recent ILO study of job evaluation, the use of this technique to bring about enforcement of the equal pay principle has been very limited for a variety of complex reasons, of which a major one seems to be that it is used essen-

---

ILO/W-5/1980 (Geneva: ILO, May 1980); and "Equality of Treatment between Men and Women in Employment: Changes in the Legislation in Australia, Canada, United States, Japan, and New Zealand," ILO/W-4/1981 (Geneva: ILO, May 1981).

tially as a management instrument.[10] Concern for equality of remuneration does not appear to be a significant motivation for its use.

Job evaluation is not a neutral exercise; the careful selection of criteria to assess jobs is essential if the equal pay principle is to be implemented. Therefore, it is very important for more women to become familiar with such procedures and to serve on job evaluation committees. This is another aspect of the role trade unions can play in the promotion of equality for women workers.

Family Responsibilities

At a time of shrinking public expenditure, will governments consent to allocate more resources to child care and other social services? As long as these are considered to be services for women only, their necessity will continue to be questioned. One step forward seems to have been taken in some countries with the recognition that family responsibilities should not be seen as falling solely on women's shoulders.

The ILO contributed to the development of this concept in 1981 by adopting a Convention and a Recommendation urging governments to make it an aim of their national policy "to enable persons with family responsibilities who are engaged in, or wish to engage in, employment to exercise their right to do so without being subject to discrimination and, to the extent possible, without conflict between their employment and family responsibilities."[11] The Recommendation provides, for example, that within a period immediately following maternity leave, either parent should have the possibility of obtaining a leave of absence (parental leave) without relinquishing employment and with employment rights safeguarded.

Experience has shown that changes in attitude come slowly. Recent studies show that even in a country such as Sweden, where the introduction of parental leave has brought about a change in the attitudes of some men, the number of hours spent by women on family work is approximately double the amount spent by men.

---

10. International Labour Office, "L'évaluation des emplois" (Geneva: ILO, 1984).

11. International Labour Office, Convention (No. 156) and Recommendation (No. 165) concerning Equal Opportunities and Equal Treatment for Men and Women Workers: Workers with Family Responsibilities (Geneva: ILO, 1981).

Equality versus Protection

A delicate issue that is still at the core of the debate in several countries and which has been a focus of attention in the ILO is the dilemma between the protection of women and the promotion of equality between the sexes.

Except for suitable forms of maternity protection, protective legislation is suspect in many quarters. When women are excluded from certain types of work, their occupational choice is thereby restricted; many see this as incompatible with the principle of equal opportunity. Some governments have dealt with this problem by renouncing international conventions they had formerly ratified. Since 1964, no fewer than twelve countries have renounced the ILO Convention concerning the prohibition of nightwork for women in industry.[19]

There are usually two major reasons for these renunciations. In developing countries, it is argued that this Convention is incompatible with industrial development. For instance, Sri Lanka considers it essential that women be employed in the third shift in the electronics industry. The second reason put forward is that the prohibition of nightwork for women only is a form of discrimination because it restricts their access to many jobs. In addition, some governments refer to the improvement of working conditions in recent years, and some note that a nightwork prohibition is not imposed in all sectors of the economy. Nobody has questioned the suitability of nightwork for nurses.

A tripartite consultative meeting was convened in 1978 to examine the possibility of revising three ILO Conventions concerning the prohibition of nightwork for women in industry. The consultation resulted in the usual confrontation between those who believe women need such protection and those who object to it on the grounds that it deprives women of equality of opportunity. Those present could not agree on any action other than to direct the ILO to pursue further studies.

The way in which tripartism functions in the ILO is clearly illustrated by the position taken on this issue by the groups involved. The workers' representatives strongly supported the idea of adopting new

---

12. Bulgaria, Burma, United Kingdom, Albania, Netherlands, Chile, Hungary, New Zealand, Luxembourg, Ireland, Sri Lanka, and Uruguay.

standards on nightwork in general, independent of the sex of the worker or the branch of activity. The employers' representatives did not want to adopt new standards or revise the existing instruments; they declared themselves opposed to any international action aimed at restricting nightwork other than that necessary to protect children, adolescents, and pregnant women. The majority of the government representatives expressed a preference for the adoption of new international standards.

A second consultation in 1983 concerned maternity protection. The ILO took note of the small number of countries that had ratified the two Conventions dealing with this issue and consulted with member states on the need to revise them. The consultation had two aims: (1) to identify all obstacles to ratification, and (2) to ascertain if the Conventions were still in line with developments in the protection of maternity in some member countries' recent legislation. The ILO proposed that more flexibility be introduced by modifying the provision on the scope of the instrument, on compulsory postnatal leave, and on the protection of employment. The discussion that took place on these proposals resulted in consensus. Instead of revising the Conventions, the representatives of the workers, employers, and of some of the governments agreed that the ILO should encourage more member countries to ratify and implement them.

The position taken by Sweden and Norway suggests the future direction of maternity protection. Sweden argued that one important shortcoming of the existing Convention is that it refers only to the role of the mother in the child's upbringing and overlooks the role of the father. In Norway it is considered almost as important to allow both parents to be with their child as it is to protect the mother's health. Any proposed increase in the duration of maternity leave should take that principle into account. Leave to care for adopted children should also be examined.

What I have tried to demonstrate in this short review is that never in the history of the women's movement has there been such a developed and egalitarian set of institutions to promote women's rights. Nevertheless, because of economic recession, technological revolution, and the imbalance in economic growth between the North and the South, women's position is precarious. Although women's right to employment is now fully recognized, the cultural and institutional support to enable them to exercise this right is still insufficient if they have children. It is also precarious because their participation in the labor market is based on a division of work that keeps them in a subordinate position vis-à-vis men. Now that there is greater competition for employment, women more than ever must be made conscious of the need to adapt their skills to the requirements of postindustrialized society.

Discussion

Shifts of Industry

ILO studies have been undertaken to assess the effects of the shift of industries from the North to the South but it has proved to be difficult to show a direct relationship between the shift of industry to the South and the growth of unemployment in the North. There is a unit in the ILO devoted to the study of multinational corporations; its projects will certainly include a focus on women workers. (Marion Janjic)

High Technology

The changes in the work force predicted for the future make it clear that fewer workers to do low-skill jobs and more workers to do high-technology work will be required. It is crucial to get young people of both sexes to think about their potential in a different way—to get women into high-skill training and get men to do their share of the domestic work so that women can achieve. (Avis Cohen)

In considering the development of new technology, we must be skeptical of "advances"—developments in computer technology, for instance—that will make it possible for a woman to have full responsibility for home and children and also do full-time work on her home computer. (Judith Buber Agassi)

Interdependence

When we distinguish between the situation of urban women and rural women in Europe, we must take into account that the cities have developed the way they have in part because of policies initiated elsewhere in the world. All countries are interrelated. In Bangladesh, 80 percent of the national budget comes from foreign assistance. In Venezuela money is abundant, yet the national budget is dependent on foreign aid—50 percent comes from outside sources. (Shelley Feldman)

2.
The Soviet Union
Gail W. Lapidus

AN EXTENSIVE RELIANCE on female labor has been a central feature of Soviet economic development over several decades, with important consequences for virtually every aspect of political, economic,
and social life. The highest female labor force participation rates of
any industrial society are to be found in the USSR—over 51 percent
of all workers and employees are women—at the same time that
sharply declining birthrates have already made the single-child family
the norm in the urban regions of the European USSR. Moreover, important regional and ethnic variations, linked to sociocultural as well
as economic differences, make the Soviet Union a fascinating universe for comparative analysis. The economic and demographic patterns characteristic of the European regions of the country contrast
sharply, for example, with those which prevail in the largely agricultural Moslem republics of Soviet Central Asia.

Until the mid-1960s high levels of female labor force participation in the modern sector of the economy were viewed as unambigu-
ous evidence that socialism and sexual equality went hand in hand.
Soviet policy, official sources claimed, had created optimal conditions
for the harmonious combination of female work and family roles; if
no feminist movement had emerged within the USSR, it was because
these questions had been happily resolved.[1]

This paper is adapted from Gail Warshofsky Lapidus, ed., *Women, Work, and Family
in the Soviet Union* (Armonk, NY: M. E. Sharpe, 1982). A slightly different version was
presented at the conference in the author's name by Caryl Emerson, assistant professor
of Russian literature, Cornell University.

1. A typical example of this genre, intended for foreign as well as domestic audi-
ences, is Vera Bilshai's *Reshenie zhenskogo voprosa v SSSR* (Moscow, 1956). An English
version was issued in 1957: *The Status of Women in the Soviet Union* (Moscow, 1957).

Beginning in the mid-1960s, however, ritual self-congratulation began to give way to serious discussions of "shortcomings" and ultimately of "contradictions" in Soviet everyday life. A growing array of scholarly studies began to document in some detail the lower level of skill, mobility, and income of women workers, the heavy and conflicting demands of their dual roles, and the harmful effects of poor working conditions and inadequate social services on the health and well-being of working mothers and their families.[2] Rising divorce rates and declining birthrates provoked particular concern, challenging as they did the comfortable assumption that under "developed socialism" economic progress and social stability went hand in hand.

Trade union and party meetings as well as scholarly conferences began to devote themselves to discussions of female labor and everyday life. The Twenty-fourth Party Congress officially proclaimed the need for a comprehensive national demographic policy, while the Twenty-sixth Party Congress explicitly inaugurated one. Party Chairman Leonid Brezhnev himself, addressing the Trade Union Congress in 1977, admitted: "We men . . . have thus far done far from all we could to ease the dual burden that [women] bear both at home and in production."[3] Increasingly social planning became explicitly incorporated into the Soviet policy agenda.

Official public discussion formed only the tip of a far larger iceberg of private dissatisfaction. In 1969, in a short story entitled "A Week Like Any Other," Natalia Baranskaia gave fictional expression to the stresses and conflicts faced by millions of her counterparts in daily life.[4] A decade later the *samizdat* publication of the first Soviet feminist journal, with its implicit repudiation of the official view that the "woman question" had been solved, was greeted by the expulsion

---

2. The initial contribution to this reassessment came from labor economists. Four pioneering studies of female labor in the USSR, all by female authors, were published between 1964 and 1970: N. I. Tatarinova, *Stroitel'styo kommunizma i trud zhenshchin* (Moscow, 1964); V. I. Tolkunova, *Pravo zhenshchin na trud i ego garantii* (Moscow, 1967); E. Z. Danilova, *Sotsial'nye problemy truda zhenshchiny-rabotnitsy* (Moscow, 1968); and V. B. Mikhailiuk, *Ispol'zovanie zhenskogo truda v narodnom khoziaistve* (Moscow, 1970). The fine study by A. G. Zdravomyslov, V. P. Rozhin, and V. A. Iadov, *Chelovek i ego rabota* (Moscow, 1967), includes some important findings on male-female differences in work orientation and job satisfaction; translated into English as *Man and His Work* (White Plains, 1970).

3. *Pravda*, March 22, 1977, p. 2.

4. Natalia Baranskaia, "Nedelia kak nedelia," *Novy mir*, November 1969, no. 11, pp. 23–55, translated into English in *Massachusetts Review*, Autumn 1974.

from the USSR of its four founding editors—a dramatic revelation of the extent of official sensitivity and the limits to public discussion.[5]

The reassessment of earlier assumptions and policies which began in the mid-1960s was prompted by the emergence of two serious and interrelated problems. First and foremost was the declining birthrate. Its ominous implications for future political and military power, for the supply of labor, for the balance between productive and dependent age cohorts, and above all for the ethnic structure of the USSR brought demographic problems to the forefront of political concern. At the same time, the virtual exhaustion of the vast labor reserves which had traditionally fed the expanding Soviet economy compelled a shift from an extensive to an intensive strategy of economic development. Future economic growth was now heavily dependent on increased labor productivity and the optimal utilization of all available labor resources. Given the irreplaceable contribution of women to both production and reproduction, the conflicting requirements of these two overarching priorities created profound policy dilemmas and established the framework for subsequent debates.

Soviet discussions of these issues turn on five distinct but interrelated questions. What is the optimal level of female labor force participation consistent with demographic and social needs? How could female labor be better distributed among different economic sectors and occupations? What changes need to be made in the elaboration and enforcement of protective labor measures to improve the working conditions of the female labor force? What is the impact of female labor force participation on family structure and fertility? Finally, what changes in present policies are needed to achieve an optimal balance between female work and family roles?

Female Labor Force Participation

The causes and consequences of high rates of female labor force participation in the modern sector of the Soviet economy are a subject of sharp controversy among Soviet authors. The heavy reliance on female labor which has characterized the Soviet pattern of industrialization had as its rationale the ideological conviction, originating in

---

5. The journal has been translated into English as *Woman and Russia* (London: Sheba Feminist Press, September 1980). See also Tatyana Mamonara, *Women and Russia* (Boston: Beacon Press, 1984).

Marxist-Leninist theory, that the full entry of women into social production held the key to genuine equality. However, it was the inauguration of the First Five-Year Plan which provided its real impetus. Female employment outside agriculture was further accelerated in subsequent decades by the interaction of economic, demographic, and social pressures created by Soviet policy, and above all by the enormous deficit of males. The cumulative effects of war and civil war, of collectivization, purges, deportations, and then of World War II transformed wives and widows into heads of households and deprived a large proportion of Soviet women of any opportunity to marry. In 1946 there were only 59 men for every 100 women in the 35-to-59-year-old age group.

Although World War II made especially heavy demands on female labor, female participation rates have not declined in recent years but have actually risen in response to deliberate efforts to alleviate the growing labor shortage. A campaign launched in the early 1960s, and accompanied by increases in minimum wages and in pension benefits, raised the cost of *not* being employed and brought an additional 25 million women into the labor force by the mid-1970s (see table 2.1). Today almost 90 percent of able-bodied adult women are employed or engaged in study, virtually all full time.

The only remaining major untapped reserves of female labor are found in the Central Asian and Transcaucasian republics where female participation rates outside agriculture—particularly among the local nationalities—are much lower than the national average. Since the recruitment of native women into industry has encountered great difficulties in these regions, a high proportion of women workers and employees in Central Asia are Russian and Ukranian.

While no Soviet analysts would publicly challenge the view that high levels of female employment in the modern sector are a progressive phenomenon, and indeed a major achievement of socialism, not all see current participation rates as either natural or desirable. Taking issue with the view that current patterns reflect positive and irreversible changes in the social position of women, some authors argue that present levels are abnormal and excessive, the result of extraordinary but temporary economic and demographic conditions.[6] Likewise, a number of demographers argue that long-term demographic

---

6. A. E. Kotliar and S. Ia. Turchaninova, *Zaniatost' zhenshchin v proizvodstve* (Moscow, 1975), p. 8.

TABLE 2.1
Female Workers, USSR, Selected Years 1922–83

Year	Total Workers (in thousands)	Number of Women Workers (in thousands)	Percent Women
1922	6,200	1,560	25
1926	9,900	2,265	23
1928	11,400	2,795	24
1940	33,900	13,190	39
1945	28,600	15,920	56
1950	40,400	19,180	47
1955	50,300	23,040	46
1960	62,000	29,250	47
1965	76,900	37,680	49
1970	90,200	45,800	51
1973	97,500	49,959	51
1976	104,235	53,632	51
1979	110,592	56,678	51
1980	112,480	57,700	51
1983	116,100	58,910	51

Sources: Tsentral'noe statistichesko upravlenie pri Sovete Ministrov SSSR, *Narodnoe khoziaistvo SSSR; 1922–1972* (Moscow, 1972), pp. 345 and 348; idem., *Zhenshchiny SSSR* (Moscow, 1975), pp. 28–29; idem., *Narodnoe khoziaistvo SSSR za 60 let* (Moscow, 1977), p. 470; "Zhenshchiny v SSSR," *Vestnik statistiki*, 1980, no. 1, p. 70; Tsentral'noe statisticheskoe upravlenie pri Sovete Ministrov SSSR, *SSSR v tsifrakh v 1978 godu: kratku statisticheskii sbornik* (Moscow, 1979), pp. 178–79, idem., *Narodnoe khoziaistvo SSSR v 1979 godu* (Moscow, 1980), pp. 387–88, 391; idem., *SSSR v tsifrakh v 1980 godu: kratkii statisticheskii sbornik* (Moscow, 1981), p. 160; *Vestnik statistiki*. 1984, no. 1, p. 65.

needs are being sacrificed to short-term economic priorities and advocate measures to reduce the level and intensity of female employment in regions where it is especially high.

Surveys conducted to ascertain the attitudes of women themselves have been marshaled in support of both points of view. According to Soviet sociologists the overwhelming majority of women interviewed attached great importance to the contribution of work to economic independence, social status, and personal satisfaction; relatively few indicated they would withdraw from the labor force even if that were to become economically feasible. At the same time, economic need was repeatedly cited as a more central motivation in employment than "broadening of horizons" or "civic satisfaction."[7] A number of Soviet analysts therefore conclude that the "participation of women in social production is, under the conditions of socialism,

7. Between 75 and 80 percent of respondents reported they would continue to work even if their income were no longer vital, with the proportion higher among white-collar than blue-collar workers. See Mikhailiuk, p. 24; Z. A. Iankova, "Razvitie lichnosti zhenshchiny v sovetskom obshchestve," *Sotsiologicheskoe issledovanie*, 1975, no. 4, p. 43; Pimenova, pp. 36–39; Osipov and Szczepanski, pp. 444–46; Kharchev and Golod, pp. 38–69.

dictated to a significant extent by economic necessity."[8] The policy implications of this perspective are clear. To the extent that the Soviet leadership encourages further rises in incomes and in public consumption funds, it may facilitate a slight reduction in what analysts view as an excessively high level of female employment.

However, the fact that participation rates have risen sharply despite the palpable economic improvements of the past twenty years suggests that other forces are also at work. "Economic need" is relative; if rising aspirations outrun rising incomes, a second income may still appear essential. Moreover, rising wages increase the opportunity cost of *not* being employed, encouraging women to prefer employment to either larger families or more leisure. In addition, rising education and professionalism further strengthen labor force attachment. For all these reasons it is unlikely that Soviet female participation rates will undergo a substantial decline in the years ahead in the absence of vigorous pronatalist policies. However, the intensity of female participation may be diminished slightly if part-time work and more flexible work schedules are actively encouraged, since there is much evidence that they would be warmly welcomed by working mothers.

The Distribution of the Female Labor Force

Women in the USSR are heavily concentrated in certain types of economic activity and significantly underrepresented in others. They account for three-fourths or more of the labor force in the service sector and only one-fourth of the labor force in construction and transportation (table 2.2). In industry, where women represent almost half of all production personnel, they constitute over 80 percent of food and textile workers and over 90 percent of garment workers.

Shifting from economic sectors to occupations, we find that women predominate in the lower and middle levels of white-collar and technical employment but are underrepresented in supervisory and managerial positions. Moreover, within any given occupation or workplace, women are concentrated at lower levels of the job pyramid. In agriculture, the overwhelming proportion are engaged in heavy manual labor, while men move into the newly mechanized jobs. A similar situation prevails in industry, where women predominate in low-skilled, nonmechanized, and poorly paid positions.

---

8. Mikhailiuk, p. 24.

TABLE 2.2
Women by Industrial Sector, USSR, 1975

Industrial Sector	Number of Women Employees	Women as Percentage of Labor Force
Construction	3,002,000	28
Transport	2,211,000	24
Manufacturing (production personnel)	1,662,000	49
Science and scientific services	2,015,000	50
Credit and state insurance	423,000	82
Apparatus of government and economic administration	1,457,000	65
Agriculture	4,530,000	44
Communications	1,042,000	68
Education	5,904,000	73
Trade, public catering, materials and equipment, supply and sales	6,763,000	76
Housing and municipal economy, every-day services	2,010,000	53
Arts	207,000	47
Public health, physical culture, social welfare	4,851,000	84
Culture	747,000	73

Sources: Tsentral'noe statisticheskoe upravlenie, *Narodnoe khoziaistvo SSSR v 1975 g.* (Moscow, 1976), pp. 542–43; 546–47.

This situation cannot be attributed to the predominance of an older generation of women with limited education and few skills; the educational attainments of the female labor force now match and even exceed those of males. Moreover, a recent study of industrial enterprises in Taganrog found that 40 percent of all female workers with higher or secondary specialized education occupied low-skill industrial positions, compared to only 6 percent of males with comparable educational attainments. Most striking of all was the finding that the distribution of the male labor force without respect to education was more favorable with respect to high-skill positions than the distribution of the highly educated female contingent.[9]

The tendency for the proportion of women to decline as the level

9. E. B. Gruzdeva, "Osobennosti obraza zhizni intelligentnykh rabochikh," *Rabochii klass i sovremennyi mir*, 1975, no. 2, p. 94. The discrepancy between the educational attainments of workers and the content of the jobs they perform has been a serious general concern in recent years. The authors of *Chelovek i ego rabota* report a typical statement by a woman worker: "In the shop no one looks to see who has an education, but they put you where they think best." The authors comment: "It is obvious how abnormal the situation is in which a female worker with secondary education stands on the assembly line . . ." (pp. 280–81).

of skill, responsibility, and pay rises is as characteristic of the professions as it is of industry. Women have moved upward into technical and specialist positions but not into supervisory roles in the proportions one might expect on the basis of their training and work experience, even in professions such as teaching and medicine in which women predominate. When we bear in mind that women constitute almost two-thirds of the key administrative age-cohort, their absence in managerial roles is especially striking.

As a consequence of occupational segregation, women's earnings in the Soviet Union are considerably lower than those of men's. While there are no published national wage data which would permit precise comparisons, the evidence of fragmentary local samples suggests that average female earnings are about 65–70 percent of those of males, higher than for the United States but lower than for Scandinavia.

While numerous Soviet studies document the disparities in male and female earnings, they flatly rule out direct wage discrimination as a possible explanation. Starting from the premise that wage differentials are essential to the efficient allocation of labor resources and that existing differentials reflect objective differences in the quantity and quality of labor, Soviet writings tend to focus on the reasons why women choose particular kinds of jobs rather than questioning the prevailing structure of wages or the low value placed on women's work.

Soviet discussions of occupational segregation begin with the assumption that sex-linked differences in abilities and preferences, largely rooted in biology, shape prevailing patterns of employment; the effects of differential socialization receive relatively little attention. Although the rationale for particular classifications may be questioned, there is widespread acceptance of the distinction in principle between "men's work" and "women's work." Labor economists take for granted that "the psycho-physiological makeup of women permits them to carry out certain kinds of work more successfully than men, as for example, work demanding assiduity, attention, accuracy, and precision."[10] Consistent with this assumption, each of the 1,100 occupations for which training is offered at Soviet technical-vocational institutions is explicitly designated for males, females, or both sexes;

---

10. A Kotliar and A. Shlemin, "Problemy ratsional'noi zaniatosti zhenshchin," *Sotsialisticheskii trud*, 1974, no. 7, p. 111.

only 714 are accessible to women.[11] The central concern in Soviet discussions of occupational segregation is to encourage the transfer of women out of unsuitable jobs and into more appropriately feminine positions.

Soviet discussions of why women tend to be heavily concentrated in unskilled and low-paid occupations have recently begun to reveal increasing recognition that both the system of formal education and the heavy reliance on continuing education through combining work with study act to limit the occupational mobility of women. Family responsibilities, which fall heavily on the shoulders of women, aggravate the problem still further. A vicious cycle is thus created: women have lower expectations of occupational mobility than their male counterparts; they gravitate toward jobs which are most compatible with their domestic responsibilities; they have less time than men for study to improve their qualifications; they tend to become stuck in less rewarding and stimulating jobs with few incentives or opportunities for upward mobility; and they are viewed by managers as less promising and productive, which reduces their leverage and opportunities still further.

This problem has not gone unrecognized in political circles. Complaints that insufficient attention is paid to recruiting women to responsible positions occur with monotonous regularity in official pronouncements. Dubious of the value of mere exhortation and impatient with the slow pace of change, one labor specialist recommended a radical solution: the adoption of sex quotas, with the number of women in managerial positions to be proportional to the number of women working under their jurisdiction.[12]

Working Conditions and Protective Labor Measures

One subject on which virtually all Soviet authors agree is the need for substantial improvements in the working conditions of the female labor force, and particularly its blue-collar contingent. Despite the elaborate provisions contained in Soviet labor legislation for the protection of female labor, complaints abound that existing regulations are inadequate and their requirements widely violated. Although many

---

11. E. L. Manevich, ed., *Osnovnye problemy ratsional'nogo ispol'zovaniia trudovykh resursov v SSSR* (Moscow, 1971), pp. 168, 39.

12. Tolkunova, p. 103.

managers show little concern for observing protective legislation concerning female workers, they are rarely punished severely for their negligence. Managers often prefer to "compensate" for bad working conditions through additional pay instead of attempting to improve the conditions. Trade union organizations and local factory committees share the responsibility for violations because of their failure to protest them.

While the need for better enforcement of existing protective measures is widely recognized, the rationale for some of these measures has been questioned. Some regulations ostensibly designed for the protection of female labor serve in fact to remove women from the most highly rewarded jobs. Moreover, it is not always clear whether it is medical research or administrative fiat that explains the classification of many highly paid occupations as hazardous or unsafe for women. In response to widespread criticism that the 1932 list of occupations considered strenuous or harmful and therefore closed to women was obsolete, a revised and expanded version was issued in July 1978 and new regulations came into effect in January 1980 banning women from some 460 occupations. Nevertheless, unsafe and unhealthy conditions abound in occupations considered especially suitable for women. A recent study of health and living conditions among female textile workers, for example, found the incidence of illness and of health-related absenteeism to be significantly higher among spinners and weavers than among white-collar workers of comparable age in the same enterprises.[13] Rising infant mortality rates may also reflect the increasing exposure of women to hazardous working conditions. However, in the absence of sophisticated medical research in this entire area, occupations closed to women are more likely to reflect traditional stereotypes about male and female work than a scientifically grounded recognition of hazards engendered by new technologies.

One way to reduce the discriminatory effects of protective measures on women is to extend their coverage to men; but this suggestion has not been seriously taken up in Soviet publications, where more emphasis has been given to the need to adapt new technologies and work norms to the physiological and psychological characteristics of women. Particular attention has been devoted to the needs of working mothers. In addition to urging that part-time work be ex-

---

13. N. V. Dogle, *Usloviia zhizni i zdorov'e tekstil'shchits* (Moscow, 1977), pp. 77–93.

panded and more flexible work schedules introduced, some specialists advocate the creation of a preferential work regime for mothers of young children to allow more time for family responsibilities. Some even advocate a shortened workday with no loss of pay for working mothers, arguing that because the development of day care services has failed to keep pace with the expansion of female employment, they should be compensated for their "double shift" in the workplace and at home.

The advocates of a shortened workday with no loss of pay appeal to more traditional forms of legitimation as well. Lenin himself can be cited in defense of the principle that the intensity of female and male employment need not be identical. This line of argument illustrates the way in which conventional formulas can be used on behalf of new and socially progressive purposes. By refusing to exclude women's domestic chores from the definition of work, and by arguing that women have a right to be compensated for the nation's failure to provide sufficiently supportive conditions for their employment, the advocates of such measures are not only insisting that socially valued work be adequately rewarded, they are also holding policymakers accountable for existing shortcomings.

The Impact of Women's Work on the Family

The impact of women's employment on the family has become a major subject of controversy in the Soviet Union in recent years. Until the mid-1960s Soviet writings routinely assumed that the increased participation of women in economic and political life would have a direct and favorable impact on their role within the family. In a striking parallel to Western sociological and feminist writings, the conventional Soviet wisdom assumed that rising educational and occupational attainments among women would lead to greater sexual equality within the family, a more democratic pattern of family relationships, and a higher degree of family stability.

In recent years, however, rising levels of female education and labor force participation in the urban and industrial regions of the USSR have been accompanied by lower rates of marriage, later marriage age, rising rates of divorce, and declining birthrates. These trends have become the focus of anxious discussion, challenging as they do the expectation that in a socialist society sexual equality and family stability went hand in hand. For the first time since the 1920s,

Soviet writers are compelled to confront the prospect that female liberation and family stability may prove to be "at odds," to draw on the title of a recent American work.[14]

Current Soviet trends appear to support the view that female education and employment are inversely associated with family stability. With 3.5 divorces per thousand population, the Soviet divorce rate is exceeded only by that of the United States. Regional differences, however, remain pronounced. In the highly industrialized and urbanized republics with high rates of female labor force participation the proportion of married women is lower, the mean age at marriage higher, and divorce rates considerably higher than in predominantly agricultural regions with low female participation rates outside agriculture.[15] There is also a growing tendency for women to initiate divorce actions, and the fact that they are less willing than formerly to hold together a marriage at any price or to marry irrespective of the cost is evidence of the wider range of options which economic independence has created.

Female employment also affects the family through its influence on childbearing. Declining birthrates in the urban and industrial regions of the USSR have been attributed to excessively high levels of female employment. An inverse relationship between female employment and fertility in the USSR was first established in the 1930s with the finding that housewives bore twice as many children as working women.[16] More recent studies have shown that while the gap has narrowed, nonworking women have 20 to 25 percent more children than do their working counterparts, and the latter have 2.5 times as many abortions.[17] The fact that the one-child family has become the norm in the urban regions of the European USSR has led to calls for reducing the level of female labor force participation and for restricting abortions in order to increase the birthrate to a socially optimal level.[18]

---

14. Carl Degler, *At Odds: Women and the Family in America from the Revolution to the Present* (New York: Oxford Press, 1980).

15. Based on figures given in Tsentral'noe statisticheskogo upravlenie pri Sovete Ministrov SSSR, *Itogi vsesoiuznoi perepisi naseleniia 1970 goda*, vol. 2 (Moscow: Statistika, 1972), pp. 263–68.

16. S. G. Strumilin, *Izbrannye proizvedeniia*, vol. 3 (Moscow: Nauka, 1964), p. 140.

17. Sh. Shlindman and P. Zvidrin'sh, *Izuchenie rozhdaemosti* (Moscow: Statistika, 1973), p. 74. A smaller difference is reported by V. Nemchenko, "Mezhotraslevoe dvizhenie trudovykh resursov," in *Narodonaselenie*, edited by D. E. Valentei et al. (Moscow: Statistika, 1973), pp. 35–36. For abortions, see I. M. Musatov, *Sotsial'no-ekonomicheskie problemy trudovykh resursov v SSSR* (Novosibirsk: Mysl', 1968), p. 321.

18. One recent example is Boris Urlanis in *Nedelia*, December 1–7, 1981, p. 16.

While recognizing the need for slightly higher birthrates, others point out that a decline in the *quantity* of children is associated with greater investments in their *quality*, and that future economic growth depends less on large additions to the labor force than on higher skills and productivity. Rejecting proposals for legal or administrative regulation of family size, they call instead for the adoption of a comprehensive demographic policy that corresponds to the specific circumstances and needs of different social and ethnic groups; provides more substantial social and economic support to families; and is congruent with broader economic and social priorities.

A third way in which female employment affects the family is through its impact on the sexual division of labor. According to Soviet data, men and women devote roughly equal time to paid employment, but women devote an additional 28 hours a week to housework, compared to 12 hours for men. As a consequence, men enjoy 50 percent more leisure than women. Although the share of women's time devoted to housework has diminished over several decades, and is lower among women with higher levels of education, this trend is less the result of greater male sharing of chores than of the availability of new technologies, household appliances, and services that higher incomes make possible. The household continues to be viewed as preeminently a female domain, and the family as a female responsibility. The fundamental assumption of Soviet economic and family policy—that women, and women alone, have dual roles—is a continuing barrier to fundamental improvements in women's position.

Optimizing the Balance of Work and Family Roles

At the heart of current Soviet discussions of women's work and family roles lies a central controversy and a major policy issue for the 1980s and beyond: how to achieve an optimal balance between women's work and family roles. The irreplaceable contribution of women to both production and reproduction militates against measures which would seriously circumscribe their roles in either domain. At the same time, there is widespread agreement that the present situation gives rise to profound contradictions between women's roles as workers and their roles as wives and mothers, contradictions that bear a very high economic, social, and demographic cost.

Although Soviet analysts share a common alarm over current trends and agree that new policy departures are essential, they diverge both in their assessments of the causes of current problems and in the policy recommendations which flow from their divergent diagnoses. Three distinct orientations can be discerned in current Soviet writings.

A first orientation, which might be termed *social feminist*, is relatively orthodox in its assumptions and moderately reformist in its policy recommendations. It views the present balance of work and family roles as optimal and focuses on reducing the tension between the two by expanding the availability of consumer goods and services—from supermarkets and laundromats to day care—and by modest reforms in the conditions of female employment. It proposes an agenda for slow but incremental reforms in the expectation that the combination of technological progress and socioeconomic reform will obviate the need for more far-reaching changes in the structure of family or work.

A second orientation, which is strongly *pronatalist*, reflects a sharper concern about current demographic trends. Critical of policies that subordinate women's primary roles as wives and mothers to short-run economic needs, it advocates an all-out effort to increase the social status and material rewards of motherhood, urging the Soviet leadership to assign highest priority to a comprehensive population policy designed to achieve higher birthrates.[19] The central and most controversial aspect of this position is its proposal to transform maternity into paid social labor, using substantial financial subsidies based on forgone wages to induce women to withdraw from the labor force in order to have children. The short-term costs of such a program, in the view of its supporters, would be more than offset by its long-term contribution to labor supply and by more immediate savings generated by a cutback in nursery facilities.

A third orientation, which echoes Western *radical feminist* concerns, opposes such a diminution of women's role in production and considers any such reversion to traditional maternal and homemaking roles a step backward. Emphasizing both the critical importance of female labor to the national economy and the equally critical importance of economic participation to women's social status and personal development, its advocates call for an extension of women's roles in economic and political life and a reduction in the family burdens that inhibit it. The solution, in this view, lies in a fundamental redefinition of male-female relationships characterized by a more

---

19. Boris Urlanis, *Problemy dinamiki naseleniia SSSR* (Moscow: Nauka, 1974), p. 283.

equal sharing by men and women of functions, responsibilities, and rewards.

For some who share this orientation, the problems of working mothers with young children could better be solved by an expansion of part-time work than by extended maternity leaves. Part-time employment, in this view, would have two benefits: it would create employment opportunities for women who are currently at home because family responsibilities prevent them from taking full-time jobs, and it would permit working mothers to reduce their workday to create more time for childcare, for personal and professional development, and for leisure. By enabling women to maintain continuity of employment with reduced strain during the years of family formation, part-time work would prevent the loss of skills and promotion opportunities which would result from extended maternity leaves.

However, the introduction of part-time work on a large scale is far more feasible in routine white-collar and service occupations than in skilled technical or supervisory positions. In industry it would require the creation of special sections and assembly lines that would segregate part-time workers from the regular labor force. It might increase the concentration of women in low-skilled and poorly remunerated jobs, and is also likely to impede a more equal division of domestic responsibilities between males and females.[20]

The economic and demographic issues that surround questions of female employment have come to occupy an increasingly important place on the Soviet political agenda of the 1980s, but it is too soon to ascertain the precise direction Soviet policy will ultimately take and what resources will be committed to sustain it. Nonetheless the Eleventh Five-Year Plan, announced at the Twenty-sixth Party Congress in 1981, and the decree of January 22, 1981, "On Measures to Strengthen State Assistance to Families with Children," indicate that a decision has clearly been made to commit additional resources to the implementation of pronatalist measures. The new decree has two key provisions. The first is the introduction of partially paid maternity leave, initially promised in 1976. Working mothers are scheduled to receive 35 rubles a month for a full year after the birth of a child, and 50 rubles a month if they reside in Siberia, the Soviet Far East, or cer-

---

20. For a more comprehensive treatment of this issue, see Joel Moses, "Women and the Politics of Alternative Work Schedules in the Soviet Union and in the United States," Monograph series, Institute of International Studies, University of California at Berkeley, 1981.

tain northern regions of the USSR. These payments are to be introduced in stages, with their scope and timing left unspecified. Women may also choose to take an additional half-year of unpaid leave, to be eventually extended to a full year.

The second major feature of the new decree is a regionally differentiated population policy in the form of new child allowances that pay 50 rubles at the birth of a first child and 100 rubles for a second and a third child, with no further payments for subsequent children. This new plan will be superimposed on the existing system of state benefits, so that the resources now flowing to the large families which predominate in Soviet Central Asia will not be reduced. The clear intent of the new payments is to encourage single-child couples in the urban regions of the European USSR to have second and third children. Whether the size of the payments offers sufficient incentive to offset existing impediments remains open to question.

Taken by themselves, these measures are too limited to have a substantial impact on current patterns of female employment or reproductive behavior. They are significant, rather, as indications of the high priority the Soviet leadership has begun to attach to demographic and family policy; of the pronatalist direction which future measures are likely to take; and of the growing role of social science in the formation of public policy. The irreplaceable role of Soviet women in both production and reproduction makes it virtually certain that the questions of women's work and family roles will remain central issues on the Soviet political agenda in the years ahead.

Discussion

The Soviet Model

The picture presented by Gail Lapidus mirrors in many ways the experiences of women in Western countries, where labor market policies have never been fashioned to bring about equality for anyone. Why has the Russian model in which so many had faith been so singularly unsuccessful? One explanation often advanced is that this model was first tried out in a culturally, economically, and politically disadvantaged country whose priorities were to modernize the economy and build an industrial base rather than to create services for the population. According to this point of view, the problem can be expected to take care of itself as the industrial potential of the Soviet Union improves. That explanation is often put forward in Eastern European countries when there is criticism of the lack of progress. However, if that were the case, we would see improvement over time rather than the deterioration we do see. Moreover, the same model has been used in Eastern European countries such as Czechoslovakia where the level of development is higher than in the Soviet Union, yet there has been no decrease in the gap between women's and men's pay, according to my studies.

There is disagreement about how much the Soviet government was—or is—committed to the principle of equality. How can we evaluate Soviet social policy—family law, education, child care—which actually undergirds labor market policy? We must recognize that the Soviet Union captured the imagination of two generations of women in Europe, at least so far as the amount of day care, health care, and education they provided at a time when similar programs have not been developed in most Western countries. The Soviet model is still very attractive to many people, especially in the third world, and is not something that can be lightly disregarded. There is a need for a complex analysis of the tension between the Soviet commitment to equality, which I believe did exist and does exist, and the resort to political and economic opportunism.

Can the Marxist model of incorporating women into the production process and taking household work and child care out of the home bring about equality in any society? Can the relationship between men and women be totally subsumed under "production"? That is a solution that is attractive to many men in Eastern European countries because it does not imply any effort on their part. They just have to wait for "society" to take over these tasks; their position will not have to be affected in any way.

This leads me to key questions: Are women to be involved in production, as production is defined by men? Is the dichotomy between "productive" work and "nonproductive" work a totally false one? Is a society built on such a value system ever likely to give real priority to taking housework out of the home, to child care, or to other reforms that would relieve women and that women could afford? When push comes to shove, even in the most advanced industrialized countries, the solution to economic problems is to resolve them at the expense of women. (Hilda Scott)

Women's Role

The emphasis on biology is a relatively new phenomenon in the USSR. When women were first incorporated into the labor force, it was believed that they were physically capable of doing the same jobs as men, and they did work in the mines and in heavy industry. The emphasis on biology came about only because of worry over the lowered birthrate. It is not a belief that women cannot do heavy work; the concern is that heavy work interferes with women's capacity to bear children. (Hilda Scott)

Russian women have done heavy work in agriculture for two hundred and fifty years. There was a movement in the 1920s and 1930s to put women in more responsible positions because they drank less than men and thus could be depended upon to turn up and to push the right buttons in the right way. Perceived differences between the sexes were not seen as detrimental to women. On the contrary, women were seen as more responsible. Of course, this was not viewed as contradicting the general attitude that women should take second place. In the party system today it is difficult to get reliable statistics, but the available evidence suggests that women are fully represented only at the lower levels. (Caryl Emerson)

The family is sometimes seen as a source of resistance to totalitarian society, as a sort of "defense unit." There is evidence from some sociological studies that women are underutilizing communal facilities for laundry and food. Are there forces within a totalitarian society seeking to preserve some intermediate institution like the family that provides a resource for resistance? Are these pressures coming from women? I don't find this point in Lapidus's work but I do see evidence of it in the People's Republic of China studies. (Hanna Papanek)

In many European countries, the family has become an escape from the rigidity of outside society. The family, which was no longer supposed to have economic functions, continues to serve as an economic unit in the sense that everybody needs a family to keep everybody else going. Someone has to stand in the lines; somebody has to deal with the bureaucracy; somebody has to find out about the gas bill—all these tasks are so time-consuming that the more people there are in the family, the better for its members. I have not seen any reports of underutilization of communal facilities. If they are underutilized, it could well be because they are not adequate. (Hilda Scott)

I perceive a backsliding in the provision of child care close to factories since the 1930s. At that time—and over the next decades—some children even lived in nurseries and took vacations separate from their parents. It was almost an effort to break up families, to change the socialization of Soviet children so that they would grow up independent of the influence of their parents and be "New Soviet Citizens." In the 1980s in the USSR I detect a return to the recognition of strong family values and away from State socialization of children. (Edward Devereux)

I have just returned from the Soviet Union where I observed two trends of interest. First, many Soviet women retire with pensions at age 50 or 55, as do some men. However, the women continue to work at home caring for grandchildren, while the men, by tradition, enjoy retirement. A second more ominous trend was clear at the Moscow State University where I attended three lectures offered by sociologists, all of which emphasized "equality in the family" for women but none mentioned equality in the work force. There were discussions of the importance of fathers taking on additional tasks at home to free up the mothers, but what made me uneasy was the differentiation between father's and mother's roles: the father should stimulate the children intellectually while the mother should provide emotional warmth and nourishment. (Sandra Pollack)

The persistence of traditional sex roles in the Soviet Union is a continuing problem. A study of recent Russian émigrés in terms of their attitudes toward childbirthing procedures suggested that Soviet women are horrified to hear of the movement in the United States to have men present at births. Such a practice would be harmful to the fetus, some of the Russian women said; others referred to it as an "evil eye." It is ingrained in certain Slavic cultures that men should not even be present at "women's work." What we would term, with a certain resignation, "women's responsibilities," Soviet women would defend, with a certain pride, as their realm.

Also, the issue of childbearing in the Soviet Union is not only related to work; it also involves housing space, which is severely limited—nine square meters a person in the cities. Is there adequate space to raise a child? If you have a child, can you get additional space? If you divorce your husband, you can't necessarily get him out of your room because both of you have been assigned to it. Sometimes couples who split up, partition their room, and one former spouse starts a new family in half of the divided room. Many persons often marry to get rights to live in a certain city. The problems of housing are critically related to reproductive decisions. (Caryl Emerson)

Soviet literature is full of references to the fact that most divorces are initiated by women and that one of the main causes for these actions is alcoholism among men. In the early years after the war, the shortage of men was so acute that women were less demanding of their husbands. A man could always find someone to marry him. Now, conditions have changed; this is no longer the case. (Hilda Scott)

One Soviet woman told me that she would rather seek a divorce and try to rear her children alone rather than have another child in the household. (Andrée Michel)

3.
The People's Republic of China

Margery Wolf

MAO ZEDONG SAW WOMEN as a necessary part of China's economic transformation even before liberation.[1] He also set equality for women as one of the goals of revolution. The first paragraph of the first major law to be promulgated after liberation stated flatly that women were no longer subjugated to men. Implementing this bold pronouncement, however, was another matter. Women in traditional Chinese society were considered inferior in every way—intellectually, physically, and socially. One does not erase by decree the attitudes and institutions developed over centuries of male supremacy. Although Mao repeatedly said that revolution could not be accomplished without the aid of China's women, he also said, prophetically as it turns out, that women were a vast reserve labor force. In time he used women in the same way that the capitalist societies he so denigrated used their female reserve labor force, drawing them into production when needed and sending them away when they were not.

During the war with Japan and the civil war that followed, getting women in the liberated areas out of their homes and into factories was an absolute necessity if the troops of the People's Liberation Army were to be fed, clothed, and equipped. But village men who were to-

---

1. Two excellent accounts of the varying policies toward women in the People's Republic of China between 1949 and the late 1970s can be found in Kay Ann Johnson, *Women, the Family and Peasant Revolution in China* (Chicago: University of Chicago Press, 1983) and Judith Stacey, *Patriarchy and Socialist Revolution in China* (Berkeley: University of California Press, 1983). I am heavily indebted to both authors for my summary of this period.

tally committed to revolution had second thoughts when they saw their wives and daughters among nonrelatives, including some males, sewing uniforms for other men in makeshift factories. When political cadres began to teach women to read and write and talked to them about the events of the world and their place in that world, village men and local cadres alike expressed those second thoughts rather forcefully. The women cadres were soon told to focus their attention on women's health needs and work skills. Those who showed signs of letting feminist ideas interfere with socialist goals were reprimanded and, if that was not sufficient, were reassigned to less desirable jobs.

After the civil war was won, women were urged to seek their own liberation through labor. In the rural areas there was still much grumbling among the men, but on this aspect of women's liberation the state was finally willing to hold firm, making concessions to male anxieties by assigning women to single-sex work groups and to tasks requiring no special training. In the cities, where the economy had not developed sufficiently to absorb all the women who responded to the party's call, women were encouraged to further the revolution as good socialist wives and mothers helping their husbands in the struggle by providing peaceful homes and happy, healthy children.

But in 1957, only a few years after women had been sent back to the sidelines, Mao called for the "Great Leap Forward." China began a frenetic period of activity in which the entire nation seemed intent on working itself to exhaustion to transform a flagging economy and a stagnant agricultural sector. It was during this period that rural women got their first taste of real partnership in collective labor. In order to free them to spend all day every day in the fields or in reclamation and water conservancy projects, collectives were ordered to organize canteens so that individual households need no longer cook meals; to establish crèches for more efficient child care; and even to set up mending stations. Unfortunately, inexperience, poor planning, and insufficient supplies caused most of these facilities to close before they were fully operational. But the most frequent problem remained that of male opposition. Although women were rarely given the same workpoints as men, the men complained, criticizing women's lack of skill or strength, but what really seemed to bother them were women's new roles. When the Great Leap slowed to a stumble in the early 1960s, brought down by a combination of fatigue, overcommitment, and a cycle of weather disasters, many rural women's gains fell with it. What remained was a grudging acceptance of women's membership on production teams.

In the cities, recruitment of women into the labor force during the Great Leap was not as threatening to male sensibilities as in the countryside. There was precedent for women working in factories and they were hired for simple routinized tasks that would free men to perform more technically advanced processes. Women workers were not in competition with men. Small neighborhood factories or workshops were organized by groups of housewives to manufacture consumer items from industrial waste materials or to engage in preliminary processing of a factory's raw material. Although the state encouraged these neighborhood collectives, they received no help from the government in the way of funds, raw materials, equipment, premises, or workers from state factories. If they could still manage to put together a productive enterprise, they were assured that they would be doing their country a service. It is a tribute to China's women that twenty years later many of these neighborhood workshops are still in operation. Some of them were so successful that the state took them over, no doubt putting men in charge and certainly changing the nature of the working conditions. After the Great Leap Forward was abandoned, many women were sent home but, as in the countryside, the idea of women working had been firmly established.

Without tracing the rise and fall of China's economy, it is fair to say that the state has managed its unemployment problem over the years at considerable cost to women. Women have not been accepted as workers who need jobs and their benefits are not equal to those of men. This is not to say that women have seen no improvement in their lives and in their access to productive labor, for they have, and those women who lived through the transition are sincere in their appreciation of what the socialist transformation has meant to them personally. But as we turn to the situation I observed in 1980–81, it will become clear that equality is still a long way off.[2]

In the countryside, as in the city, the slogan "Equal pay for equal work" has been heard since liberation, but in the countryside few even pretend that it has been achieved. All over rural China the basic daily "wage" for men is 10 to 12 workpoints, but for women it varies from a low of 5.5 workpoints to a high of 8. This is reflected in the wage ratios for 1,154 people that I obtained in five rural communes. The

---

2. During my field research in China in 1980–81, I interviewed some officials and administrators, but most of my more than three hundred interviews were with working women. I spent three months in Beijing and four to six weeks in four rural communes and the smaller city of Shaoxing. I also made brief visits to a number of cities, towns, and villages along the way.

earnings of women who worked strictly in agriculture "whenever work was available" ranged from a low of 44 percent of the wages of similarly employed men in Fujian to a high of 87 percent in Jiangsu. The Jiangsu figures are extremely high—the ratios in the other three provinces were 60, 66, and 70 percent—because the only Jiangsu men still working in agriculture were elderly or otherwise disadvantaged.

Some rural workers are employed in local industry rather than in agriculture. Rural collectives are encouraged to develop such enterprises as pig bristle brush factories and workshops that make cloth shoes or bookbags. For collective members, work in these shops is steadier; is considered more skilled hence higher status; and therefore is more likely to be done by men. Women's wages in rural enterprises range from a low of 30 percent of those of men to a high of 79 percent.

To give the state due credit, a local cadre in one area told me that the party had sent a Women's Federation member from the county seat out to their commune to tell them they had to give the same number of workpoints to women as men when they did the same work as men. The commune leaders agreed, but as soon as the official left they announced that they would continue to use the old system. The means used by different collectives to assure that women are paid less than men are often ingenious, but the most common method is to devalue work usually assigned to women, such as teapicking or weeding, and to upgrade that assigned to men, such as plowing or harvesting grain. A subtler means of achieving the same end was described to me in a model commune in Shaanxi province. Most of the women were assigned to workteams called field crop groups and most of the men were assigned to one of several technical groups, such as the irrigation group or the forestry group. The workpoints of technical workers had a higher value that those of workers in the field crop groups, so even though men might work side by side with women at harvest or planting, at the end of the year payout their workpoints were worth nearly 40 percent more in hard cash than women's.

Young unmarried women receive the highest workpoint ratings of their sex, but these drop considerably as they take on the burdens of marriage and parenthood. Although most young married women live with their mothers-in-law, they are expected to do many of the domestic chores of the household, such as grind wheat, boil the day's water, and prepare the morning gruel for the family. As a result, they usually cannot participate in the first two-hour stint of work before breakfast. According to the cadres, in justification of females' lower workpoint ratings, women also take off early from the fields in order to start dinner and are generally poorer workers because they have other things on their minds. It is inconceivable in rural areas that a man might sweep a floor or wash a bedcover. When I asked one elderly lady if her son ever helped his wife with the laundry, she was indignant—I had obviously implied that he was under his wife's thumb.

Although one of the rights guaranteed to women is half an hour morning and evening in which to nurse their babies, nursing mothers who did so in one brigade I interviewed were routinely docked half a workpoint a day. Women are also guaranteed relief from wetwork and time off if necessary during their menstrual periods, but they are docked workpoints if they exercise these rights. Women are required to take at least a month off after childbirth for they are considered unclean and ritually dangerous to others. They are not paid during this period, either. When work is scarce, women don't work. Few complain since their wages are so low anyway and they view men as the main earners in the family who should have whatever work is available.

Although one finds nurseries on showplace communes, even the model communes I worked on had only temporary facilities during agricultural busy seasons. Most women depend on their mothers-in-law for child care. Since this is a reversal of the traditional relationship in which the younger woman is expected to be her mother-in-law's servant, I was surprised to discover that the older women withdraw readily from work on the production team. As soon as they get themselves a daughter-in-law to take their place, as they put it, they retire. Although they claim they retire because of the extra household duties their enlarged family entails, I discovered that the real reason is that they can earn considerably more—often twice as much—working in sideline production, raising rabbits and chickens, weaving, and so forth. In collective labor, middle-aged women are the least well paid, but in sideline activities, an ambitious older woman can net as much or more in a year as a young male engaged in collective labor.

There are women on China's communes who are enthusiastic workers and who would much rather work in the fields or in other collective work than earn more in the relative isolation of their homes. Many of these women are bitter about their treatment at the hands of their male comrades, and some are cynical about the state's avowed commitment to providing them with equal work—let alone equal pay. But even the most disgruntled woman remembers the days before liberation when she could not work even if she wished to and still retain her respectability. Really hard times could mean starvation or the selling of herself or her children in order to preserve the lives of other family members, usually males. Few women, or men, would want to return to those days, but equally few women express much interest in the latest government programs, which they assume—and rightly— are designed for men.

The attitudes of urban Chinese women toward their jobs are quite different from those of their rural sisters. This comes in no small part from the fact that for the last decade most urban women between the ages of 20 and 50 have had full-time employment. The younger women in particular have come to think of themselves as workers rather than as wives or daughters of workers. In the countryside, women still take their identity fully from their family relationships, but in the cities the state has coopted many of the old functions of the family and vested them in work units. Permission to marry or to bear a child, ration cards for buying scarce consumer items, housing assignments, job transfers—all of these things that were once in the domain of the head of the household now are decided in an individual's work unit. Aside from diminishing the authority of the patriarchal family, this change has given women, if not autonomy, at least a new sense of themselves as individuals separate from the family.

Unfortunately, this separate identity is not accompanied by equality in pay. My urban informants were all selected for me by the officials in charge of my research so I assume that they were better paid than average.[3] Nevertheless, they and the women family members for whom they could give me wage information were paid only 78 percent of what the men in their families earned. In discussing these wage discrepancies with cadre, I was told that they were the result of past discrimination prior to liberation when women were not educated, did not work outside the home, and were not competent to hold the skilled jobs men occupied. However, when I analyzed the data by education, I discovered that women who had middle school

---

3. For a fuller description of the women I interviewed in China, see Margery Wolf, *Revolution Postponed: A Study of Women in the People's Republic of China* (Stanford: Stanford University Press, 1985); See also Martin King Whyte and William L. Parish, *Urban China* (Chicago: Chicago University Press, 1984).

and higher education earned less than men who had no more than a primary school education.

When young men and women are assigned to jobs after leaving school, they usually start out with equal pay if assigned to the same job; the youngest cohort of women in my sample received only a few yuan less per year than their male contemporaries. In a few years, however, earnings equality disappears. Men are quickly moved out of routine factory jobs into skilled work or into apprenticeships for jobs in heavy industry, which are better paid. These jobs are not considered suitable for women who instead occupy most of the lower paid slots in textile mills or light assembly plants where they perform the usual female tasks requiring patience, good eyesight, and manual dexterity. Older women who did not have any education or work experience before liberation, work in neighborhood collectives where they earn far less than any factory worker and receive few or no benefits.

Another source of wage disparity that reflects devastating basic attitudes toward women industrial workers is the unavailability of the bonuses, overtime pay, and promotions that are men's normal lot. Women are denied these benefits not on the basis of their sex but because they are considered poor workers. According to my informants, women do not stay for afterwork meetings that will upgrade their skills or their political influence. If a unit needs to surpass its quota for one reason or another, women cannot be counted on to work overtime, especially if to do so means coming back after the evening meal or on Sunday. Administrators and their foremen told me that women simply do not have the same commitment to their jobs as men because their attention is divided as soon as they marry. When children are born, the time a man spends thinking about ways to increase production women spend worrying about their children and domestic affairs. They also take more time off when they or their family members are sick, absences which are viewed as further indication of poor work attitudes.

Chinese women are not likely to criticize their government or its policies to a foreign researcher, but they are willing to complain about their double day. Woman after woman in China's cities spoke to me of exhaustion. "You know," they would say, "rush in the morning, stand in line at noon, headache in the afternoon, angry in the evening." Others described their weekends with another frequently heard saying, "Tense Saturdays, struggling Sundays, exhausted Mondays."

Like most issues that are considered women's issues, the socialization of housework, supposedly a major goal of the socialist transformation, has been sorely neglected in the People's Republic. Showplace factories have showplace child care facilities, but smaller units have either minimal child care services or none at all. Most parents find places in neighborhood crèches or with relatives. Some parents must add long bus or bicycle rides to already lengthy commutes to work in order to find suitable caretakers for their children. Canteens are scarce; although many workers can manage their own midday meals at work, their children may not be able to get meals at school. Even the process of buying food takes an inordinate amount of time; some women estimate waiting in line as much as two hours a day. Laundry is a miserable chore since it must be done by hand, often after carrying buckets of water up several flights of stairs. Editorials in government-controlled newspapers and study-group materials urge husbands to share the long list of chores a household faces after the day's work and on the one day off, but it is clear to all that these are basically women's responsibilities. Some men make a great show of doing their own laundry, but wives told me men were hopeless with household laundry because they wouldn't touch diapers, refused to use enough rinse water to remove soap, and wrung clothes so poorly that it took days for them to dry. This kind of domestic sabotage is familiar to all women.

If women are distracted from their roles as workers by worries about their families and homes, it is not difficult to understand why. Even the most politically advanced cadre assumes women have a special relationship with things domestic that men do not. A woman who devotes herself to her work in the way that a man does may get more social and material rewards from her work unit, but her family and neighbors will be critical unless she can also somehow manage to do her domestic work well. In other words, although many women now view themselves as workers, they are also wives and mothers, roles that involve many more duties than do the roles of husband and father.

Nevertheless, from the perspective of a rural woman, urban women have a good life. They work indoors in the main, and the wages and benefits associated with most urban jobs are impressive to rural women. Maternity leave is a minimum of 56 days with full salary and in many industries it is six months. Retirement with a pension of 80 percent of final wages is at age 50 for female manual laborers and age 55 for clerical workers, five years earlier than men. Good as this looks to rural women, female retirement pensions come in a poor second to those of males, since men have high wages and retire five years later. As a matter of fact, most men do not retire at age 60 and those who do are often reassigned to other jobs in the same unit paying wages that, when added to their pensions, bring their earnings to their preretirement level. Women seem to be encouraged to retire both by their units and their families; their jobs are needed by younger workers and their services are needed as babysitters for younger family members.

China has a national organization of women, called the All China Women's Federation, with regional branches that place representatives at nearly every level of society. I met many of these people during my travels; they are dedicated, hard-working women. They themselves, and the women on whose behalf they work, recognize Federation representatives as an arm of the government and their organization as a wing of the party. In no sense is the Women's Federation an advocacy group. This is not to say that it does not represent women's interests, since its representatives will firmly confront male factory managers who want to close nurseries or cut back on the number of women workers hired. But they do so as government cadres, not as representatives of the people. I asked a representative in a brigade on a rural commune how she went about advising the Women's Federation headquarters in Beijing about rural women's needs. She looked puzzled and finally said, "We get information and orders from them, but we never give information to them." Women can hope that the Federation will plead their case when new policy is being developed, but the primary role of the Women's Federation has always been to mobilize women to carry out government policy. During the Cultural Revolution, the Federation was closed down completely and has been back in full operation only since late 1979.

Trade unions cannot be considered advocacy groups for women *or* men. Party membership is required for union leadership roles and most of the top union leaders also hold government leadership positions. The main functions of a Chinese trade union seem to be that of overseeing welfare, organizing recreational events, and encouraging political study.[4] Unions do not appear to be considered important by

---

4. Martin King Whyte, *Small Groups and Political Rituals in China* (Berkeley: University of California Press, 1974).

the average worker. For example, one young person said, "I don't join because I don't want to have to go to any more meetings."

When I was in China in 1981 it was again in the process of revising its economic system. Large sections of rural Guangdong and selected areas elsewhere in China were withdrawing from collective farming and instituting a new program called the "family responsibility system" or the "household production system." The change was basic. Instead of production teams of twenty to forty households holding land, draft animals, and major tools in common, working the land together, and sharing the profits at the end of the year, individual families now bid for rights to work particular plots of land. After turning over their share of the state grain quota and taxes, they are free to dispose of the excess produce in any way they wish.[5] If a team has less easily divided enterprises, small factories, fish ponds or the like, these remain collective property for which individuals or groups bid, paying the collective for the right to use the facility including, in some places, the right to choose employees, even workers from other collectives.

Under the communal system, women and men did not receive equal treatment from the male-dominated management of the commune, brigade, and team. Nonetheless, supervision by the production team rather than by autocratic eldest males in their households protected young women through social pressure and state regulations. Older women, whose powerlessness was not as extreme as that of the young women, left collective labor with the arrival of a daughter-in-law in order to work full time on sideline activities. Since the men of their households were either sons or aging husbands and were usually completely involved in the activities of the production team, these older women experienced considerable freedom in their economic activities.

I suspect that the new household responsibility system will have a detrimental effect on the limited independence of rural women. No longer will younger women report to the team office for their work assignments, electing to stay home only as their own or their children's needs require. Instead, they will be at the beck and call of the male head of their household and of their mothers-in-law. The pro-

---

5. For an interesting discussion of some of the systems tried on one commune in Guangdong, see Jack Potter, "The Implementation of Production Systems in Guangdong, 1978–81, and Their Social and Economic Consequences" (unpublished paper, Department of Anthropology, University of California, Berkeley, n.d.).

ceeds from their labor are even less likely to come into their possession than under collective labor. While protective legislation contributed to women's lower workpoint earnings, it also improved their health and reduced infant and maternal mortality. Under the new program, every head of household becomes the head of his own production team and, if he is shorthanded, he is not going to bother with the niceties of government regulations, nor is his young daughter-in-law likely to remind him of them or discuss her physical condition with him. Older women may find their sideline activities totally incorporated into the new domestic economy, and what were once their decisions alone may become part of the general family strategy. In effect, the state has handed back to men as individuals their full patriarchal authority over women in what amounts to a decollectivization of Chinese agriculture.

The new economic policies have resulted in major changes in urban employment as well. For the first time in nearly thirty years, some people are no longer being assigned or transferred to jobs at the will of a bureaucrat who often neither knew nor cared about the interests of an employee or the skills required by an employer. Employers are now encouraged to advertise for the kind of workers they need, and employees who have been assigned to jobs that do not fit their skills or training are free to search for more suitable work. Workers and managers in some factories now sign a contract establishing wage rates, production levels, and the conditions under which the contract may be terminated. Employees who do not do satisfactory work will be told to find jobs elsewhere. As the current slogan puts it, "The iron rice bowl is broken."

This new flexibility does not do much to solve China's continuing unemployment problem, however; in fact it may exacerbate it. To attempt to alleviate that ongoing woe, unemployed youths and anyone else interested are being encouraged to start private enterprises; apparently they are doing so with exuberance. Quick food shops, middlemen who bring farm produce or consumer items to more convenient locations for resale, and various service providers are blossoming in China's cities along with, according to recent visitors, youth gangs who use strong-arm tactics to coerce farmers into selling their produce at reduced rates, and protection rings that threaten small factory cadre with beatings unless they sell their products to specified middlemen.

In a major shift the government has changed the manufacturing emphasis from heavy industry to consumer goods, sensing correctly that, after the costly tragedies of the Cultural Revolution with morale at an all-time low, it was time to reward workers with material goods in the form of better clothing, small appliances, and other modest luxuries. In order to supply these goods, as well as to create more employment, even urban governments are being urged to organize collectives. These urban collective enterprises showed a growth rate in 1982 twice as large as that of state-owned factories.[6]

What do the new economic policies mean for urban women? The freedom factory managers now have to choose their own employees and the opportunity employees have to look for more suitable jobs also means that the government no longer takes full responsibility for job placement. In the past, factory managers in some industries objected to the number of women assigned to them, and in heavy industry many managers successfully refused to employ women. One Women's Federation representative told me in 1981 that they had struggled hard to get women workers into the labor force of a new factory being built in their city but because of the new productivity requirements the managers were adamant about the work being inappropriate for women. She would not identify the industry but said it was one in which women have been employed elsewhere. Her suspicion was that the managers did not want to bear the cost of building and maintaining child care facilities; of paying salaries during maternity leaves; and of the purportedly lower productivity of women employees.

Now that workers are no longer assigned by a government authority, it may well be that the only industries that will willingly hire women are those requiring fast, dextrous workers who do not rebel against monotony—textile mills, handicraft producers, and assembly lines in light industry. The neighborhood workshops that were set up by groups of housewives during the Great Leap Forward continue to employ women primarily. The new municipal collectives, which offer few of the benefits such as pensions and maternity leaves that state-run industries provide, are also specializing in work at which women are supposed to excel. Women probably are being shunted into these new jobs as well as into other traditionally low-paid women's jobs, allowing them even less opportunity to overcome the existing wage inequality than formerly. If, as government records indicate, there

6. *Xinhua* News Agency, May 1, 1983 (FBIS).

was only a 3 percent increase in women's share of the labor force in the last four years, but the increase in jobs in urban collectives is twice as great as the increase in jobs in state enterprises, I suspect that a good many women formerly employed by state enterprises are being shifted into the low-paying collective enterprises.

In a very thoughtful article, Marlyn Dalsimer and Laurie Nison-off draw out some of the worrying implications of the new material incentives for Chinese women working within traditional women's industries.[7] In the first place, women-dominated industries work at a faster pace than other industries. Women are not likely to shut down looms or stop work to watch a foreign tour group pass through their plant, but time and again I have seen men halt production activities on such occasions. Work that requires nimble fingers cannot be laid aside. Dalsimer and Nisonoff fear that the new requirements for profitability will encourage factory administrators to attempt speed-ups, and individual incentives will tempt workers to accept them.

In addition, women are victimized by various bonus systems that start with a production quota and a basic wage for meeting it, and pay a bonus either per annum or per piece for exceeding the quota. A recent innovation is the "floating wage"—exceeding the assigned quota produces a wage increase equal to a percentage of the basic wage; with a drop in productivity, the wage returns to the original level. As Dalsimer and Nisonoff point out, because women's bonuses are tied to their basic wages and since they are on a lower wage scale than men from the outset, they will still not be paid as much as less productive men no matter how productive they are.

There is another more threatening trend developing that predates the current set of economic revisions but is clearly related to them. Beginning in 1978 with the National Women's Federation Congress, the first since the organization was disbanded during the Cultural Revolution, women were told in so many words that the attainment of equality was going to take a long time. Rather than discussing how to resolve the sexual division of labor in the household until full socialization of housework could be achieved, women were applauded for being service workers and reminded that they had special responsibilities to the home and the family. In 1980, leaders of the Beijing

---

7. Marlyn Dalsimer and Laurie Nisonoff, "Implications of the New Economic Readjustment Policies for Chinese Urban Working Women," *Review of Radical Political Economics*, in press.

Women's Federation and, in 1981, leaders of the All China Women's Federation told me that their organization was concerned with the welfare of women and *children*, a broadened scope that was new to me. The Beijing Women's Federation in particular seemed far more interested in talking about a new unit concerned with the quality of the pre-school experience in the home than in women's working conditions.

Many recent official discussions of women's working conditions in Chinese newspaper articles and editorials are concerned with adjusting women's role in social production to their more pressing domestic duties. From one perspective, longer maternity leaves, part-time jobs, and split shifts seem to be an advance, an attempt by a concerned state to alleviate the burden of the double day. From another perspective, however, they look very much like a return to the view of women as a reserve labor force. In 1982, women represented about 36 percent of the Chinese work force.[8] Faced with growing unemployment, it seems possible that the government will send many women back to unpaid domestic labor in order to make room for younger, primarily male, jobseekers. Currently, most urban Chinese women between ages 20 and 50 are employed and thoroughly identify with their role as workers.[9] It will be a tragedy for them to be once again demoted to the status of men's helpers. For employed rural women whose numbers cannot be estimated, the tragedy is compounded since they will be returning to subordination within a family system that has for centuries viewed them as expendable.[10]

Discussion

Child Care
Resolution of the problems of women workers in China is entwined with the quality of child care. In Shanghai, there is a direct relation-

---

8. *Xinhua* News Agency, Beijing, May 1, 1983 (FBIS).

9. See Wolf, *Revolution Postponed.*

10. For an attempt at an estimate of rural women's employment, see Marina Thorborg, "Chinese Employment Policy in 1949–78, with Special Emphasis on Women in Rural Production," in *Chinese Economy Post-Mao,* prepared for the Joint Economic Committee, Congress of the United States (Washington, D.C.: GPO, 1978).

ship between the number of women working in a factory and the quality of the child care available to them. If the facility for child care is good enough, women are willing and able to go to work. (Lee C. Lee)

The Family
Wolf is exactly right about the sexual division of labor in the home in China. In my samples in Shanghai and Beijing, a third of the families were three-generation households and the remainder had two generations living together. There is a sharp difference in the way household work is done in these two types of households. Women in the three-generation families continue in the old tradition, doing all the washing, cooking, shopping—all the tasks except those involving spending money. In the two-generation households, women still do most of this work but there is a greater tendency for men to perform at least some of these tasks. What I find disturbing about Wolf's paper is her report that Chinese society is returning to the three-generation model. If so, Chinese women are in trouble. Young couples can try to change their ways but, if there are maternal or paternal grandparents in the household, such changes become much more difficult to bring about. (Lee C. Lee)

With the return to domestic autonomy, it is clear that the more workers there are in a family, the better off the family will be. On the other hand, a policy that permits urban couples to have only one child and rural families only two means that the birth of daughters is a tragedy. In a rural area the birth of a daughter dooms the parents to poverty in old age. This is known to the parents and to all the neighbors. (Margery Wolf)

But if the child is a daughter, she can work. We have heard from Wolf's paper that some women, at least, earn 79 percent of men's wages. That is something. Thus, in the cities in China, a daughter is more highly valued than she would be in the rural areas—not as highly valued as a son, to be sure, but more welcome than in the past. In the past, mothers could not invest emotionally in their daughters but today, because women are economically useful people, mothers can take pride in girl children. (Janet Salaff)

Will the move away from collective farms toward family farms increase women's isolation? As the Chinese go back to the old traditional family, women will be cut off from public life even more. (Janet Salaff)

The Chinese family in the rural areas is "alive and well." Its family form has survived thousands of years. In a sense, in the countryside, the family has won; in the cities, in contrast, the state has won because it has taken on so many of the functions of the family. (Margery Wolf)

Education

Most Chinese girls leave school in the sixth grade. Boys are encouraged to continue because there is a need for "scientific farmers." There is no migration in China, so no mobility in that sense. There is, of course, imbalance in the professions: for example, there are many women physicians but all the surgeons are men. (Margery Wolf)

The Elderly

In the countryside, the elderly woman with no son is in deep trouble. The welfare system (known as the "Five Guarantees"—provision of water, food, clothing, shelter, and a coffin) is designed to take care of women who do not have sons to live with. Incidentally, many women told me they wished they could live with their daughters, but that is not done. (Margery Wolf)

Feminism

Every now and then, a window is opened on the problem of the "double day" in the media. Then, there comes a blast of fresh air as women tell what it is really like. I think of a recent book, *The Stories of Nine Chinese Women*, which details the problems. (Margery Wolf)

I attended a meeting of women workers in Shanghai in 1980. At the time, there was unofficial pressure for women to give up their jobs and go home. Those women came on like thunder. "No!" And again, "No!" They were not willing to give up their jobs. (Anne Nelson)

As carefully as I have looked, I can find no trace of a feminist movement in China yet. Until there is, there can be no liberation for women in China. At the moment, the movement consists of a handful of women in jail. For real change to come about for Chinese women, the traditional family system must be changed. Not the family itself, but the traditional system. Will it be replaced by the state, by what some have termed "public patriarchy"? The traditional family system which has dominated Chinese thought and Chinese culture since long before the revolution—that is what must change. How and when I cannot say. (Margery Wolf)

4.
Yugoslavia
Olivera Burić

THE SIGNIFICANT ENTRY OF WOMEN into the sphere of production in Yugoslavia began immediately after World War II. From 1945 to 1960, a period of economic and social upheaval, labor force participation increased at a high rate. The impressive quantitative data for that period suggested that equal employment rights had been achieved and thus that one of the basic principles of socialist society had been realized: equal remuneration for working women and men and equal rights to participate in all decisions affecting work, home life, and family. It seemed that the problem of women's status was solved and that there was no need for further empirical and theoretical investigation.[1]

However, the great economic emancipation of women brought in its wake a number of difficulties that impeded the realization of social equality between the sexes. Not infrequently, these problems created a discrepancy between the principles proclaimed and everyday reality.[2] In this regard, the International Year of the Woman proclaimed by the United Nations in 1975—and the subsequent establishment of

1. These were the statements Eva Berković used as starting points in her research on employment as a factor in the realization of social equality for women. That research is part of the project, "Social Position of Women in SR Srbia," presently being undertaken at the Institute of Social Policy, Belgrade.

2. I undertook systematic analysis of this phenomenon in a paper prepared for the Twelfth International Seminar on the Family, organized by the International Sociological Association, Moscow, 1972. See also, Olivera Burić, "Položaj žene u sistemu društvene moći u Jugoslaviji," *Sociologija* 2 (1972): 61–76 (summary in English); and "Change in the System of Social Power: Conditions for the Social Equality of Women," in *The Changing Position of Women in Family and Society*, Eugen Lupri, ed. (Leiden: E. J. Brill,1983), 173–83.

the "Decade of Women"—provided an opportunity for summing up the efforts that had been undertaken to improve the social status of women. They also provided a stimulus for a more energetic approach to overcoming the obstacles that stood in the way of equality.

Early in 1978, the Executive Council of the Yugoslav National Assembly passed a "Resolution concerning the Betterment of the Social and Economic Position of Women."[3] Implementation of this resolution is the responsibility of various organizations but especially of the Conference for the Public Activity of Women and of the trade unions. At many meetings developments have been discussed, new problems identified, and relevant actions planned and initiated. Let me turn to a brief review of some of the problems uncovered, the way they are being handled, and with what success.

In Yugoslavia, the rate of increase in labor force participation has been higher for women than for men. According to the 1981 census, women constitute 36.7 percent of all workers, up from 23 percent in 1952.[4] Overall social planning in Yugoslavia suggests that there will be an annual increase of 3.8 percent for women by 1985, compared to a total rate of 2.5 percent.

Related to this phenomenon is the reality of different occupations pursued by women and men, a problem the world over. This is one of the main causes of inequality between the sexes. The industries where a great many women have been traditionally employed are lagging behind other industries economically, not because women are inferior workers, but because technology in female-dominated industries is outmoded. Statistics show there has been little change in occupational segregation by sex in Yugoslavia in the last three decades. This can be seen in the textile industry, where about 70 percent of workers throughout the country are women and as much as 80 percent in more industrialized regions. Similarly, women constitute about 80 percent of those employed in nonindustrial economic activities, as public servants in social work and health care, for example.

A redress in this imbalance is expected to be brought about by a reform in educational strategy. Until recently, the educational system in Yugoslavia was not very well adjusted to the demands of a developing country, but the reformed school system now being developed is

---

3. Official *Gazette* of SFR Jugoslavia, No. 18, 1978.
4. Women employed in the public sector only. An additional 32.4 percent work in their own private agricultural and other small-scale enterprises.

expected ultimately to encourage more girls to train for careers in the manufacturing sector, instead of opting as they have, by and large, for clerical or administrative work. Actions in Yugoslavia that have served to raise wages in manufacturing and to diminish pay in other careers have been seen as vital to the national effort to bring about economic stabilization.

The steadily mounting number of women applying for jobs considerably exceeds the demand. There are now three times as many applicants for jobs as there were thirty years ago, and 57 percent of the total applicants for work are women. It is interesting to note the linkages between education and employment. For women, a high level of education is reflected in a high rate of employment, whereas for men the correlation does not appear to be so clear. Perhaps this is the case because it is presumed that men should work anyway, whether or not they are educated.

Young, unmarried women from the countryside try to obtain work in the cities because they are dissatisfied with their position and work conditions in traditional rural communities dominated by small family farms. In recent years, however, food production has received much national attention. If the economic recession can be stemmed and the conditions in the rural villages improved, it is hoped that young women as well as young men will be more likely to remain in their native villages. There is evidence that this is happening and that young people are returning to their native villages when their expectations for life in the cities are not met.

New opportunities for employment for young women recently have been opening up in small businesses, many in the private sector—artisans' workshops, restaurants, domestic services, and the like. Discussions are going forward on the provision of part-time jobs and job-sharing for both women and men and for the development of small-scale businesses.

Dismissal from work in times of recession does not occur in Yugoslavia. Permanent tenure on the job is guaranteed by law to man and woman alike. Dismissal from work occurs only for serious offenses. However, sex discrimination does occur in hiring. If a man and a woman apply for the same job, his chances of being hired are better than hers. This happens because businesses and industrial organizations are discouraged from hiring women, especially young mothers, because the law guarantees a long maternity leave as well as leaves to care for ill children under the age of seven. As a result, young mothers are often absent from work and thus are seen as less desirable employees. The discrimination in recruitment is somewhat subtle. The advertisements do not say, "No women," but sometimes they do say, "Candidates must have completed their military service." Nevertheless, the official policy on equal employment opportunity appears to have been implemented overall, since the ratio of newly hired women is higher than that of men.

The constitution of Yugoslavia guarantees equal pay for equal work without regard to sex. The principle is never questioned or departed from. Yet statistical data indicate that women and men with the same professional qualifications earn different salaries, with women's average salary lower than the male average. This is true even in the branches of industry where women workers constitute the majority. Women's salaries are lower because they perform less demanding tasks; seldom are in important decision-making posts; and are absent from work for family reasons more often than men.

The 1978 Resolution of the Yugoslav National Assembly in connection with the International Year of the Woman called for much activity in the realm of protections for mothers and children who, according to the Yugoslav constitution, should benefit from "special public care." In the last few years, an impressive number of child care institutions have been opened but there are still not enough. It is estimated that 25 percent of children who need child care do not receive it because there are not enough facilities.

The child care facilities are in communes, at the neighborhood level. The quality of the facilities depends on the size of the commune and, even more, on the extent to which the women are active. There is also money flowing from the national government to underdeveloped communes to help them set up day care. In one study, I asked women about services that would help them, such as child care, help with housework, and so on. Virtually all wanted day care for their children but very few wanted services to help them inside the household. I was surprised because I had imagined that they would all welcome household help. I don't know if they thought such services would be too expensive or if they really want to do their own cooking and cleaning. It could also be that sometimes they have no feeling of fulfillment in the jobs they do outside, whereas at home they can see the results of their labor immediately.

There is a strong effort to improve health care and social services in Yugoslavia. There are comparatively few women who do not take advantage of such services as well-baby clinics. The maternity leave provision was expanded from 180 to 270 days by the 1983 New Law on Working Relations when it was demonstrated that liberal sick leave granted by doctors to mothers of newborn babies was, in effect, maternity leave lasting more than 230 days. Mothers of infants also were given the right to work shorter hours until their babies reach twelve months of age.

Much less has been achieved in terms of lightening the burden of the housewife. It is true that the work of housekeeping has been somewhat eased with the invention of household appliances, but it is also true that the household of the working mother is an issue that deserves more public attention. Our studies reveal, however, that there is stubborn resistance to a closer connection between families and public institutions, with some arguing that a closer relationship would endanger the privacy of family life. The prejudice against the socialization and institutionalization of the family is ill founded. It depends very much on what kind of institutions and what kind of socio-political system the family is linked to. Family privacy is not at risk if the family is not just an object of bureaucratic interest but is actively engaged in creating family and social policy, in decision making, and in using self-management effectively. The process should begin in the factory, where decisions are made as to how much money shall be allocated to public social services and end in the local community, where such services are organized on a community-sharing basis.

Equality between the sexes will not be realized until social relationships between men and women are restructured both inside and outside the family, and it is a mistake to wait for the government to do it. But then we come again to the difficult question of the relationship between the family and the sociopolitical system in which it exists. These systems vary from country to country. In my opinion, the issue needs to be researched by political scientists, who have tended to neglect the family as outside their concerns on the ground that it is a private social group separate from the political system. Thus the family has been studied by scholars of anthropology, psychology, sociology, and the law, all of whom have focused mainly on relationships inside the family. When they looked outside the family, it was only at other kin groups or informal networks, almost never at the relationship between the family and the larger sociopolitical system.[5]

The self-management system in Yugoslavia does not mean the

---

5. I try to clarify this aspect of family life in my book *Family and the Social System*, which is based on empirical research on the position of the family in a self-managed soci-

participation of workers in the division of income only. Self-management requires participation in a whole range of decisions that directly or indirectly affect the position of women and their families. Each worker makes decisions which affect not only his or her own social security but that of others as well. Unfortunately, not enough women are active in such decision making, possibly due to some shortcomings in the self-management system. It is clear that the self-management system needs to be improved; but since it has no other model to follow and no long tradition, the system is flexible and open to change. The process of improvement and reexamination is continually going forward in Yugoslavia. This will presumably have a favorable effect on women's social participation and bring about a gradual improvement of their status in society.

In conclusion, I should like to emphasize that despite the difficulties that occur in efforts to realize equality between women and men during a time of recession, women should never be viewed as recipients of charity. "This is not a question of 'helping women'; it is an issue of bringing about socio-economic change which is vital to overall human development.[6]"

Discussion

Women's Role in the Yugoslav Economy
The economic and political system in Yugoslavia is substantially different from those operating in the other socialist countries. Yugoslavia has tried to introduce an industrial democracy, which we call the "labor managed" system or self-management. This is a social as well as a political concept. A business enterprise run by workers is both an economic organization and a social organization. The implications are twofold. First, the most complex and comprehensive self-management takes place at the factory level; second, what happens in factories and businesses is of fundamental importance for social relations throughout the society.

---

ety. Olivera Burić, "Porodica i drustveni sistem" (Belgrade: Institute of Social Policy, 1980).

6. Vida Tomišić, "Women of Rural Pluri-Activity" (Ljubljana, Yugoslavia: FAO, European Commission on Agriculture, 1983).

The point here is that men and women have equal rights and equal responsibilities in Yugoslavia's self-managed society. Of course, all citizens cannot participate in each decision in every department. Therefore, they elect a Worker's Council, which in turn elects a general manager or a board of managers. The size of the council depends on the size of the business; it meets once or twice a month and considers all important decisions. The general manager has the responsibility for implementing the decisions made by the council. About 70 to 80 percent of the members of Workers' Councils are workers; the rest are top and middle managers and supervisors.

To what extent are women represented in these councils? Business and industrial organizations in Yugoslavia are classed into five groups, by size. Let me focus on the smallest and the largest. In the smallest businesses, there are 33,000 council members, of whom 46 percent are women. The largest scale enterprises are run by 9,000 members of Workers' Councils, of whom 14 percent are women. Overall, women account for 30 percent of council members.

How about promotion to top managerial positions? Overall, 6 percent of top managers are women. Again this varies by the size of the business. In small businesses, women are 10 percent of top managers, while in the biggest operations, there are either no women at the top or very few.

In my opinion, the self-management system offers a new start towards equality for women in Yugoslavia. To be sure, there still remains a gap between legislation and practice, but it is apparent that Yugoslavia is not the only country with this problem.

Each Workers' Council decides how it will allocate the money it earns. Some councils choose to build roads or to construct new housing developments; others choose to provide child care facilities. The decisions depend in part on the age, rather than the sex, of those making the decision. Young women, of course, would vote for child care, but I don't think that older women would. (Miroljub Labus)

Male Emigration to Western Europe

The effect on their families of men working in other countries has been researched. One of my own studies had begun with the hypothesis that the father's absence would have a bad effect on children. What I found was that the effect varied by social class and by region. If a father left his family in a city with no other kin around, for example, the effect of his absence on his children was not good. On the other hand, if he left his family in a rural village, the effects were not as bad and in some cases even positive. The women became more independent and the men brought back new ideas and goods which helped in the development of whole villages. It should be noted, however, that the divorce rate goes up when the men go away to work.

I found an interesting village in Eastern Serbia where the women were managing very well. Emigrants from that village all went to work in a certain iron factory in one city, Innsbruck, Austria. When a family needed money, one member would go to Innsbruck and switch places with a relative—the father, an uncle, brother, grandfather, sometimes the mother. It is unskilled work so nobody needs special training. As families get some money together, they buy a bus for transportation. They don't learn to speak German at work; they just go to Innsbruck, work, get the money, come home. And now every house in that village has a bathroom with running water; there are better roads, health services, and schools. As I have said, there are bad effects sometimes. The trade unions have taken an interest in this problem and have tried to develop good relationships with the companies in foreign countries where Yugoslavs go to work. The unions try to ensure that the workers can come and go freely, that is, come home regularly. (Olivera Burić)

Children

Abortion is free in Yugoslavia. The constitution provides every citizen with the right to a free decision on childbearing. Both parents have the right to decide on the number of their children and the spacing of their births. In order to realize this right, the state provides free birth control and free abortion, as well as free services for parents with problems of infertility.

The birthrate is declining—the extent of the decline varying by ethnic group. At present, we are below the replacement rate. In adjacent cities, we have the highest birthrate in the world and the lowest. In some villages, there is a tradition of one-child families in order to keep the property in the family; women have used birth control methods for centuries, sometimes dangerous methods of self-abortion that have resulted in death. There are other traditional villages where families are very large. For this reason, unitary family planning policy for the whole country of Yugoslavia is difficult to develop. We are one country and, according to our constitution, we are committed to free choice in the matter of family size. (Olivera Burić)

5.
Japan
Hiroko Hayashi

HISTORICALLY, MOST JAPANESE WOMEN workers were employed in agriculture and forestry, primarily in family enterprises. Recently, the occupational structure for women has changed significantly. The number of women in agriculture and forestry has declined while the number in nonagricultural industries has increased. Between 1950 and 1981, the proportion of women in agriculture and forestry dropped from 62.3 percent to 11.9 percent. Accompanying this decline was a decrease in the proportion of women working in family businesses—from more than 50 percent in 1965 to 35.6 percent in 1981. Nevertheless, more than one-fifth of Japanese women currently work in family businesses, a relatively high rate that is characteristic of many Asian countries (table 5.1). Women have represented about 40 percent of the Japanese work force each year since World War II. In 1980, over 22 million women, almost half of all females beyond the age of 15, were working either as salaried employees or family workers.

TABLE 5.1
Distribution of Working Women by Occupational Status, Selected Countries (in percent)

Country	Year	Occupational Status			
		Self-employed	Family Worker	Employed	Other
Canada	1982	6.1	2.2	91.7	
USA	1981	5.2	1.1	93.6	
West Germany	1981	4.8	9.2	86.0	
Japan	1981	13.2	22.4	64.4	
Phillipines	1978	27.9	30.8	40.9	.3
Korea	1981	22.8	39.1	38.1	

Source: ILO, *Year Book of Labour Statistics*, 1982.

The average age of Japanese working women has been increasing since the 1960s. In 1949, the average age of working women was 23.8 years and that of working men, 32.5 years; in 1981, the average age of women workers had risen to 34.8 years, of men to 38 years. The distribution of Japanese women's employment by age forms an "M" curve: the point of greatest employment is the 20- to 24-year-old group; the low point comes between 30 and 34 years of age; and another high point is reached between 40 and 50 years of age. Since the average age at women's first marriage was 25.3 years of age in 1981, these data indicate that great numbers of Japanese women work in their early twenties, withdraw from the labor market at marriage or at the birth of their first child, and return to paid employment after the age of 40.

Since 1980, most Japanese women have entered the labor market as part-time workers; currently, 19.6 percent of all women workers are employed part time. For statistical purposes, "part time" is defined as fewer than 35 weekly working hours, but persons classified as part-time workers may work the same number of hours per week as full-time workers or even longer. Of the 2.7 million Japanese women classified as part-time workers—most of them married and middle-aged—more than one-fifth work the same hours per week as persons classified as full-time workers. Since there is no legal definition of a part-time worker, there is a good deal of overlap between the part- and full-time categories. At the other extreme, although a 48-hour maximum workweek is stipulated by the Japanese Labor Standards Act, this regulation is not strictly enforced in small businesses. As a consequence of loose definitions and lax law enforcement, therefore, the range of hours worked by Japanese women is wide but difficult to specify accurately.

Employment Practices affecting Working Women

Despite the increase in the number of working women, opportunities open to them are still unequal to those offered to men. In Japan, there is no legal prohibition against discrimination in hiring. Legal protection against discrimination exists only after one has been employed. Research by the Ministry of Labor shows that many industries discriminate against women not only in hiring but also in wages, job assignments, on-the-job training, promotion, and retirement age. For example, a 1981 business survey found that only 24 percent of firms employing new graduates from four-year universities employed both sexes (71 percent hired men only and 5 percent, women only). On-the-job training was provided in 68 percent of the businesses surveyed, but 21 percent of these firms provided no training for women and an additional 39 percent provided different training to men and women. Nevertheless, the number of firms offering the same training to men and women showed an increase: from 30 percent in 1977 to 40 percent in 1981.

Eighty-three percent of the businesses surveyed in 1981 had positions that were not open to women, a slight improvement from 92 percent in 1977. Obviously, sex discrimination remains deeply embedded in general employment practice in Japan. When asked why certain positions were closed to women, 51 percent of employers surveyed cited women's "lack of physical strength"; 36 percent, their "lack of skill"; 27 percent noted requirements for work outside the office and on official tours; 23 percent referred to the need for publicity and for frequent contact with people outside the office; 18 percent, to the need for overtime work; and 15 percent, to women's "lack of good judgment."

Of the businesses surveyed, 45 percent gave women no opportunity for promotion. Where retirement systems were in place (86 percent of the businesses with more than thirty employees), the retirement age differed for women and men in 19 percent of these companies. Enforced retirement at the time of marriage, pregnancy, or childbirth was official policy in 2 percent of the businesses in 1981, down from 7.4 percent in 1977.

Legal Status of Working Women

The Japanese Constitution stipulates that "All of the people are equal under the law and there shall be no discrimination in political, economic, or social relations because of race, creed, sex, social status, or family origin" (Article 14). Under this principle, related labor laws prohibit sex-based discrimination. For example, the Trade Union Act outlaws sex-based discrimination in admission to membership in labor unions, and the Employment Security Act requires equal treatment of the sexes in vocational guidance, employment, and the like. The Labor Standards Act provides for equality between men and women in the matter of wages (Article 4), and states that "No employer shall discriminate against or for any worker by reason of nationality, creed, or social status in wages, working hours, and other working conditions" (Article 3). Since sex is not mentioned in Article 3, most court decisions concerning discrimination against women have held that the principle of equality in the Labor Standards Act could not be applied except in cases of unequal pay. An employer who violates the stipulations of Article 3 or Article 4 can be punished with penal servitude not exceeding six months or with a fine not exceeding 8,000 yen ($35).

The Working Women's Welfare Act of 1972 lays down the fundamental principle that women workers shall not suffer from any discrimination on the basis of their sex. Unfortunately, this act has no penalty clause so there is no real guarantee that equal treatment will be provided.

Both legal theory and recent court decisions hold that the constitutional guarantees of equal rights can be applied only indirectly to labor relations in the private sector. In the public sector, however, the Government Official Act and the Local Government Official Act mandate equality between men and women in regard to all working conditions so that constitutional guarantees can be invoked directly. For example, since 1981, new regulations have opened several types of government jobs formerly closed to women. In the private sector, the lack of the word "sex" in Article 3 of the Labor Standards Act has made the legal fight for equality for Japanese women more complicated because judicial interpretation is required.

A landmark case was decided by the District Court of Tokyo in 1966 when Setsuko Suzuki won reinstatement at the Sumitomo Cement Company as an office clerk. She had been dismissed because she had been married; the court ruled the action illegal and granted her back pay. Since the Sumitomo decision, women have brought a number of other suits. In most cases, the company's right to force women to take early retirement has been at issue. Also under litigation has been unequal pay for equal work. Women workers have charged that these policies were violations of their constitutional guarantees of equality in economic life, freedom of marriage, and of equal working conditions as mandated by the Labor Standards Act.

Some fifty sex discrimination cases have been decided since the Sumitomo Cement decision. In several of these, at issue were clauses from collective agreements permitting discrimination in wages and retirement age, or bias in promotion, which suggests that the trade unions have been traditional rather than progressive in terms of helping working women. In almost all the cases decided in favor of women employees, the courts have ruled that any part of individual contracts, work rules, or collective agreements that include sex-based discrimination are null and void because they violate good public order. In 1981, women constituted only 28 percent of the membership of Japanese trade unions; about one-third of the unions had no women delegates. If union attitudes are to change, women must become more active in these organizations in the future.

In a number of countries, the government has been a moving force in promoting equality for women. In Japan both the House of Representatives and the House of Councillors adopted resolutions in June 1972 calling for the banning of any and all discriminatory treatment of women workers because of sex and provided for necessary actions to achieve this goal. In 1977, the Ministry of Labor announced a five-year plan to eliminate discrimination, consisting of three steps: (1) a general survey of discrimination in 1977; (2) elimination by 1978 or 1979 of the practice of enforced retirement of women workers for marriage, pregnancy, or childbirth and of the practice of requiring women to retire early, i.e., before the age of forty; and (3) elimination by 1980 or 1981 of policies requiring retirement of women before the age of fifty-five.

In the courts, the practice of requiring women to retire at marriage was declared illegal at an early stage. Thereafter, that decision was invoked in subsequent litigation involving sex discrimination. In 1981, the Supreme Court struck down any retirement systems that differentiated between women and men. More complex issues involving sex discrimination in job opportunity, job assignment, and opportunity for promotion have yet to be decided.

Government Control over the Labor Market

The Labor Standards Act Research Society, a group that is advisory to the Minister of Labor, reported to the minister on the status of working women in 1978. The report recommended abolition of all special protections then provided for women, with the single exception of maternity leave. The government set up a Committee of Specialists on Equality in Employment in 1979. Three years later, the committee submitted draft guidelines for ensuring equality of men and women in employment.

The International Women's Decade officially ends in 1985. The

Japanese government has announced that it will ratify the Convention on the Elimination of All Forms of Discrimination against Women by that target date. Before the convention can be ratified, it will be necessary to amend the Labor Standards Act to include a clause banning all forms of sex discrimination or, alternatively to introduce new legislation to eliminate sex discrimination in employment.

The tension between protection for women and the provision of equality in employment is well symbolized by legislative discussions over amending the Labor Standards Act, since the act includes many clauses prohibiting women from nightwork, holiday work, overtime, and the like. Between 1978 and 1983, many Japanese political parties put forward bills banning sex discrimination. Each of the bills stressed the protection of working women from discrimination as a necessary condition for the realization of equal employment opportunity. None of them passed.

Despite the statutory requirement for equal pay for equal work and Japan's ratification of ILO Convention No. 100 regarding equal remuneration, equal pay is not a reality in Japan. Quite the contrary. Most women workers feel that they are not paid fairly. Women's earnings average 53.8 percent of men's, while in England the comparable figure is 69.7 percent; in France, 87.3 percent; and in West Germany, 72.4 percent. The pay gap between men and women in Japan is one of the largest in the industrialized world.

Law and practice diverge in Japan. It was not until twenty years after the date of the enactment of the new Constitution and the Labor Standards Act (1947) that the first working woman sued her employer for sex discrimination. Since that case, there have been about fifty others concerned with unfair treatment of women.

It is expected that the Employment Equality Act will be enacted in 1985. This new legislation will, it is hoped, provide effective mechanisms that can be applied to the private sector for the first time in the history of Japan. Its provisions follow closely the recommendations of the Labor Standards Act Research Society. Various forms of protection granted to women under existing legislation are eliminated—with the exception of those related to pregnancy and childbirth. However, the act does not include any punitive provision, since it was feared that such a provision would be counterproductive. I believe that the lack of such a provision greatly weakens this legislation, and many women workers believe that the legislation favors management unfairly. The experience of Japan suggests that without workable enforcement mechanisms the legal guarantee of equality is like a pot of gold at the end of the rainbow: a dream, not a reality.

Discussion

Background

The situation of the Japanese woman in the 1970s and 1980s has not been well understood internationally and remains enigmatic to many people outside of Japan. This is partly due to the specific nature of Japan's twentieth-century history, particularly the last fifty years. While Japan has not undergone the upheaval of a mass-based social revolution such as that experienced by China, it has nevertheless seemed to careen from extreme to extreme. There was the Pacific war, which mobilized Japanese women and men under the banner of the state as family; the world's first nuclear holocausts; the American occupation; and twenty-five years later, Japan's emergence as a leading economic and technological power. If we look at the popular Western image of the Japanese woman during this period, we find the "Madame Butterfly" stereotype surprisingly consistent, whether it be in the childlike, docile GI bride epitomized by the film *Sayonara* in the 1950s or the beautiful Mariko with her ersatz mysticism and selfless adherence to male authority. With the popularity of the movie *Shogun* in the United States has come a new romanticization of the compliant, gentle Japanese woman. Even the famous "education mama" is seen as focusing entirely on her family.

Such images are far from the reality. Yet it seems to be difficult for those outside Japan to reconcile the kimono with high tech and to understand how women have positioned themselves, both socially and psychologically, in the increasingly cosmopolitan, hybrid culture of contemporary Japan. Professor Hayashi's paper serves as an antidote to the image of fragile Japanese feminity by showing that the sturdy labor of Japanese women has been a consistent and crucial component of the Japanese economic miracle. (Brett deBary)

An Equal Rights Amendment was inserted by the occupation forces into the constitutions of both Japan and West Germany after World War II, even as it was resisted in the United States. [One participant commented that it must have been seen as a punishment!]

There was an extraordinary woman sergeant in the Women's Army Corps who was appointed to do "women's work" in Japan when she was released from the army after the war. She went about the country, interviewing women in villages and cities about their needs, and she ultimately was responsible for the introduction of protective and equal pay legislation between 1946 and 1952. This was at a time when virtually nobody else in the industrialized world was thinking in terms of protecting women workers or granting them equality. (Alice Hanson Cook)

There are important differences by class and by region (rural-urban) in Japan. After World War II, developments paralleled closely what had happened in the United States much earlier. As production moved out of the home, lower-class women went to work but middle-class women stayed home, in part because those with college degrees had great difficulty finding employment as late as the early 1970s. Women were active during the war and when peace came there was a concerted effort on the part of urban women to break away from certain old traditions: living in a three-generation family dominated by the mother-in-law, for example.

Legislating morality is slow work. During the occupation of Japan, the legal underpinnings of the traditional family system were swept away by the new constitution. Nevertheless, after the occupation, the family unit came back strong—in rural areas, fully half of the families were traditional in structure and custom right after the occupation. (Edward Devereux)

Legislation

Women trade unionists are strongly protectionist in Japan. Protective legislation was put in place between 1946 and 1952, long before anybody else in the industrialized world was thinking of either protecting women workers or granting them equality. Now Japanese women do not want to lose the protective legislation, which they see as the one defense against total exploitation. This is understandable, considering that such a small proportion of the total Japanese labor force is protected by union agreements. Even if the unions were concerned with equality between the sexes, which they are not, their efforts would affect only a relatively small group of women. (Alice Hanson Cook)

The pro-protectionist stand now popular in parts of Japan has affected legislation in other countries. The Japanese occupation of

Southeast Asia left a heritage of protectionism in Indonesia, Korea, and elsewhere. (Hanna Papanek)

A major problem for women workers in Japan is that salary is linked to age. When a woman seeks to return to the labor force after her children have grown, she has great difficulty getting work because her age entitles her to a higher salary than an employer may want to pay a person who has been absent from the work force. [This policy, it was suggested, may be the cause of the high proportion of middle-aged women working part time.] (Anne Nelson)

In the mid-1970s, an advisory committee on women was created at the level of the prime minister, headed by Rioko Akamatsu, later Japanese Minister to the United Nations. A considerable cleavage developed between the trade union committee members and the legal authorities and scholars over the issue of protectionism versus equality. I believe that the reason the Japanese government is moving toward equality is that the advisory committee ultimately recommended taking that direction. Akamatsu was instructed to sign the UN Convention at Copenhagen for Japan although the government knew that education, labor, and some justice legislation would have to be changed to conform to the resolution. That was a great symbolic moment. (Alice Hanson Cook)

Status of Women
A paradox Professor Hayashi elucidates is the gap between legal status and practice in Japan. Although Japan has had an Equal Rights Amendment since 1947, in many ways this apparently progressive aspect of the postwar constitution has remained very much a formality. Indeed, the phenomenon of progressive changes being wrought by fiat—from above or outside rather than from below or within—is seen by many Japanese as a distinctive feature of their history, their politics, and their culture since the Meiji Restoration of 1868. Professor Hayashi has pointed out the legal loopholes in current legislation that permit injustice towards women to continue. Take the case of menstrual leave, as described in Alice Cook's and Hiroko Hayashi's book, *Working Women in Japan*: "The Japanese law allows for leave where 'a woman suffers heavily from menstruation' or is employed on a job 'injurious to menstruation.' In such cases, the woman requests leave from her employer. But the law says nothing about whether it is to be paid leave and in most cases it is not."

Other aspects of the status of Japanese working women should be noted. The first is that, due to her heavy responsibilities at home, the woman worker pays a high penalty in exhaustion. Second is the fact that child care facilities have not been developed in Japan as in other countries. It is still widely believed that "nobody can substitute for mama" in rearing children. Moreover, women are still largely excluded from public life with the typical business meeting held over dinner where saki is drunk and entertainment and companionship are provided by geisha. (Brett deBary)

On a recent trip to Japan, the top woman expert on pension policy was very kind to me and introduced me to experts in the field in the Ministry of Labor. When I tried to express my appreciation to the Japanese woman, she responded, "Don't thank me. I have always wanted to meet the pension expert but have never been able to arrange it until you came to visit. So it is thanks to you that I now know him." (Anne Nelson)

Feminism

The women's liberation movement in Japan grew out of anti-Vietnam sentiment, mainly in what was called the "New Left" in the late 1960s and early 1970s. To some extent, the women in Japan who are politically active feminists have had close ties with men who were associated with the antiwar movement. However, the women found themselves in subordinate positions in these larger movements. Their strong need for feminism grew out of tensions between themselves and the very men who were advocates of progressive change. (Brett deBary)

My recent contacts with Japanese women journalists suggested that there was general despair about the women's movement. One told me that there were only about thirty women in the whole country of Japan who could be counted on to support feminist causes. (Anne Nelson)

Today only 2 percent of Japanese companies report forced early retirement for women and that reform can be traced to the staying power of the women plaintiffs in the sex discrimination cases. (Roberta Till-Retz)

No Japanese woman could have carried through a legal case alone. Not many took as long as the *Nissan* case, but none was resolved quickly. The plaintiffs' suits were supported either by a *minor* union in their own plants or by the Communist party. A support group is essential for any grievant in a sex discrimination suit. This is as true for a woman academic in the United States as for these plaintiffs in Japan.

Moreover, feminist issues are publicly debated in Japan due to the efforts of women journalists. Women hold relatively high posts on all four national newspapers, which are excellent sources of information on the progress of the feminist movement in Japan. These journalists were responsible for giving coverage to the legal cases that Hiroko Hayashi described. Women have made progress because of these cases, but progress takes time. The *Nissan* case, in which the issue was differential retirement ages, was in the courts from 1948 to 1982. (Alice Hanson Cook)

6.
Israel

Rivka W. Bar-Yosef

ISRAEL HAS BEEN USED as a case to prove that gender equality *is* attainable and that gender equality is *not* attainable. Paradoxically there is some evidence to support both of these contradictory opinions.[1] Probably more than many modern countries, Israel harbors sharply contrasting value systems and ideologies, which are especially conspicuous with respect to the position of women.

In order to describe the status of women in any society it seems useful to refer to two dimensions: a measure of relevance, indicating the extent of sex division beyond biological differences, and a scale of ranking indicating how attributed differences affect the roles allocated to each sex. The combination of these two dimensions produces three feasible types of status:

1. *Similar and equal* deems the sex criterion as irrelevant, considers the sexes to have similar attributes, and excludes hierarchical considerations.

2. *Dissimilar and equal* accentuates the significance of qualitative differences between the sexes but does not use these as a basis for ranking.

3. *Dissimilar and unequal* is the original "ascriptive" pattern in which sex differences are used to denote variety and determine ranking, in this case ranking women lower than men.

These three patterns are logically exclusive, but it does not follow

---

1. Michal Palgi and Menachem Rosner, "Equality between the Sexes in the Kibbutz: Regression or Changed Meaning," in *Sexual Equality: The Israel Kibbutz Tests Theories,* M. Palgi et al., eds. (Norwood, Pa.: Norwood Editions, 1983), 255–96; Lionel Tiger and Joseph Shepher, *Women in the Kibbutz* (London: Harcourt Brace, 1975); Selma Koss Brandow, "Ideology, Myth, and Reality: Sex Equality in Israel," *Sex Roles* 6, no. 3 (1980):403–19.

that each society has to be characterized by only one of them. Israel is an example of the coexistence, albeit not always comfortably, of each of these patterns, even within the formal legal system.[2]

Similar and Equal

A series of Israeli legislative acts proclaim the irrelevance of sex attributes and the equality of women with regard to certain rights and duties in the orbit of political, economic, and educational institutions. The most general statement in this direction appears in the constitution: "The State of Israel will maintain equal social and political rights for all citizens, irrespective of religion, race and sex."[3] This basic principle has been elaborated through more specific definitions of similarity and equality of the sexes in various institutional spheres, in cluding the labor market.

The Women's Equal Rights Act of 1951 defines the equal status of women with respect "to all legal activity," and it states that "any legal act which discriminates against woman for being a woman, should not be acted upon." Women have the same right to be gainfully employed as men. Seniority, severence, and other rules pertaining to "job property" do not distinguish between men and women. A specific law ensures equality of remuneration, stating that "equal pay should be paid for equal work." In 1981, an Equal Employment Opportunities Law was passed by the Knesset, specifying nondiscrimination in hiring and in job training. Nevertheless, it allows refusal to hire "on the grounds of sex, where the nature of the job . . . so requires. . . ." It remains to be seen how the "nature of the job" will be interpreted. The law does not try to tackle the difficult question of promotion. An important innovation is the prohibition of gender-specific advertisement of job vacancies. Given the nature of the Hebrew language, which distinguishes among the genders in nouns, adjectives, and verbs, nondiscriminatory advertisement demands special awareness and effort.

The common factor in these and other Israeli laws is the egalitarian ideology that characterizes modern industrial democracies in general. This ideology did not grow out of the social conditions of the Israeli society but was the product of European revolutionary thought

---

2. For a comprehensive although not updated summary of laws concerning the status of women see Plea Albeck, "The Status of Women in Israel," *American Journal of Comparative Law* 20, no. 4 (Fall 1972):693–715.

3. Basic Law, Knesset, 1948.

and was brought to Israel in the early days of Zionist settlement by groups of young intellectuals intending to build a new type of society. Their three main objectives were the national emancipation of the Jewish nation by building an independent state; the social emancipation of the working class through a socialist system; and the personal emancipation of women through legal equality and social recognition. This approach did not represent the value system of the entire population—neither in the Jewish nor in the Arab sector. It was an elite ideology, propagated by select groups that acquired leadership roles and consequently were able to shape the legislation of the new state.

At the time of independence, when legislative power went to the elected representatives of this population, the ideological political struggle for the legal emancipation of women was already over. Subsequent legislation gave general validity to tenets of equality which already existed in parts of the society, and these were incorporated in the political platform of the Labor party, which was the governing party during the first thirty years of the state.

Dissimilar and Equal

Besides an egalitarian orientation that categorically rejects the ascriptive criterion, there runs a parallel trend in Israel that recognizes sex differentiation as a legitimate basis for differential treatment. These "ascriptive" laws have a protective tendency, their rationale being the assumption that women are more vulnerable than men due to their biological attributes, hence formal equality based on assumptions of complete similarity results in discrimination. The gender-specific laws contain protections that can be interpreted as restrictive, stereotyped, or privileged, depending on one's value premises.

The Defense Service Act is an example of restrictive protection: women serve two years in the military while men serve three; they perform different types of training and service; married women, pregnant women, and mothers are exempt from service; marriage of women during service automatically discontinues further military obligations, while men have yearly reserve duties to the age of 55.

Another example of the same type is the Employment of Women Law, which empowers the minister of labor to restrict the types of work in which women may be employed since "there are activities liable to be especially injurious to the health of women." The act also forbids women to work on nightshifts, a restriction which is much criticized, especially in view of many exemptions permitted in female occupations. The parliamentary majority opposing the repeal of this law used stereotypic justifications such as nightshifts being detrimental to family life and mothers not sleeping after working nightshifts. The number of women actually affected is very small, thus it seems that the symbolic importance of maintaining the stereotypic approach is greater than the effective application of the restriction.

Pregnancy and motherhood are surrounded by a protective fence of rights. A pregnant employee is allowed to be absent from work upon her doctor's recommendation, and she is permitted a shorter workday without loss of income. The law also guarantees that a woman's job be held for her while absent due to childbirth, and it is illegal to dismiss a woman on maternity leave. A pregnant woman is granted a total of twelve weeks paid leave of which a minimum of three weeks must be taken after the child's birth. The Employment Severance Compensation Law assures a woman pay if she resigns from her job within nine months of giving birth or of adopting a child who is not yet nine months of age, if her resignation is to care for her child.

The rationale for these rights is a combination of the general welfare ideology of collective responsibility for the health and well-being of the individual as expressed in compulsory health measures and the idea that equality is safeguarded by unequal treatment for dissimilar needs. Nevertheless, there are also strong stereotypic elements, such as the coercive aspect of maternity leave beyond the medically prescribed time, or the child care leave granted only to women and not to men.

In some instances the protective restrictions produce peculiar results, as in the case of retirement age. There is no universal mandatory age of retirement but there are three patterns: in the public service, 65 is the age of retirement for both sexes; in academic institutions, retirement age is 68 for academic personnel; trade union collective agreements set the age of retirement at 60 for women, at 65 for men. This discriminatory practice was established by the socialist Histadrut (General Federation of Labor), which claimed it to be a privilege desired by women. Recently the Histadrut leadership was persuaded that restriction of choice is not a privilege and started to replace the old formula with a new policy of flexible retirement age for both sexes.

The National Insurance Act follows the former Histadrut pattern and defines 60 and 65 years as the ages of female or male eligibility for Old Age Benefits. Old age insurance is a sort of intermediate solution insofar as it is obligatory for employed men and women, while it is voluntary for homemakers. The position accorded to the homemaker role is a test problem, the dispute being whether she is a "working woman" and whether home and children are her "business" alone or are common to both spouses. The response to these questions is not clear. Housewives are now included in the work-accident insurance plan, and fees in child care centers run by women's organizations and subsidized by the government are progressively correlated to the mother's income. There also is a lobby of women demanding that the wages of household help should be deductible from the income tax of an employed wife. These facts suggest that homemaking and child care are considered to be the business of women. At the same time, alimony and maintenance rights are becoming more symmetrical.

Dissimilar and Unequal

The peculiarity of the Israeli legal system is its duality. Parallel to the secular system, there is the system of religious jurisdiction. The two systems are not combined but act as separate, partially autonomous structures. The authority of the two systems is divided according to institutional areas, and there are far-reaching differences, even contradictions, between the two systems. The religious laws are recognized regulations of family and personal status. The authority of the religious jurisdiction in these matters was given universal legal basis by the secular legislature. The secular legislation is universalistic and egalitarian. Its legitimation is secular-legal, hence it is changeable.

The religious system is particularistic and nonegalitarian. It draws legitimacy by virtue of its sanctity and tradition; in principle it is unchangeable. The recognition of the legal authority of the religious traditions results in the parallel validity of several legal systems. There are fourteen recognized denominations in Israel each having its own legal system, courts, procedures, and legal experts. The major denominations are the Jewish, in certain aspects having the status of "state religion"; the Moslem (mainly the Sunni branch); the Druse; several Christian denominations; Samaritans; and Karaites. The primacy of the secular laws is recognized, and since they do not include *expressis verbis* limitations, they have more general legal validity than the religious laws.

The religious authorities, while accepting the legal status proffered them, do not accept the idea of secular primacy. This conflict is particularly relevant to the question of the status of women. The secular law proclaims equality of status of the male and the female, while the religious systems are patriarchal. The operational problem is whether women's status is relevant to the "principle of universal equality" or to "freedom of worship and tradition."

The dual legal system has considerable political clout. Although the majority of the Israeli population is composed of nonobservant or only mildly religious Jews, small religious parties often have a decisive role in determining the government leadership and can use their position to influence secular policies. As a result, some crucial aspects of the position of women have come under attack.

One of the most important of these issues is the compulsory draft of women, which has been controversial since the establishment of the state. The solution was acceptance of a modified concept of the conscientious objector: exemption from compulsory draft of Arabs, religious students, and young women who declare that army service is not compatible with their religious way of life. The definition of a "religious way of life" was vague and could be extended on demand. Under the Labor government, eligibility was based on a test of religious knowledge, a signed declaration of observance of specified norms, and an interview with the draft exemption committee. Under the subsequent Likud government the procedure became much simpler and vaguer with no tests, definitions, or personal interviews. This exemption of women from army service has had far-reaching consequences for the self-image and the behavior of young women in all spheres of life and specifically in the labor market.

The analysis has thus far been confined to the level of formalized values as expressed by the legal system. It was shown that the legal universe contains two contradictory systems: the modern secular and the traditional religious. The patterns of traditionalism and modernity observable on the legal level are paralleled by a traditional-modern continuum along which various groups of population can be ordered.

Traditional versus Modern

Israeli society is multicultural and the attitudes and norms relevant to behavior are influenced by many groups. Besides the formal value system there are three variables that consistently influence the position of women in the labor market. The first is the general cultural background of values, norms, and social customs which appear as a continuum from traditionalism represented by the rural Arab society to extreme modernity represented by urban native-born Israelis, and immigrants from Western Europe and the United States. In between are immigrant groups originating in Eastern Europe and South America who tend towards the modern pole and immigrants from Islamic countries who tend towards the traditional pole.

Rural-urban differentiation is the second variable. This in its obvious form of town versus farm has less importance in Israel than in many other countries, because only about 14 percent of the population live in rural areas and only about 5 percent work in agriculture. The rural population is highly differentiated. Many Jewish and Arab villages are similar to traditional peasant societies; yet beside them resides a large farm population organized in socialist cooperative and collective settlements based on modern egalitarian ideas. In these cases, the type of organization is a stronger factor in determining the culture and the institutional structure of the social unit than the environmental factor. A third dimension is religion and ideology, both in their cultural aspects as belief systems and in their social-institutional aspects.

These three variables are less than perfectly correlated. Religiosity heightens the level of traditionality; membership in a kibbutz strengthens modernity. Women from Eastern European communist countries show an interesting mixture of traditional attitudes and modern behavior. The traditional-modern scale is significantly correlated with demographic characteristics such as age of marriage, number of children, years of schooling, and rate of labor market activity.

Women in the more traditional groups are characterized by fewer years of schooling, lower age of marriage, higher rates of fertility, and lower rates of participation in the labor market. In the younger generation, there is a marked tendency of convergence of all these demographic characteristics, but the differences are still significant.

In both modern and traditional groups there has been a dramatic decrease in the work participation of the younger age groups.[4] During the last decade, the rate of participation of young males in the 18 to 24 year age group decreased from 46 percent to 40 percent, and that of women of the same ages fell from 46 percent to 38 percent.

4. The following statistics are from the Statistical Abstract of Israel (Jerusalem: Central Bureau of Statistics, 1983).

The main reason for this trend is the rapid increase in the level of education of the population. The peak of female labor force participation is in the 25 to 44 year age group, 54 percent of whom are in the labor market compared to 89 percent of the males.

The correlation between age and labor market activity varies with education. Among the women there are two critical points in this correlation. The group with only elementary education (less than nine years) is "low participator—about 20 percent," although they show a tendency to late entry into the labor market after their childbearing years. The high school educated have a higher rate of participation (40 percent to 65 percent) and longer careers—from the age of 18 until age 54. Women who have achieved higher education have nearly the same pattern of occupational behavior as men; 80 percent to 90 percent of them are in the labor market and 65 percent until the age of 64. Obviously, the careers of women have been affected by collective agreements which impose retirement at the age of 60. Now that a more flexible retirement pattern is being tried by the trade union, it can be expected that in this group the male and female patterns of retirement will be even more alike.

The majority of employed women are married and mothers. The number of children and the age of the youngest child are significant factors in reduced participation in the labor force. Sixty percent of Jewish women with one child are working outside their homes compared with only 27 percent of mothers of four or more children. Having more than four children is correlated with other facets of traditionality like low educational attainment, low income, strong religiosity, and patriarchal family systems.

Women are concentrated in clerical and administrative jobs (31 percent), professional and technical jobs (24 percent), and the services (18 percent). Males are mainly blue-collar (36 percent) and clerical workers (11 percent). Similar ratios of men and women are in scientific and academic jobs (8.5 percent of the male and 8 percent of the female labor force). Many Israeli women prefer part-time work (41 percent), about 36 percent of whom give family responsibilities as the reason for this choice. Undoubtedly, part-time work deters promotion and restricts the choice of occupation. The dilemma between career orientation and the relative comfort of part-time work is not alien to the majority of the working women.[5]

---

5. Anita Griffel and Haim Kaufman, *Part-time Work and Women: The Case of Israeli Nurses* (Hebrew University of Jerusalem, Work and Welfare Research Institute, 1977).

As in many other countries, Israeli women tend to earn less than men. Woman's average hourly pay is 80 percent of the male average.[6] This is true not only in general but also in specific sectors such as the civil service and industry. There has been no definitive explanation of the reasons for the income differential. A study of the civil service, with a large percentage of women employees, shows the women are not deficient in human capital: at each rank they are better educated than their male colleagues; have only slightly less seniority; and generally are employed continuously. Some of the difference stems from the definition of their jobs and their ranking, from differential fringe benefits, and probably a combination of several other factors.[7]

Several studies have probed the attitudes of women toward work outside their homes.[8] The findings show that women rank family interests higher than career interests. Even in the kibbutz, which is a strongly work-oriented community, work is less central in the lives of women than in the lives of men. Israeli society has strong family values which are maintained among both those with traditional and those with modern orientations. While norms of behavior, the structure of the family, and its position in the community vary according to the level of traditionality, the common denominator is the valuation of the family on both the collective and the individual level. Because of this general orientation, societal organization is insufficiently prepared to cope with the modern pattern of dual-career families. The majority of women, even in the most egalitarian, modern families, see their commitment to their families as stronger than that of their husbands. Many employers recognize this sentiment as part of the characteristics of the female labor force, but because they need women workers, they try to cope by establishing day care centers and holiday camps and are seeking additional ways of integrating family and work commitment.

The demographic data point out that variations due to cultural factors are decreasing as the society moves toward a standard that re-

---

6. Dafna Nundi Israeli, "Israeli Women in the Work Force," *Jerusalem Quarterly* 27 (Spring 1983):58–80.

7. Linda Efroni, *Promotion and Wages of Women in the Israel Civil Service*, Ph.D. thesis, Hebrew University, 1980 (Hebrew).

8. Rivka Bar-Yosef, Ann Bloom, and Zvia Levi, *Perception of Women's Roles among Seventeen-Year-Old Girls* (Institute for Work and Welfare, Hebrew University of Jerusalem, 1976); Bilha Mannheim, *Job Satisfaction, Work Role Centrality and Work Place Preference of Male and Female Industrial Workers* (Haifa: Technion, Israel Institute of Technology, 1981).

sembles the modern "Western" mode in educational and occupational areas but is more familial with respect to age at marriage and fertility. The education of girls does not differ from that of the boys, and education is the great modernizing factor.

Women who formerly had a strong egalitarian orientation lately have been developing more of an identification with the characteristic feminine role of homemaker and mother. They take equality for granted but they seek recognition for a life style that integrates the feminine role with a societal (political, occupational) role. They do not try to enter every type of occupation and often prefer typical women's jobs. The feminization of the self-image of women is especially evident in collective settlements where it leads to changes in the life style of the community.[9]

The modernization of the traditional image in Israel mainly affects Moslem women and Jewish women from Moslem countries, both raised in groups in which the traditional image of women emphasizes extreme inequality between the sexes. Their dominant role has been placed in the home and in the family. This image is changing slowly. In urban areas, younger women in these groups have developed a new sort of intermediate pattern that is more family oriented and less egalitarian than the so-called modern image, but allows for greater autonomy and responsibility than has been traditional. While these women do not show a strong orientation toward occupational roles, they are ready to work in order to raise their standard of living. Many of them are "target workers" who intend to earn money in order to buy a home, a car, a vacation, or an education for their children. They usually do not see themselves as "earners" responsible for family support, and the "targets" used to legitimate their work roles typically are tied to modern consumption goods. Women in rural Moslem areas have been slower to accept change, but even there the feminine image is changing.

The norms of sex equality are being slowly established among more traditional groups at the same time that new patterns are arising influenced by the recent welfare ideology of differential treatment according to specific needs and by the feminization of the role image of modern elements in the population. This seems to be leading toward

9. Uri Leviatan, "Why Is Work Less Central for Women," in *Sexual Equality: The Israeli Kibbutz Tests the Theories*, M. Pagli et al., eds. (Norwood, Pa.: Norwood Editions, 1983), 174–205.

the strengthening of the "dissimilar and equal" pattern, which protects the biologically and socially prescribed feminine roles.

At present it is difficult to predict the form of the new pattern or the time it will take to overcome existing legal and cultural diversity, assuming that tendencies toward homogeneity are powerful and will affect each institution and ethnic-cultural group with the same intensity. It may well be that new plural patterns are emerging which are basically redefinitions of the former traditional-modern continuum.

Discussion

Women on the Kibbutz

Although Israelis living on a kibbutz constitute only 4 percent of the population, they are often seen as representing all of Israel; they do not. Another misconception is that the kibbutz movement was founded on a completely egalitarian basis with respect to the sexes. This misconception arose because of the complete abolition of the family as the consuming unit on the kibbutz, a move intended to free women for other pursuits. What really happened was that all the communal domestic services, the most important of which is child care, became the virtually exclusive preserve of women. It is not considered appropriate for a man on a kibbutz to perform any kind of work involving small children. Some men may devote a little time to teaching high school students, but nobody younger. This has resulted in maximum occupational segregation on the kibbutz. One lesson from the kibbutz experience is that, if men are not drawn into child care occupations, women have to do those jobs and there is no reduction in sex inequality.

Occupational segregation by sex is a major Israeli social problem because it has been used as a shield for sex discrimination. Under the mantle of segregation, the law has been circumvented again and again. On the kibbutz where nobody is paid a wage or salary and, technically, everybody has the same standard of living, there actually is great inequality in the area of work. There is a narrower range of occupations open to kibbutzim than to people in the rest of Israel. The challenging jobs that carry prestige on the outside are comparatively few and are jealously guarded by men. Quite consciously, the men relegate the lesser tasks to women. I know of cases where groups of young men have cooperated in attempts to oust young women from their jobs as technicians.

The kibbutz is no longer exclusively an agricultural society; a large part of its income comes from industry. In what could be important experiments, factories are being operated in combination with agriculture in these small communities. From the point of view of women, however, these industrial experiments have been less than successful because they have not employed women in technical or managerial jobs. In fact, in terms of opportunities for women, agriculture has been somewhat more open than the new experiments with industry. (Judith Buber Agassi)

Opportunity Structure

I undertook a comparative study of men and women in three low-level service occupations in Israel, which showed a higher incidence of promotion for men. Some employers I interviewed acknowledged that the lack of opportunities for promotion is particularly acute for women. A store manager who said he had a policy that women who work part time are not eligible for promotion admitted that it was "arbitrary" but was policy nonetheless. Since the majority of saleswomen in Israel work part time, that is, a six-hour day, this makes it possible for all promotions of salespeople to supervisors or managers to go to men. I believe we need to study the issue of part-time work and eligibility for promotion, even in low-status occupations. (Judith Buber Agassi)

I am skeptical of findings that suggest that women don't care about promotion. If they don't care, this may be because the chances are so slim that women will be promoted that they are resigned to that reality. (Barbara Bergmann)

It is nowhere written that everybody has to aim for advancement, that "success" is the only value worth striving for. There are women—and men—who have many interests outside their work; they find their challenges there rather than in competing for advancement. This comes as a shock to people at the top of the occupational hierarchy, but it is true. Studies done in France, England, and elsewhere suggest that this is not just an Israeli phenomenon: some workers everywhere have alternative interests that absorb them more than their jobs. There is a decrease in the number of workers of both sexes who are willing to work overtime. When we talk of reducing the workday, we may be ahead of ourselves. We need to think about the need to reduce the necessity for working overtime. In some occupations, willingness to work overtime is directly linked to promotion. Women are said to be ineligible for promotion because "they always want to run home at four o'clock." (Rivka Bar-Yosef)

Working Hours
I favor the six-hour working day, across the board, even if the result might be that only an idealistic minority of parents will really be doing equal parenting. (Judith Buber Agassi) This might help the demographic problem of supporting the elderly. (Marion Janjic)

I believe that the workday has become rigidified because of the need for a "family wage." However, given that a high proportion of families now have two earners, the need for one earner to work a long week has been diminished. I think feminists should call for proportional reduction in hours and proportional reduction in wages, even if the unions don't favor this. (Barbara Bergmann) I don't believe that unions will advocate a reduction in weekly hours of work but they will favor a reduction in the number of hours worked per day. (Marion Janjic)

Childbirth
We must work to counteract the enormous public pressure on young women in Israel to be married and have a first child by age 25. Traditionalism, familialism, chauvinism, and militarism act together in telling young women, "It is your duty to keep the home fires burning and to replenish the Israeli population." Young women need to be supported and helped to recognize that they need their own identities, their own education, and their own life work before they get into the family bind. (Judith Buber Agassi)

7.
Low-Income Countries
Hanna Papanek

MY SPECIAL INTEREST is in the development of an analytical framework that will encompass patterns of female labor utilization at various levels of national income and in various types of economic, social, and political organization. Given the huge problems faced by low-income countries, why and how does women's work even matter? I believe that researchers and policymakers have erred in not paying more attention to major shifts in female labor utilization that have occurred in these countries over the past thirty years. These shifts are a key feature in the process of class differentiation and social mobility.

Let me begin with some indicators: In the United States the adult literacy rate in 1981 was close to 100 percent and the annual per capita income was $12,820. In the same year, in Bangladesh, the literacy rate was 26 percent and the average annual income, $140; in India the literacy rate was 36 percent and the annual income, $260; Egypt had a literacy rate of 44 percent and an annual income of $650; and Yugoslavia had a literacy rate of 85 percent and an annual income of $2,790. Moreover, while 11 percent of the enumerated labor force in Bangladesh works in industry and 74 percent in agriculture, in the United States 32 percent works in industry, 66 percent in services, and 2 percent in agriculture. These figures include both male and female enumerated workers.

These statistics suggest the range of conditions that analyses of female labor utilization must cover. No simplistic general theory can

---

Further discussion of these ideas can be found in Hanna Papanek's articles, "Class and Gender in Education-Employment Linkages," *Comparative Education Review*, forthcoming 1985, and *Soziale Welt* (Goettingen) 35 (1984), Heft 1/2 (in German).

encompass such diversity. Additionally, I find that a feminist perspective is indispensable to such an analysis. In the present case, this means broadly defining "women's work" to include activities paid for in cash or in kind, unpaid family labor, and other work I call "family status production." Family status production includes those tasks in which women invest time, effort, and learned skills to enhance the competitive advantage of the family and its wage earners, now or in the future. Since the rewards of status production are indirect and often deferred, the family must control enough resources to enable it to deploy its female labor in work that has no immediate payoff.

The data on several low-income nations show a clear bifurcation in female labor force participation, largely based on shifts in the demand for female labor, with the demand for educated women having risen sharply in recent years and that for uneducated women having declined. Family strategies for the utilization of female labor have also changed, partly in response to changes in demand, partly as a result of other factors. Poor families, always dependent on women's and children's work because they have only labor to sell, have lost ground as technology displaces women from traditional occupations. Middle-class families, on the other hand, can afford to educate daughters as well as sons. Now that newly "respectable" jobs are available to women with high school educations in the growing modern sectors of these economies, middle-class families are encouraging daughters to seek paid work even though this was not "respectable" in the past. The occupations these young women enter on the basis of their higher education are not only education-dependent but also rapidly become feminized. In low-income as in industrialized societies, the range of occupations available to women is typically much narrower than that available to men.

As a result of these opposing shifts in the utilization of women's labor, not only have class differences widened, but the place of women in the process of class differentiation and social mobility has become more salient. One crucial element in these changes is formal education. In these countries, however, with their low rates of adult literacy, formal schooling is not a universally accessible means of social and geographic mobility. The barriers to educational access are high for those who are poor, rural, and female.

Let me begin with the example of Egypt. (The statistics available for many of these countries are suspect, but they constitute the best evidence we have.) Egypt's measured female labor force has been transformed in the last twenty years by a great influx of high school and university educated women. Although about 80 percent of Egypt's adult females are illiterate and only about 60 percent of its young girls were enrolled in primary school in 1980, employers increasingly have been asking for educational prerequisites and certificates, even for industrial employment. In previous generations, industrial employment for women, although small, was the preserve of wives and daughters of industrial workers, many of whom lived in housing areas adjacent to their jobs. Today something important has happened: jobs that were previously open mostly to illiterate women are reserved for people who have nine or ten years of education.

In 1976, according to Egypt's Census of Population, 47 percent of all the women reported as "economically active" had high school or university educations—a huge proportion for a country in which only 5 percent of the female population over 10 years of age has attained these levels of schooling. This means that nearly half the measured female work force is drawn from a tiny sector of the population. We also know that many highly educated women still come from the middle- and upper-income groups. What has happened to uneducated Egyptian women? They almost certainly have not stopped working and earning, because their families need the income. Instead of having regular jobs with predictable earnings, as some of them did before, a much larger number of them are now working at the margins of the economy in the informal sector, often under illegal working conditions at illegally low wages. Some women are even reported to be "renting" steady jobs from those who legally hold them, doing the work but collecting only a fraction of the wage, perhaps plus tips.

A reported rise in male and female dropout rates from Egyptian primary schools may be due to the fact that as the earnings of adult women decrease, more children must work and earn. Because of spot shortages of skilled male workers, who emigrate to high paying jobs in the Gulf states, young boys are being hired as low-paid "apprentices" in jobs defined as being "men's work."

Proceeding to developments in India, we find that there has been an overall decline in the measured female labor force over at least the last twenty years from 23 percent of the female population in 1951 to 12 percent in 1971. Indian analysts attribute the decline to the reduced demand for unskilled labor, the introduction of technological innovations, a declining share of household industries, and a reduced reliance on intermediate marketing systems. Expanded female employment occurred in occupations requiring educational preparation, particularly technical and professional jobs. In India as in Egypt, educational credentials are increasingly required for employment. But because the poor, uneducated population of India is so enormous in relation to the very small educated sector, an increase in female participation in professional jobs does not begin to offset the sharp decline in women's paid employment in so-called unskilled jobs that require little or no formal schooling.

In Bangladesh, the chance of a woman's becoming highly educated is also very small. In the 1970s, only 5 percent of rural females aged 15 to 19 were attending school compared with 20 percent of urban girls of similar ages. Of rural boys in that age group, 30 percent were in school; of urban boys, 40 percent. Investment in female education in Bangladesh is a high risk effort, which a family can take only when it can afford it. The chances that a girl growing up in an isolated village will become a doctor are so remote that a family would very, very seldom invest in her education beyond the required few years of primary school, if that.

Throughout South and Southeast Asia, as well as in Egypt, women qualify for modern sector employment mainly through high school and university educations. But achieving this level of education is a *mark* of family status, and usually not an effective means of improving family status. While some young men from poor village families may eventually make it through high school and university, often with the help of a wealthy patron to whom the boy is then indebted, this is very rare for young women. Even though education is free and supposed to be universally available, women from poor families are not likely to become highly educated. Only when a family has made it up the social ladder, especially if it has moved to the city, will daughters enter higher education.

There are considerable variations among countries and within each nation, however. To take the example of Bangladesh, for every three female university students in the country as a whole, there are one hundred males, but in the country's top university, located in the capital city, fully 25 percent of the student body is female and there are some female professors. In other words, while low-income countries can boast of some extremely highly educated women—and have highly visible women in positions of political power and in the professions—the *number* of highly educated and professionally active women is very small in comparison with the total population. This is clearly related to the fact that the size of the middle and upper classes in these countries is also very small.

Women's economic activities in low-income countries are proportionately more important in poor families than among higher income groups. Labor force statistics may be especially misleading on this point because poor people are more likely to be working in unrecorded occupations and in poorly studied parts of the economy. Where people have only their labor to sell, most members of a household, including women and children, must work and earn to survive. Where family households control other resources besides labor, some persons—usually adult women and female children—withdraw from wage labor.

Evidence from Indonesia strongly suggests that women's economic contribution is proportionately much more important at the lower end of the socioeconomic ladder. Among landless workers, women and men make approximately equal contributions in terms of time worked for pay. At a higher level, where families have a surplus production of rice which can be sold, women contribute little cash or none, but many more hours of unpaid work.

It must be emphasized that to be a housewife and *only* a housewife is something many women in many low-income countries devoutly desire. It is a mark of economic progress and family status. While studies of industrialized societies suggest that paid employment is important to women's self-esteem and feelings of autonomy, much of the population of the world lives in societies where this is not true.

As noted earlier, the definition of "working woman" has to be reexamined when we study low-income countries. My own belief is that housewives and mothers are "working women" whether they have paying jobs or not. Consider the rural women of Bangladesh who spend about 40 percent of their time in secondary processing of agricultural crops, in animal care, and in the preparation of food for sale, yet none of this work is currently counted in that country's labor force statistics. I believe that in all countries where there is a large agricultural sector, the work output of women is high but it may be entirely invisible. This is especially true in societies where women are in purdah, that is, secluded from the eyes of men outside their own families or otherwise limited in their contacts with men. These women usually work hard, especially in rural families engaged in agriculture, but since their work is carried out within the homestead, it tends not to be counted by census takers.

It is interesting to consider whether we should count as work those activities that people themselves consider simply "being a good wife" and that sociologists think of as being "part of the wifely role." I think these terms are evasions and that feminist scholarship must direct attention to defining and measuring women's work in all sorts of innovative ways, not only to broaden its own research horizons but also to develop a better understanding of the place of women's work in the process of change and development. Furthermore, claims for greater equality for women in the work force depend on making a strong and accurate case for both obvious and hidden labor contributions.

My concept of "family status production" by women explains the persistent significance of many kinds of work that women do, often in preference to paid work. Their choices in this respect show that women's opportunity costs are not zero, even though in the terminology of economists or labor statisticians, they are "not working." Family status production includes those activities by which women provide unpaid support, often indispensable, for the paid work of men and for the schoolwork of children. In Japan, as is well known, and to a lesser extent in a great many other countries, women work very hard at tutoring children and motivating them to do well in school and on the job. This is a crucial ingredient in the family strategies of the upwardly mobile middle class. These support activities, as in the "two-person career" (e.g., minister and minister's wife), take women's time and effort and require learned skills, criteria by which many people define "work." Yet in the case of women's work at status production, rewards for work are indirect (improving men's competitive advantage) and delayed (until children are grown).

Families able to invest women's time in status production must have two things: first, the resources required to divert women from wage labor; and second, some realistic sense that upward mobility is both possible and desirable. Being able to allocate women's labor to status production may be a much more profitable strategy, from the family's point of view, than having them work for low wages often accompanied by loss of face.

Other activities I include under women's status production are collecting and disseminating information in the community (status politics), participating in religious rituals required to maintain status in many societies, and arranging advantageous marriages for their children. All of these activities may pay off in enhanced status for the family; hence, they have significant economic consequences.

I think of the production of family status as real *work*, in a way that most sociologists and economists do not. This concept is particularly relevant to societies where the family as a collectivity is responsible for its joint strategies of advancement and survival, where the land is owned by a family as a collectivity. Increasingly, some of this collectively owned property or its rent is directly transferred to an individual in another form—as advanced education. This has tremendously important consequences, especially for women. A woman with advanced education and professional employment, such as a doctor, usually has considerable control over her options. Contrast her situation with that of a woman living in a large family dependent on income from land. In the latter circumstances, the woman may have very little to say about the pattern of labor allocation in the family. Since she is entirely dependent on the family for survival, she has few alternatives to doing what she must.

In other words, women whose labor takes the form of status production may belong to families that are highly respected and have high status in their communities, while women who do wage labor are at the bottom of the social hierarchy. Poor female wage earners may have much more influence than richer women on how to dispose of the little income the family has, but the family as a whole is powerless. Yet, while women who belong to middle- and upper-class families partake to some extent of the status and power of their families, they may have less decision-making power within the family than poorer women. These distinctions have to be carefully drawn so that we do not equate "working" with women's power and "non-working" (a really meaningless term) with lack of power.

Some people say that middle-class and lower-middle-class families are now starting to encourage their daughters to enter paid jobs because the middle class in low-income countries is in an economic squeeze. I do not find this argument entirely persuasive. The real income of middle-class families in these parts of the world probably has not declined. What has changed are their aspirations, that is, "the contents of the status basket"—those consumer items and styles of life that mark a family as belonging to a particular status level in its community or reference group. In part, this is related to the growing availability of consumer goods even in very poor countries. In part, these changes reflect changes in social and political relations.

Although the changing role of women in both education and employment in these countries has not been *primarily* due to changes in political consciousness, gender differences are gaining a new importance in social transformations in these societies. The focus that governments and international agencies have placed on "women and development" is the *result* and not the *cause* of the shift in female labor utilization. Only after the shift caught the attention of policymakers, came political mobilization and changes in the investment policies of bilateral and international development assistance agencies, and the process has snowballed.

In conclusion, let me stress the importance of identifying the various trends in female labor force participation in low-income countries that become clear only when one factors in differences in education, class background, and mobility strategies. In these countries where labor force statistics are often unreliable, it is crucial to the analysis of women's work to include their activities in the informal sector, at the margins of the economy. The development of innovative concepts and new theoretical frameworks that will enable us to transform the study of women's work so that it has more relevance to the totality of women's lives is the prerequisite to achieving more equality.

Discussion

Bangladesh

In an underdeveloped state in the third world, there are simply not enough resources to offer education or employment to all women. In Bangladesh, there has been a concerted effort to be sure that women are included as recipients of extension education. All the extension agents were men so there was an attempt to recruit women agents. But then it was decided that it would be unsuitable to have women agents roaming the countryside so they confined women agents' work to the cities.

While in Bangladesh, I visited a potters' village and was surprised to find that some villagers weren't sending their children to the nicely equipped school there. One mother explained that in school her child would not learn pottery skills but might learn how to read. If he learned to make pottery, he would have something usable on the labor exchange; reading would only prepare him for the lowest level job in the very small civil service sector. People obviously are making rational choices about the kind of training that is useful to them. (Shelley Feldman)

Ghana

Foreign aid can have an adverse effect on women. An example is American aid to Ghana, where women are cocoa farmers. An American analysis of needs there resulted in only men being given scientific training in farming, thus cutting women off from possible improvements in their traditional occupation. (Margaret Feldman)

Singapore

Shifts in demand change women's work. In Singapore, women with a little education have tended to enter capital intensive, foreign-owned industries such as electronics, while those with less education have entered textile factories paying even lower wages. Women's education determines much about their lives. The textile workers tend to drop out of the work force at marriage and can never get back in. The electronics workers, in contrast, are in demand even if married, because of their experience. As a result, women's work sharpens the difference between social classes in Singapore. This may well be taking place in South Korea and Taiwan as well. (Janet Salaff)

8.
Great Britain
Emma MacLennan and Nickie Fonda

*If the good Lord had intended us all having equal rights to
go out to work and to behave equally, you know he really
wouldn't have created man and woman.*
> —Rt. Hon. Patrick Jenkin, M.P.,
> Secretary of State for Social Services

LABOR MARKET POLICY and its effect upon women can be evalu-
ated only in light of the goals one wants to achieve and in terms of
one's vision of the respective roles of men and women. The foregoing
comment of Patrick Jenkin on the BBC "Man Alive" program in
1979 leaves little room for active intervention in the labor market in
order to promote women's employment or to encourage them to
learn nontraditional skills. A successful set of policies, from Mr. Jenkin's point of view, might instead promote the work of women in the
home, as housewives and mothers. Indeed, Mr. Jenkin has been out-
spoken in his concern for "latchkey kids."

Our evaluation of labor market policy in Britain is based on
somewhat different criteria. Although in the short term the success of
any measure must be judged by what is achievable within given constraints, we, unlike Mr. Jenkin, do not see any constraints inherent in
the nature of men and women themselves. The nature of inequality,
however, places very real constraints on the achievement of sex equality. If women fulfill a certain role in the labor market, they must either be replaced by other disadvantaged groups or the dynamics of
the labor market must be transformed. The first, in our view, solves
nothing; the second takes time.

It is necessary, therefore, to have a clear idea of one's long-term
goals. Our aims are fivefold: (1) to enable women and men as far as

possible to pursue their desired careers, with respect to both the type of work chosen and the life-cycle pattern of employment; (2) to desegregate the jobs done by men and women in and outside the home; (3) to assure women the same rewards as men from their participation in the labor market in terms of pay and occupational benefits; (4) to provide women with a fair share of economic and political power and a fair representation within labor organizations and at all levels of government; and (5) to extend the issue of women's equality in the labor market beyond a narrow view of fair competition. Since women work in the lowest paid, least powerful, and most poorly organized sectors of the economy, we see the achievement of greater equality between men and women as part of a desire for a society in which all members participate and are rewarded similarly. Our analysis of the effects of British labor market policy on women's employment must be seen in this context.

In this paper, we examine the main trends in women's employment over the past decade or so and the impact of labor market policies on these trends. We note two distinct policy climates during this period. The first, during the early to mid-1970s, might be described as an era of employee protection. The second, coinciding with the election of a conservative government in 1979 and continuing to the present day, might be described as a period of deregulation. As we shall show, women have made certain gains in both periods almost despite labor market policy, but we are concerned with the longer-term impact of the current policy climate.

1970–79: Equal Pay, Employment Protection, and the Growth of Women's Employment

The 1970s were a growth period for women's employment in Britain. In 1971 women constituted 36 percent of the work force; by 1979 this figure had risen to 41.5 percent. Much of this growth can be accounted for by the increased participation of married women in the labor market. While the economic activity rate for all males dropped by over 3 percent during the 1970s and the rate for nonmarried females aged 16 and over remained more or less stable at 50 percent, the rate for married women increased from 42.3 percent to 49.6 percent in just eight years.[1] This increase in the labor force participation

1. Department of Employment *Gazette*, December 1975, table 5; April 1981, table 4.

TABLE 8.1
Part-time Workers, Great Britain, 1971–83

	1971	1972	1973	1974	1975	1976	1977	1980	1983
Total (000)	21,648	21,650	22,182	22,297	22,213	22,048	22,126	22,008	20,179
Male part-time (000)	584	600	665	689	697	699	681	—[a]	—[a]
Female part-time (000)	2,757	2,877	3,163	3,421	3,551	3,585	3,617	3,726	3,803
Female part-time as percent of total workers	12.7	13.3	14.3	15.3	16.0	16.3	16.3	16.9	18.8
Female part-time as percent of total female workers	33.5	34.5	36.3	38.3	39.5	40.0	40.0	40.6	43.3
Male part-time as percent of total male workers	4.3	4.5	4.9	5.1	5.2	5.3	5.2	—[a]	—[a]
Female part-time in service industries as percent of total female part-time	80.0	81.4	80.9	80.2	82.6	83.7	84.0	85.9	88.9

Source: Department of Employment *Gazette*, July 1979, February 1980, October 1981, October 1983.
[a]Figures unavailable.

rate of married women during the 1970s was not unique to Britain. Throughout its member countries, the OECD points out, "The most profound changes in labour market activity rates relate to women, and in particular married women."[2] What may be unique to Britain is the extent to which the increased participation rate of married women was accompanied by a growth in part-time work; the number of female part-time workers increased by nearly one-third between 1971 and 1979 (table 8.1).

At the same time that women's labor market participation was growing, women's earnings were increasing relative to those of men. Women's gross weekly and hourly earnings improved in relative terms by some 15 percent during the 1970s, achieving a peak in 1976–77 (table 8.2). Moreover, this increase represented an improvement in the female/male earnings ratio which cannot be explained by changes in the industrial, occupational, or age distribution of men and women in employment, or by changes in hours worked.[3]

However, women's employment growth during the 1970s occurred almost entirely in sectors already dominated by female employment. In 1959, the distributive trades and service industries together employed 58.1 percent of the female working population; two

TABLE 8.2
Women's Wages as Percentage of Men's Wages, All Industries, Great Britain, 1970–83

Year	Percentage of Men's Gross Weekly Wages	Percentage of Men's Gross Hourly Wages
1970	54	62
1971	55	63
1972	55	64
1973	55	64
1974	56	65
1975	61	70
1976	64	73
1977	64	73
1978	63	72
1979	62	71
1983	65	72

Source: New Earnings Survey Part A, table 15, April 1979, and Department of Employment *Gazette*, October 1983.

---

2. OECD, *Present and Prospective Employment Situation and the Functioning of Labour Markets* (Paris: OECD, 1982), p. 24.

3. Chiplin et al., "Relative Female Earnings in Great Britain and the Impact of Legislation," in *Women and Low Pay*, ed. P. Sloane (London: Macmillan Press, 1980).

TABLE 8.3
Female Employment in Selected Industries, Great Britain, 1959–83 (in percentage)

Industry (SIC)	1959	1969	1979	1983
Distributive trades	18.3	17.4	16.5	16.6
Insurance, banking, finance and business services	3.8	5.3	6.5	8.0
Professional and scientific services	17.6	22.4	27.1	28.6
Miscellaneous services	13.4	12.6	14.6	16.5
Public administration and defense	5.0	5.6	6.7	6.6
Total	58.1	63.3	71.4	76.3
Females as percent of all workers	34.1	37.2	41.3	43.5

Sources: Department of Employment continuous employment estimates; Department of Employment *Gazette*, March 1975, July 1979, and October 1983.

decades later, this figure had increased to 71.4 percent, most of the increase having taken place in the latter decade (table 8.3). During this period women were not squeezing men out of service sector employment but filling a labor shortage in an expanding public and private service sector. There was little change in occupational segregation of women during this period. In 1979, women remained only 13 percent of employers and managers, 11 percent of professional and scientific workers, 5 percent of foremen, and 9 percent of skilled manual workers. However, the large majority of all junior nonmanual and personal service workers were women, as were nearly half of all semiskilled and unskilled manual workers.

A final major growth area for women during this period was their representation in trade unions. From 1968 to 1978, the total number of female trade union members increased by 36 percent.[4] On the whole, increases in women's representation occurred most markedly in large unions in the public sector, although notable increases also occurred among organizations of shop, engineering, and technical workers. Throughout this period, male trade union membership was also growing and the union density of male workers (i.e., actual membership as a percentage of potential membership) rose from 51.4 percent in 1968 to 63.4 percent in 1979. However, male po-

---

4. J. Hunt and S. Adams, *Women, Work and Trade Union Organization* (London: Workers Educational Association, 1980), p. 14.

tential union membership was decreasing over that period, so that the proportional increase was therefore greater among women. While women had been 20 percent of all union members within the Trades Union Congress in 1968, their proportion had increased to 28.7 percent by 1978.[5]

The 1970s were thus a period of change for women in the labor market in many respects. Women's labor market participation grew substantially during those years, particularly the labor market activity of married women, and there was a rapid growth in part-time working. Both of these areas of work growth were largely due to an expansion of the service sector, in which women's employment had traditionally been concentrated. Another important feature of this period was a rise in women's relative earnings unrelated to any changes in the industrial distribution of women. Finally, women's trade union membership increased both in absolute and relative terms and was accompanied by a new militancy in sectors dominated by female employment, particularly the public sector where low-paid women in nursing, the health services, local authorities, and the school meals service began to make their voices heard.

Two major pieces of legislation directly aimed at women's employment were enacted during the 1970s, and these might account for some of the changing patterns of women's employment. The introduction of the Equal Pay Act in 1970 and the Sex Discrimination Act in 1975 certainly played an important ideological role in that they represented official recognition of principles of equal treatment and opportunities for women in the labor market. In practice, however, the acts could have only a limited effect on women's employment and earnings.

The first of these laws provided for equal pay for men and women employed by the same firm and engaged in the same or broadly similar work. In addition, collective agreements and pay structures were also to be nondiscriminatory. In order to reduce the costs to employers where pay differentials were large, the 1970 act allowed for a five-year "phasing in" period, so that full implementation was not required until 1975.

The Equal Pay Act undeniably made some impact on the relative earnings of women in employment since women's relative earnings increased by some 15 percent during the 1970s, at the same time that

---

5. Ibid.

their employment was expanding.[6] But the legislation appears to have had a one-time effect. The Equal Opportunities Commission (EOC) concluded in 1980,

> that the reality is that women's relative earnings have now stabilized at around 73 percent (of men's earnings) and that they are unlikely to show any further substantial improvement. . . . The Commission is convinced that no further progress can now be made without substantial amendments to the Equal Pay and Sex Discrimination Acts, to enable them to give better effect to Parliament's original intention.[7]

The Equal Pay Act improved women's pay by forcing employers to integrate recognized pay scales in a number of industries but, beyond that, the legislation could not go, because of its nature and because of the prevalence of job segregation. Section 1(2) of the Equal Pay Act allows for a claim of equal pay if the jobs done by men and women are the same or are rated as equivalent under a job evaluation scheme. In most firms, job segregation is such that women and men are not employed in the same work, and not all firms, particularly small ones, use job evaluation. Moreover, in such jobs as typing, nursing, operating a sewing machine, and doing domestic service, the few men who are employed are, on the whole, as lowly paid as their female colleagues. Nor are all women covered by provisions related to collective agreements. According to one estimate, 44.5 percent of full-time women workers fall outside their scope and the proportion among part-time workers is likely to be even higher.[8] The law also contains no provision regarding indirect discrimination in pay whereby employees receive rewards for factors unnecessary to the performance of the job, such as length of service or a willingness to travel for which more males than females qualify.

It was hoped that the Sex Discrimination Act of 1975 would provide some remedy for job segregation by opening up nontraditional areas of work to many more women. Such hopes were also not fully realized. The Sex Discrimination Act made it unlawful to discriminate, directly or indirectly, on the grounds of sex or marital status in offering employment, training, or promotion and in other areas. The act also provided for the establishment of the EOC to monitor and

---

6. H. Neuburger, *Unemployment: Are Wages to Blame?* (London: Low Pay Unit, 1983).

7. Equal Opportunity Commission, *Fifth Annual Report*, 1980, p. 1.

8. A. Mitchell, "The Consequences of the Equal Pay Act," in *Are Low Wages Inevitable?* ed. T. Field (London: Russell Press, 1976).

promote women's equality and in some cases to enforce the legislation. As a result of the act, most forms of overt discrimination in job advertising and recruitment disappeared. In addition, test cases raised public awareness of discrimination against women. But, like the Equal Pay Act, the sex discrimination legislation had only a limited effect on women's employment.

Much of the problem lies in the difficulty of proving discrimination at work. The burden of proof is on the complainant, who is unlikely to have direct evidence of unfair treatment. A second major shortcoming of the act is in its limited aims. For example, there is no requirement that employers or other bodies undertake positive action programs, and even where discrimination in employment is proven, redress is available only for the individual applicant. A court cannot order an employer to review overall employment policies or to show future evidence of nondiscrimination.

Finally, Section 6 of the Sex Discrimination Act exempts all firms employing fewer than six persons, thereby excluding substantial numbers of women from its provisions. In the hotel and catering industry, for example, 38 percent of all firms have fewer than five employees, accounting for 10 percent of all hotel employment.[9] Assuming a proportionate distribution of female employment among smaller firms, this would mean that an estimated 63,000 women are excluded in that industry alone.

Other recent legislation of potential importance to women's employment was the Employment Protection Act of 1975 and the Employment Protection Consolidation Act of 1978. The Employment Protection Act, while not specifically aimed at women, provided protections that gave women in particular greater job security. Foremost among these provisions was a package of maternity rights that included protection against dismissal when pregnant, the right to paid maternity leave, and the right to reinstatement after pregnancy, subject to certain length-of-service qualifications. The act also provided protection against unfair dismissal by an employer. Any full-time employee who had completed at least six months' service with the same employer could apply for compensation and in some cases reinstatement if dismissed without good cause. Among automatically "unfair" reasons for dismissal is pregnancy, so that a woman who is not quali-

---

9. Hotel and Catering Industrial Training Board, *Manpower in the Hotel and Catering Industry,* June 6, 1978.

fied for paid maternity leave on the basis of length of service receives some protection against dismissal.

However, all these employment rights give part-time workers substantially less protection than full-time workers. Where a two-year qualification period applies to maternity rights and six months to unfair dismissal claims for full-time workers, part-timers working between eight and sixteen hours weekly are required to have five years' service with the same employer in order to qualify. Those with a normal workweek of less than eight hours are excluded altogether. These exceptions, as we shall see, may also have been important in influencing the pattern of women's employment.

Apart from the possible role of legislation in trends in British women's employment, other factors influencing change played a part. From the mid-1960s until the end of the 1970s, various incomes policies were in operation both by statute and voluntary agreement between government and unions as part of a social contract. Most of these policies contained some special allowance for low-paid workers. In addition, in 1974–75, the Trades Union Congress set a minimum wage target for negotiations of £30 per week (or two-thirds of average male earnings). This and the £6 flat-rate maximum pay increase allowed by the government in 1975–76 are recognized to have contributed to the peak in women's relative earnings in the mid-1970s. As the majority of low-paid workers are women, policies aimed at reducing low pay are of most benefit to women.

However, the effect of these policies was short-lived and, over the whole period of incomes policy, low-paid workers were not greatly affected. As Gill and Whitty conclude, "The main reason why low-paid women improved their position had nothing to do with 'incomes policy' as such, but was due to the eradication of the 'women's only' rates in most collective agreements during the implementation of the Equal Pay Act."[10]

During the 1970s, part-time workers had become increasingly attractive to employers as a source of labor for a number of reasons. To begin with, relatively full employment in the early 1970s meant that new sources of labor were in demand, particularly in the expanding service sector. Married women, who often sought work on a part-time

---

10. T. Gill and L. Whitty, *Women's Rights in the Workplace* (Harmondsworth: Penguin, 1983), p. 371.

basis due to constraints caused by children, were a potential source of labor to be tapped. Fiscal policy reinforced this trend. In Britain, unemployment insurance and other employee benefits are provided by the state to workers who have made sufficient employee contributions to the National Insurance Fund. In addition to employee contributions, employers must also contribute a percentage of insured employees' pay to the fund, and it is the duty of the employers to administer both contributions. Contributions are required, however, only when earnings are above a certain threshold; once that point is reached, all earnings are taxable. Hence, employers can avoid contributions by taking on part-time staff whose earnings fall below the threshold. As the threshold itself is close to 50 percent of average earnings in many lower paid, unskilled jobs, the trend toward part-time work in these jobs increased as contribution rates rose during the 1970s.

In some cases, trade union recruitment policies influenced the extent of women's union organization. For example, in the early 1970s, the National Union of Public Employees (NUPE) commissioned research into the reasons for the underrepresentation of women among union members, despite a high potential membership. The researchers concluded that this had nothing to do with a lack of interest among women workers but "with the position of women in the wider society and at work," particularly their domestic role.[11] NUPE and other unions set about reorganizing union activities to more easily fit women's needs, such as holding more meetings during worktime or providing crèche facilities. Many unions also set up women's advisory committees, appointed women as national officers, or, like NUPE, reserved seats for women at the executive level. However, other unions, particularly at the local level, were instrumental in blocking women's entry in male preserves of employment or in negotiating redundancy agreements requiring part-time female staff to be the first to go in factory closures.

Two other factors that might be expected to play a role in women's changing work patterns—the provision of child care and the provision of training—were influential in reinforcing the supply of part-time workers in traditional areas of employment during this period. The difficulty of arranging full-time day care for children meant that

---

11. Fryer et al., *Organization and Change in NUPE* (London: NUPE, 1974).

many women were forced to seek work on a part-time basis, while training policy, far from emphasizing nontraditional skills, ensured a pool of ready workers in clerical and commercial work.

The major government training instrument in operation in the 1970s was the Training Opportunities Scheme (TOPS), accounting for some 70 percent of training expenditure by the Manpower Service Commission. In 1978, women were 41 percent of all TOPS trainees, which was roughly proportionate to their representation in employment. However, "insofar as women take part in (TOPS) they do, in the main, choose training for traditional female occupations in the clerical and commercial field."[12] Three-quarters of all women participating in TOPS in 1978 were in clerical and commercial courses, compared to only 4 percent of male participants. On the other hand, the most popular male course of study was in the engineering and automotive field, involving 48 percent of all male trainees; only 2 percent of all women were enrolled in that area. In gross numbers, only 186 out of 40,000 women in 1978 trained in nontraditional manual trades in skill centers.

Thus, while women's labor market participation was increasing during the 1970s, their pattern of segregation into lower-paid, part-time jobs remained largely unchanged (table 8.4). Indeed, the growth of part-time employment meant an increasing casualization of work, as part-timers were less protected by employment legislation. Many who were earning below the lower earnings limit for national insurance contributions escaped the necessity of paying a high proportion of their earnings in insurance, but were thus trapped into low-paid work. Without the necessary contributions, these women were also rendered ineligible to receive unemployment insurance or other state allowances, such as those for sickness or maternity. While these effects of fiscal and legislative policy on women's employment status may have been unintended by governments during the 1970s, in the next period such features of women's employment were to receive official encouragement.

---

12. European Center for the Development of Vocational Training, *Equal Opportunities and Vocational Training* (Berlin: CEDEFOP, 1979), p. 9.

TABLE 8.4
Employment of Women by Occupation, Great Britain, 1975 and 1982

Occupation	1975 (percent women)	1982 (percent women)
Nonmanual		
Management (including general management)	9.7	7.0
Professional and related supporting management	12.4	16.4
Professional and related in education, welfare, and health	63.1	66.6
Literary, artistic, and sports	23.4	27.9
Professional and related in science	7.1	8.5
Managerial (excluding general management)	10.9	14.5
Clerical and related	71.3	77.2
Selling	57.5	59.6
Security and protective services	5.4	7.2
Nonmanual total	48.3	51.4
Manual		
Clerical and related	10.2	12.5
Selling	13.0	17.5
Security and protective services	10.3	19.6
Catering, cleaning, hairdressing, and other personal service	72.1	76.2
Farming	7.3	10.0
Materials processing (excluding metals)	26.9	23.6
Making and repairing (excluding metals)	37.7	34.2
Processing, making, and repairing (including metals and electrical)	5.9	4.4
Painting, repetitive assembly	48.9	46.0
Construction	0.2	0.2
Transport	4.6	4.6
Miscellaneous	6.6	5.2
Manual total	26.0	28.7

Source: EOC, *Seventh Annual Report*, 1983.

1979–83: Deregulation, Casualization, and Free Market Philosophy

In some ways, the period from 1979 to 1983 has been a continuation of trends in women's work patterns established during the 1970s. As a proportion of total employed workers, women employees grew from 41.5 percent in 1979 to 43.2 percent in December 1982.[13] This

---

13. Department of Employment *Gazette*, June 1983, table 1.1, p. 57.

growth has again taken place within the service sector so that by 1982, some 76 percent of all women workers were in this sector compared to just over 71 percent in 1979. At the same time, the proportion of women working part time increased from 40 percent to 43.3 percent—a trend that is projected to continue well into the 1980s. These increases in women's labor force participation, particularly in part-time work, have been attributed to a continued influx of married women into the labor market.

One area in which there has been little progress is women's relative earnings. In 1982, the position had changed very little from the late 1970s, with women earning 73.9 percent of the male gross hourly rate. However, while women's pay has changed little relative to men's, the earnings of both men and women have deteriorated. In 1979, 10 percent of male and 67 percent of female manual workers had earnings below the minimum "decency threshold" for wages recommended by the Council of Europe—68 percent of average male and female earnings. By 1982, these proportions had increased to 17 and 75 percent respectively.[14] Moreover, since 1979 the number of families dependent on Family Income Supplement, a state contribution to low-wage families, has more than doubled.

Unemployment has also risen sharply for both women and men since 1979. From March 1979 to March 1983, female unemployment increased from 3.3 to 8.6 percent, while male unemployment grew from 6.7 to 16.3 percent. The total unemployment rate jumped from 5.3 to 13.1 percent, or from 1.25 million to over 3 million workers.[15] These figures underestimate the extent of female unemployment due to the underregistration of unemployed women ineligible for unemployment insurance. The EOC calculated that at the end of 1982, some 350,000 persons were left out of the official statistics due to underregistration, of whom 75 percent were women.[16] Nevertheless, women remain relatively well protected compared to men largely due to continued growth of the service sector where women predominate and a relative decline of traditional heavy industries, such as steel production, that employ men almost exclusively. These trends have meant that the contribution of women's earnings to family income has become more significant since 1979.

---

14. S. Winyard, *Fair Remuneration* (London: Low Pay Unit, October 1982).
15. Department of Employment *Gazette*, June 1983, Labour Market Data, p. s22.
16. *Guardian* (London), June 24, 1983.

According to the Seventh Annual Report of the EOC one in twelve families currently has a female breadwinner whose earnings are higher than those of her husband; the proportion rises to one in seven when families in which the wife's earnings regularly equal those of her husband are included. In some 400,000 families, the wife is the sole breadwinner due to her husband's unemployment; and of the 12 percent of all families in Britain headed by a single parent, nine out of ten are headed by a woman.[17]

Unemployment may also have had the effect of altering the socioeconomic distribution of male and female occupations (see table 8.4). In 1975 government statistics showed that only 12.4 percent of professional workers supporting management were women; by 1982, the proportion had increased to 16.4 percent, and women's share of managerial jobs, excluding general management, had grown from 10.9 to 14.3 percent. Women also increased their representation among professionals in science and among workers in the arts, in security and protective services, and in agriculture. Yet, at the same time women's share of employment in more traditional sectors was growing—health, education, clerical work, sales, and catering. These changes may be due in part to a movement of female labor into new areas of work, for example junior management in such industries as banking and finance, but a greater influence is likely to have been a reduction in male employment at all skill levels. However, in some traditionally male areas—general management, manual work in manufacturing, processing, and repairing—the proportion of female employment dropped over this period.

Overall, women's employment has grown relative to men's during this period, and women have been relatively protected from unemployment; there has been some growth in women's employment in occupations where they have always been a minority; and the contribution of female earnings to family income has become increasingly important. Despite these developments, recent trends in labor market policy bode ill for women's employment, and in most respects, the period from 1979 to 1983 has not been one of optimism and progress. What gains women have made appear to have been largely a result of the shifts in the distribution of employment caused by declining male sectors rather than a reflection of progressive labor market policy aimed at women.

---

17. MacLennan et al., *Low Pay: Labour's Response* (London: Fabian Society, 1983).

The aim of government policy since 1979 has been to dismantle restrictions on the free working of the labor market as far as possible. Confidential documents leaked to the British press from a secret cabinet committee meeting in 1983 provided a candid record of government thinking. Sir Geoffrey Howe, then Chancellor of the Exchequer, noted to his colleagues that equal pay legislation "prevents employers from restricting pay to what is necessary to secure employees."[18] This distaste for any sort of legislative intervention in the labor market has affected various employment protections of importance to women.

The Employment Act of 1980 was introduced by the government in order to address some of the "burdens and barriers" inappropriate to the conduct of business that had been established under the employment protection acts of the 1970s. The length of service required in order to qualify for protection from unfair dismissal was increased from six months to one year for full-time workers, and, in small firms with no more than twenty employees, the period was extended to two years. According to one estimate, over one-quarter of full-time adult males and more than one-third of adult females have less than two years' service with their current employer, "but the proportions rise to 40 percent of males and nearly half of females in sectors dominated by small firms."[19] Maternity protections were another provision amended by the 1980 act. All firms with fewer than six employees are no longer obligated to reinstate female employees after maternity leave, and, for women who might still be eligible, the procedure to qualify for reinstatement was made more complex and inacccessible.

The Employment Act of 1980 also abolished Schedule 11 of the Employment Protection Act which provided for the compulsory arbitration of wages. Schedule 11 gave legal underpinning to nationally negotiated minimum standards of pay and working conditions but it ran directly contrary to government economic strategy. As expressed by a recently retired head of Prime Minister Thatcher's policy unit, "A rapid fall in real pay is the best hope for reducing unemployment quickly."[20] Any floor on wages was therefore seen as anathema.

Various other wage protections were also targeted for removal. Among these was the system of wages councils. Wages councils are

---

18. *Daily Mirror* (London), May 25, 1983.

19. A. Westrip, "A Study of Research into the Effects of Employment Legislation on Small Firms," Manchester Business School, 1980.

20. John Hoskyns, *The Times* (London), June 1, 1982.

statutory bodies composed of representatives of workers and employers, plus three independent members appointed by government, who
negotiate minimum pay and working conditions in certain low-paying
industries. At present, there are twenty-seven wages councils in Great
Britain covering some 2.7 million workers, of whom three-quarters
are women. Moreover, wages council minimum wages are of much
greater significance to women's than to men's pay in the same industries. On average, the minimum wages are equivalent to 60–75 percent of actual male earnings, and 75–100 percent of female earnings,
in wages council industries. As a proportion of average earnings in
the entire economy, however, the wages council minimum wages are
extremely low, ranging from 25 to 44 percent of average male earnings and from 40 to 64 percent of average female earnings.[21]

The government is prevented from abolishing the wages council
system until after 1985 when an ILO Convention requiring some
form of minimum wage machinery comes up for reratification. In the
meantime, various steps have been taken to make the system less effective. The number of government wage inspectors, whose duty it is
to police and enforce minimum wages, has been cut by one-third,
leaving 119 inspectors to police the wages of nearly 3 million workers
in close to 400,000 establishments. Moreover, attempts at more direct
intervention in the process of minimum wage fixing occurred when
the Secretary of State for Employment wrote to wages councils urging
extreme moderation in pay increases. In the case of the Licensed Residential Establishment and Licensed Restaurant Wages Council, the
minimum wage objected to was £58.80 including tips for adult workers in hotels and restaurants, for a forty-hour workweek excluding
meal breaks. This represented less than 40 percent of average earnings for all adult workers.

One glimmer of hope for women's wages has appeared, however,
in the form of a European Court ruling in July 1982. The court found
that the United Kingdom was in breach of its obligation to ensure
equal pay for men and women and must make better provision for
equal pay for work of equal value. In September 1983, an under-
secretary in the Department of Employment presented an amending
order in Parliament under the European Communities Act of 1972,
thus avoiding the need for an amending act and full parliamentary
examination. Reflecting on the occasion, the political editor of the

---

21. *Who Needs the Wages Councils?* (London: Low Pay Unit, 1983).

Sunday Times argued that the under-secretary had been forced into a push for greater equality which ran contrary to "just about all his primeval instincts. . . . It involves the government in fixing pay. . . . Worst of all, it gives rights to those most risible creatures, working women, just at the time when some Tory thinkers are pondering deeply about how to keep more of them at home."[22]

The opinion of leading counsel examining the proposals for the EOC is that such amendments fall short of compliance with the European Court ruling and were drafted in a way that renders them useless. For example, women covered by job evaluation schemes or other established forms of comparability will be prevented from claiming. The burden of proof for an equal value claim will be switched from the applicant to the employer, who is presently responsible under "like work" claims, while any "material difference" in the jobs being considered will be sufficient to justify differences in pay, unless the applicant can prove that the difference is attributable to sex. Finally, there will be no way that a claimant can challenge the criteria used by "independent experts" called in to assess the case.[23] It may be that the government will be forced to return to the drawing board in future if the European Court again finds Britain in breach of its equal value ruling.

A further restriction on wages targeted for removal by the government was the Fair Wages Resolution (FWR), which, like the wages councils, had been in operation for nearly a century. In order to protect against unfair competition for lucrative government contracts, the FWR required firms under contract to the central government to maintain standards of pay and working conditions which were no less favorable than those of other employees. The resolution, once described by Sir Harold Macmillan as the protector "of the standards of competence and honour of industry as a whole," was abolished on September 21, 1983.

The implications of this action for women's employment are likely to be great because of the interaction of the FWR with another government policy—privatization. Government directives to public sector employers have insisted upon a maximum use of private contracting firms to replace directly employed staff. The areas in which privatization is likely to have its greatest impact are in health care, ca-

---

22. *Sunday Times* (London), July 24, 1983.
23. D. Byrne, "An Act of Inequality," *Low Pay Review*, no. 13 (1983).

tering services, cleaning and laundry services—sectors which employ a large majority of women. Until the abolition of the FWR, few savings in public expenditure could be made through privatization since employers in contracting firms were still required to comply with minimum standards of pay. Now that the resolution has been abolished, the door is open to competition on the basis of low pay. Thus, a dental hospital in Birmingham has been able to replace directly employed cleaning staff earning £2.40 per hour with contracted staff earning only £1.00 per hour. This trend will not only affect women's earnings in contracting firms, but is likely to have repercussions for lower grade, low-paid staff throughout the public sector.

All of these policies have been motivated by an economic philosophy that argues that the greatest stimulus to growth lies in "unfettering" the labor market and reducing labor costs to improve the competitive position of British firms. High unemployment is in fact part of this strategy. Unemployment has stemmed the growth in union membership—between 1979 and 1981 union density dropped by some 8 percent;[24] reduced the bargaining power of labor—a reserve army of over 3 million can be called upon by employers to replace existing staff; tempered demands for improvements in working conditions, so that such goals as the provision of workplace nurseries have been largely forgotten; and served to exacerbate the problem of low pay for both men and women.

One of the groups particularly hard hit by the loss of employment opportunities is young people. In many parts of the country, unemployment levels for school leavers are running at 50 percent or more. In 1983 in response to this situation, the government introduced a new one-year Youth Training Scheme designed for all 16- and 17-year-old school leavers. In keeping with the government's philosophy, however, trainees on the scheme are only being paid £25 a week. The government clearly sees this program as an additional instrument for reducing wages. On the other hand, the scheme does include a commitment to quality and to a minimum of thirteen weeks off-the-job training for all participants. As a result, many young women are likely to gain access to considerably more formal training than they have hitherto so that the consequences of this development are hard to predict.

---

24. G. Bain and R. Price, "Union Growth: Dimensions, Determinants and Destiny" in *Industrial Relations in Britain,* ed. G. Bain (Oxford: Basil Blackwell, 1983), p. 8.

The government's general toleration of high unemployment, however, has had its costs for the exchequer. In 1982, a treasury document estimated that unemployment was costing over £15 billion in the payment of benefits and in lost productive capacity. This was adding considerably to the public sector borrowing requirement and, hence, to the money supply. Other policies therefore have been aimed at reducing these costs of unemployment and cutting public spending.

To help cover the costs of unemployment insurance, employees' national insurance contributions increased from 6.5 percent of earnings in 1979 to 9 percent in 1983. This increase was a further incentive to employers to make use of part-time labor earning below the contribution threshold. At the same time, the real value of the unemployment benefit has been reduced by some 5 percent. Public spending on services has also been cut back in health care, the provision of school meals, and facilities for managing the chronically sick, the elderly, and the disabled. In the guise of "community care," the burden of looking after invalid relatives has fallen again on women. Finally, policies aimed at encouraging part-time, casual forms of employment will in the long run cut the cost of unemployment further. The government's "job-splitting" scheme, for example, pays a subsidy to employers who divide existing full-time jobs into part-time jobs. More women will be earning wages below the national insurance contribution limit and will be ineligible to claim benefits when unemployed.

Although disproportionately affecting the employment levels of male workers due to the rapid decline of the manufacturing sector, government economic strategy has had severe effects on women's employment in other ways. Unexpectedly perhaps, there have been few demands from male workers for the return of women to the home as a means of reducing male unemployment, apparently due to two factors: The relative growth of female employment not only has occurred largely in secondary employment sectors unattractive to men, but has underlined the importance of women's earnings to family income; and the increase in women's union membership and labor militancy in the 1970s has carried over into the 1980s.

During the 1970s, the major preoccupation of the women's movement was child care and social welfare issues, such as the provision of state benefits and services. Many feminists had considered the union movement to be a bastion of male power with little to offer women. However, as more women have joined unions and moved into positions in their research departments or even as executives, the emphasis of the demands of both women and trade unions has changed. Unions, particularly in the public sector, have taken up the issues of low pay, privatization, cuts in social welfare, and reductions in statutory employment rights, at the same time that the women's movement has increasingly turned its attention to the labor market. In 1983 for the first time in its history, the Royal College of Nursing, a very conservative and traditional professional body, issued a statement that its members would be prepared to take strike action in order to defend the health service against further cuts. Such a dramatic reversal in the stance taken by a woman's profession that had always left militancy to men may be a harbinger of things to come.

The past ten to fifteen years in Britain has been a period of growth for women's relative employment and earnings and has seen some desegregation of the jobs that women do. This has occurred largely despite, rather than as a result of, government labor market policies aimed at women. The one exception to this, the Equal Pay Act, appears to have exhausted its impact, although the addition of equal value provisions may improve matters in future. Other policies have been influential although not directly aimed at women, such as those affecting the structure and development of the national insurance system. The irony of the present policy climate in which a distaste for employment protection has been combined with ministerial statements that women would be better off at home is that women have maintained their position in the labor market in face of a relative decline in male employment. Moreover, government encouragement of low wages may well serve to feed this trend. Since there is no assurance that men will take the low-paid, casual, poorly protected jobs that are becoming more prevalent, there may be further gains in women's employment, but gains made on this basis are at best a mixed blessing.

Discussion

I have always pointed to the protection against unfair dismissal as British legislation we should emulate in the United States. It is particularly saddening to hear that one effect of the passage of that law in Britain has been an increase in the extent to which women work part time because employers want to escape the law's requirements. Economist Barbara Bergmann has a thesis that men and women achieve parity in wages only at the very bottom of the wage scale in industry. The evidence presented by MacLennan and Fonda supports that thesis all too well. We also see that the expansion of the public sector is important for women, both because it provides opportunities for their employment and because it provides vital service to them. The emphasis on cutting public services and the privatization concept now favored in Britain bodes ill for women. We have learned that in the United States. (Roberta Till-Retz)

The British government has spent a great deal of money surveying the public and has found that many working-class people acknowledge that things are bad at present. One of their responses is "if we sacrifice, things will get better." The high unemployment has hit the working class harder than it has hit those in better protected sectors. In fact, low-skilled and low-paid workers are six times more likely to be unemployed than are other workers. While the middle class seems to be becoming more self-interested, there are also signs of increased unselfishness.

One survey undertaken in fall 1983 showed that 74 percent of the respondents were willing to pay more taxes so as to be able to do something about poverty in Britain and 67 percent said they were in favor of a minimum wage. If such a wage were instituted, it would affect some 7 million adults in Britain. My studies of the employment of children show that the same proportion are working now as was the case ten years ago when there was full employment. Now we are in a period of high adult unemployment and children continue to work an average of sixteen hours per week, after school and on Saturdays. So it is, in some respects, a return to the days of Charles Dickens.

Another problem is the estimated half million Asian and Carribbean women who engage in homework; they have no employment protections at all. Their wages are abysmally low—the U.S. equivalent of twenty-five cents an hour for sewing machine work. There are language barriers for many Asian workers; they have to accept whatever work they can get. Black workers in Britain are much lower paid than white workers; black women tend to be concentrated in the same occupations as white women.

The problem of industry moving to low-cost areas of the world has been of concern. Until the present, unions in general have pushed for protective tariffs in those industries which have always been low-paid and have attracted very little investment. What may be needed is not protection but a push for regeneration, retooling, and a changeover to production of a different kind of goods. The women's liberation movement did not, until very recently, address these wider economic issues.

An interesting idea has been advanced recently by British activist Sheila Rowbotham. She calls for using traditional women's jobs to generate employment. One idea being talked about is setting up a community center where a woman could go and do her laundry, leave her children, have a meal with her friends, take a class. (Emma Mac-Lennan)

9.
France
Andrée Michel

THE ENTRY OF FRENCH WOMEN into the labor market is not a
new phenomenon but their motives for doing so have changed a great
deal in the last two decades. Twenty years ago, when French women
were surveyed about their reasons for working, the most popular response was "to fill the family's needs." At that time, most women appeared to focus on the well-being of their families and to put their duties as wives and mothers ahead of any consideration of their own
needs. Today, the daughters of these women report that they hope to
have salaried jobs "to earn a great deal of money." According to their
expanded answers, it is not that they see money as an end in itself but
because it allows them the benefits of "freedom, independence, and
leisure." These responses suggest that there has been a silent revolution in women's attitudes, sharply differentiating the young women of
today from their mothers and which is predictive of growing discon-
tent with persisting sex discrimination in the French labor market. As
a result, it may well be that the young women of today will become the
main agents of change in the future.

Discrimination by Sex in the French Labor Market

When French women first entered paid work, in the nineteenth century, differential treatment of workers by sex was perceived as a consequence of woman's "natural" role in the family, as bearer and care-
taker of children and as provider of general support to all family
members. This ideology was widely accepted by businessmen, trade
unions, the state, and by both men and women workers. Only some
feminist blue-collar workers, or *bourgeoises* such as Flora Tristan, questioned the validity of women having such a constricting role.

Today, the situation has reversed itself. Almost everyone connected to the labor market (excepting, to be sure, the most conservative—the employers) believes that the subordinate position of women in the work force is due not to some naturally ordained role women must play but to discrimination against them.

There are two types of discrimination: overt and covert. The first comes about either in the work force or elsewhere in society. It is overt discrimination when parents or schools refuse to prepare girls for occupations other than the traditionally feminine ones or when a manager promotes only men, never women.[1] Covert discrimination is practiced both inside and outside the work setting. Sometimes it is in the form of "autodiscrimination," as when married women refuse to attend training courses required for promotions at work because they believe it inappropriate for wives to show interest in advancement. In cases such as this, the traditional ideology of feminine and masculine roles in the family has been accepted by women themselves. Regardless of the weights assigned to overt discrimination and covert discrimination, both are sufficiently pervasive so that French women occupy a distinctly subordinate status to men in the labor force.

Recent statistics show that France is second only to Denmark among EEC countries in the percentage of girls studying beyond high school, including comprehensive education, technical studies, and vocational training (table 9.1). In 1981, there were 95 girls for every 100 boys in higher education in France. However, 80 percent of the young women were attending 34 training and technical centers while young men were divided among no fewer than 300 such centers.[2] In 1979, of adults pursuing continuing education only 34 percent were women.

More girls are being educated than in the past but what has not changed is the nature of the studies girls pursue: very few girls are training for "masculine" jobs. Studies have shown that one reason girls do not enter nontraditional training is that they believe they will not be able to find work at the end of the training. There have been many cases where an employer will not hire a woman who wants to be a carpenter or a tool-and-die maker. Parents know this; their daughters know it, too. So young women are steered into the kind of educa-

---

1. Andrée Michel, Susan Béraud, and Marguerite Lorée, *Inégalités professionnelles et socialisation differentielle des sexes* (Paris: Cordes, 1974).

2. "L'orientation et la formation professionnelle des filles," *Citoyennes à part entière*, no. 19, April 1983.

TABLE 9.1
Number of Girls per One Hundred Boys at Each Educational Level, EEC
Countries, 1978–79 and 1980–81

Country	Total		Primary Schools		Secondary Schools		Post-Secondary Education	
	78–79	80–81	78–79	80–81	78–79	80–81	78–79	80–81
Federal Republic of Germany	93	94	94	94	98	98	68	70
France	98	97	93	94	105	106	90	95
Italy	91	92	94	94	90	92	72	77
Netherlands	88	89	93	93	90	91	52	56
Belgium	94	94	94	94	97	98	76	80
Luxembourg	92	95	94	93	100	100	48	62
United Kingdom	94	94	95	95	97	97	65	68
Ireland	97	98	96	95	107	107	73	78
Denmark	93	95	96	95	91	94	89	96
Greece	85		93		79		64	
Total	93	94[a]	94	94[a]	96	97[a]	73	76[a]

Source: Eurostat, Education et Formation, Bulletin Statistique 2- 1982, published in "Les femmes en chiffres," Supplement to *Femmes d'Europe*, no. 14 (October 30, 1984).
[a]Estimated.

tion they think will prepare them for employment. Yet, there is not always a direct relationship between the kind of training a person gets and the employment for which he or she is chosen. For example, women trained for textile manufacture are being hired to work in electronics because the skill sought—manual dexterity—is developed in both programs.

While women constituted 38 percent of the French labor force in 1975, they held only 14 percent of the highest managerial posts, 19 percent of the middle management jobs, 61 percent of the clerical posts, and 24 percent of blue-collar positions. Women were 83 percent of laborers, 73 percent of semiskilled workers, and only 24 percent of skilled blue-collar workers.[3]

Research studies show that employers concentrate women in certain specific jobs and that their work sites are separate from men's. Sex segregation at work is still defended by employers who say that women have natural manual dexterity, for example, and further, that

3. *Les femmes en France dans une société d'inégalités* (Paris: La Documentation Française, January 1982).

women prefer monotonous and repetitive jobs and are therefore not suited for promotion.[4]

In 1978, women represented 40 percent of the work force in France and 49 percent of all job seekers listed with the national agency for unemployment. Currently, 8.5 percent of French men are unemployed compared with 12.5 percent of French women.[5] When they are working, French women are still concentrated in "feminine" occupations.[6] In 1975, there was a 31.6 percent gap between the average monthly wages of men and women with variations by occupation: women in highest management earned 36 percent less than men in these posts; women in middle management, 26 percent less; women white-collar workers, 21 percent less; and women in blue-collar jobs, 29 percent less than men in those jobs.[7]

There are other signs of progress, but slow progress. The male labor force participation rate decreased from 75 percent in 1968 to 69 percent in 1980, while the female rate rose from 38 percent to 43 percent.[8] The increase among women was mainly due to the entry of married women and mothers of young children. In 1983, 69 percent of all married women between the ages of 15 and 54 were in the labor force, as were fully 58 percent of those with young and adolescent children.[9]

The work attachment of French women workers is increasingly becoming more like that of men. In 1968, there were two peaks in the pattern of women's work participation: before the arrival of children and after their departure from home. By 1983, women were showing continuity rather than discontinuity; far fewer women were leaving their jobs at the birth of children. It is expected that 65 percent of women born after 1950 will participate in the labor force without interruption from the time they are twenty years old to the age of sixty.[10] The trend of continuous participation seems irreversible.[11]

---

4. Madeleine Guilbert, *Les fonctions des femmes dans l'industrie* (Paris-La Haye: Mouton, 1956).

5. "Femmes salariées," *La Semaine Sociale Lamy*, no. 170, July 1983.

6. Maryse Huet, "La concentration des emplois féminins," *Economie et Statistique*, no. 154, April 1983.

7. Guilbert, *Les fonctions des femmes dans l'industrie.*

8. Institut National de la Statistique et des Etudes Economiques, *Données sociales*, 1981 edition.

9. Ministere des Droits de la Femme, *Supprimons les obstacles* (Paris:1983).

10. Ibid.

11. Maryse Huet, "La progression de l'activité féminine:est-elle irréversible?" *Economie et Statistiques*, no. 145, June 1982.

Between October 1981 and October 1982, the number of unemployed men increased 26 percent compared with a 16 percent increase in the number of unemployed women, and one analyst has attributed this difference to a greater demand for women workers.[12] There is no guarantee, however, that this seemingly favorable situation will continue with the advent of new technology.

Only 15 percent of French women workers hold part-time jobs compared with 2 percent of French men workers. I say "only" because this proportion is significantly lower than that in other industrialized countries. Only 10 percent of female job seekers were applying for a part-time job in 1981.[13] This suggests that French women do not like working part time, a tendency supported by many French feminists who tend to view part-time work not as a desired benefit but as an obstacle to the realization of equality between the sexes at work.

These statistics taken together show progress. They also suggest that employers are still creating two labor markets: one for women; and one for men, who have better jobs and higher salaries. Working women in France are fighting to change this situation, with or without help from unions and from feminists.

Labor Market Policy and Related Social Policies

The system of industrial and labor relations in France is affected by two major forces: the French parliament, the national legislative body, and the EEC, which issues directives that are morally, if not legally, binding. A third influence is collective bargaining agreements in each branch of industry, which cannot include any clauses not in agreement with French law.

The principle of equal pay for equal work by men and women was first introduced in France in 1918 as a consequence of the Treaty of Versailles after World War I. The concept was reintroduced in the French Constitutions of 1946 and 1958, in a ministerial decree of July 30, 1946, and in Article 119 of the 1957 Treaty of Rome.

In 1972 a law was passed establishing the principle of equal pay for work of equal value; this was reaffirmed in an EEC directive in 1975. However, there were many aspects of employment not covered

---

12. Ibid.
13. Ibid.

by these initiatives: training, promotion, hiring, layoffs, and the like. In July 1983, thanks to the efforts of the new Minister for Women's Rights, Mme Yvette Roudy, Parliament passed a law, known as "the Roudy law," to reinforce the principle of equal treatment of men and women at work. Another of her innovations was the introduction of specific affirmative action measures to bring about equality for women.

Egalitarian Social Policies

In some cases, social policies seek to remedy past inequity; in others, they are aimed at protecting mothers or maintaining traditional female and male roles at work and in the family.[14] According to the Roudy law of 1983, it is forbidden to select an employee for a job on the basis of gender, either at the time of hiring or when a work agreement is renewed, and announcements of job vacancies indicating sex are prohibited. An employer is forbidden to ask a woman job applicant if she is pregnant, and a woman employee need not reveal whether she is pregnant. Similarly, firing a woman worker for becoming pregnant is prohibited. In effect, pregnancy no longer is an obstacle to the hiring, contract renewal, or promotion of women. This law prohibits the discharge of any worker—man or woman—for a reason related to his or her private life; for example, because the worker is married or in a common-law marriage to a worker in the same industrial organization.

The Roudy law protects workers against sex discrimination in "pay, training, job assignment, qualification, occupational promotion, or relocation," and calls for equal pay for work of comparable value. It considers as comparable tasks that require similar learning from workers, proven by possession of a title, a diploma, or by experience, and that require a similar cluster of skills developed from experience or responsibilities or physical or mental capacity. Employers of fifty or more salaried workers are required to submit to shop stewards and to the work committee (*comité d'entreprise*) an annual report that compares the occupational status of male and female employees. The annual report of occupational status must be provided to each employee who applies for it. Members of the French women's liberation move-

---

14. Anne Sabourin, "La femme dans l'entreprise," *La Semaine Sociale Lamy*, no. 170, July 1983.

ment protested the exemption of employers with fewer than fifty salaried employees because large numbers of French are employed by
such organizations and thus not protected by the Roudy Law. An employer and work committee also may establish a plan for promoting
equality between the sexes for the ensuing year, but this is not obligatory. If they choose to develop such a plan, they can apply to the government for financial help in implementing it. Further, the employers are enjoined from discrimination on the basis of sex in the
selection of employees for participation in extension courses or continuing education classes.

The Roudy law also permits shop stewards as representatives of
the unions to take cases of sex discrimination to court; an individual
woman can prevent her case from being taken to court if she prefers
to take it herself or if she opposes the local's action. The law also prohibits an employer from firing a woman who takes a discrimination
case to court.

Progressive legislation calling for affirmative action for women
has been initiated, in almost every case, by the Ministry for Women's
Rights with an aim to resolve problems brought about by past discrimination against women. Very seldom have initiatives been taken by
employers without prompting. The Roudy law states that temporary
measures instituted to bring about equality between the sexes do not
violate the principle of equal treatment of the sexes. These *mesures de
rattrapage* are viewed as "positive discrimination." They can either be
specific laws regulating training, hiring, promotion, the organization
of work, or working conditions, or they can be regulations included in
collective bargaining agreements.

A major focus of the Ministry for Women's Rights is the creation
of pilot training centers for women workers. The ministry organized
more than one hundred centers in 1982 for training women in masculine fields such as metalworking, soldering, and the like. Thirty of
these centers provided training for jobs in new technologies, such as
electronic data processing. These programs give priority to women
over twenty-five years of age with comparatively little education who
are unemployed and/or heads of families with one or more children.
The workshops last nine to twelve months and participants are provided with stipends at least equal to the minimum wage. The stated
purpose of these programs is to help women workers, with priority
given to women in poverty. It is unfortunate that the program is not

large because the centers have been successful; in 1982, most women trainees completed their training and moved into employment.[15]

Contracts called *contrats emploi-formation* are employment training agreements relating to theoretical learning that are offered by employers to young people of both sexes aged eighteen to twenty-six years. The National Agency for Job Seekers (ANPE) is supposed to give priority to women so that the proportion of women workers receiving these contracts is the same as the proportion of women among all job seekers applying to local ANPE bureaus.[16] These contracts are designed to give additional training to young workers so that they can become adapted to a job or qualified to do it. Training is provided on the job by the employer, who receives financial assistance from the state. For the duration of the program, which can last from 120 to 1200 hours, the trainees receive an average salary at least equal to the minimum wage.

There are hiring priorities for specific categories of women workers. Each employer is required to hire a certain quota of widows with two children; single women not receiving child support for their children; and fathers of three children. Another hiring priority favors war widows.[17]

With regard to social policies designed to assist parents, there is differentiation between fathers and mothers. For more than thirty years it has been recognized in France that motherhood is essential for the continuation of society. However, the workers' unions and the women's liberation movement agree that the burden of parenthood should not fall disproportionately on women. This perspective has resulted in many social policies that apply differentially to the sexes. For example, when a woman interrupts her work to give birth, her work agreement or contract is automatically extended. At the same time, there is agreement that employers should not have to pay for maternity leave because, if they had to, this might be an obstacle to the hiring of young women who would constitute an extra expense if they should become pregnant. Consequently, it is the social security system that pays for a maternity leave (*congé de maternité*) of sixteen weeks, six weeks before the birth of a child and ten weeks afterward. The mother receives 90 percent of her salary before the baby is born, and

---

15. "Les stages pilotes," *Citoyennes à part entière*, no. 22, July-August 1983.
16. Sabourin, "La femme dans l'entreprise," p. 9.
17. Ibid.

some collective bargaining agreements provide for an additional 10 percent to be paid by the employer.

The work agreement is not broken by maternity leave. It is forbidden to fire a working woman when she becomes pregnant, during her maternity leave, or for four weeks after such leave. The pregnant woman can apply for transfer to other work in the same workplace if a medical certificate states that the job she holds can endanger her life. Her salary remains the same in the case of such transfer.

A postnatal leave of absence without pay can be taken by new mothers for up to one year after the birth of a child, whatever the size of the employing organization or the extent of the mother's seniority. Fathers can get a one-year postnatal leave of absence as well, but they must apply for this leave two months after the birth of the child. Employers are not obligated to rehire either parent after a postnatal leave but they are obliged to give such parents priority when there are job openings.

In addition to postnatal leave, a parental leave of absence (*congé parental*) of two years after the birth of a child is legally guaranteed under certain conditions to women or men workers who ask for it. Only employers with 100 or more salaried employees are obligated to provide parental leave and applicants must have twelve months or more seniority at the time the child is born. While postnatal leave terminates a work agreement, parental leave extends it. At the end of a parental leave, an employee can resume working at the same job at pre-leave wages. It should be noted, however, that a father can apply for parental leave only if the mother gives the employer a written renunciation of her right to apply. Despite the ideology of equality, mothers are still supposed to be more motivated than fathers to take time off for child care.

Despite the Roudy law of July 1983, some protective legislation for women remains. Such policies express the ideology supporting traditional gender roles in the family and at work. For instance, the law forbids women manual workers to be employed at night in industry, mines and quarries, and certain service jobs. Women are also barred from certain industrial jobs where the use of chemicals is perceived as hazardous to health. French women take the position that what is bad for women's health is also bad for the health of men and that such protective laws should be extended to cover men. There is also a weight-lifting restriction based on women's ages. French feminists also ask that this limit be extended to men because "what is good for women is equally good for men."

Finally, women who have reared children receive earned seniority toward retirement: Those who cared for one or more children for at least nine years while the children were under sixteen years of age have two years of seniority for each child credited toward their retirement. In this regulation, "caring" for a child means staying at home. This credit is not extended to men who stayed home to rear children, and is thus in conflict with the directive of the EEC of December 9, 1978, which states that women and men should be treated equally with respect to social security. French feminists have asked that this advantage be rectified accordingly.

Conclusions

In France, the labor market is no longer thought to be a free market regulated by the law of supply and demand. In the nineteenth century, workers fought for laws to protect themselves against long working hours and to prohibit women and young children from work at dangerous sites. In the twentieth century, these campaigns have been waged by the labor unions. However, efforts to bring about equality between the sexes have always been initiated, publicized, and carried out by French women themselves. Historians of trade unionism in England, the United States, and France have suggested that unionists have supported protectionist laws as a means of keeping women out of the labor market.[18]

After World War II, women's pressure for equality at work intensified, especially pressure for equal pay. With the creation of the EEC, some French employers granted salary increases to men and not to women because they feared they could not compete with European countries that had not yet subscribed to the "equal pay for equal work" concept. As a result, in 1957, Article 119 of the Treaty of Rome extended the equal pay principle to bind each country in the EEC.

Since 1970, the women's movements in France have exerted great pressure to improve the status of women and to bring about equality between the sexes in the family, the workplace, political and social life, and the mass media. Members of the women's liberation

---

18. Elise Boulding, *The Underside of History* (Boulder, Colo.: Westview Press, 1976).

movements (and there is more than one) pushed for and won the right to abortion in the late seventies. Women workers who seek to protest sex discrimination have been supported not only by the trade unions but by feminists. In 1975, it was established that the typical striker was a young woman about thirty years of age who did semi-skilled work on an assembly line in a textile or metalworking factory. One male shop steward characterized women workers as a treasure for unionists, a "gold mine."

Feminist analysis of women's oppression, not only at work but in the society at large, exerts a significant influence on the perspectives and actions of women workers in France, whether organized or not. Most women decision makers in industry and in the unions believe that women's oppression can be traced to two systems: (1) class stratification resulting in the exploitation of workers and (2) gender stratification resulting in the exploitation of women by men in the family and in society. These two systems are not identical but are believed to be interconnected. Therefore, French feminists are calling not only for changes in the class system to bring about more justice for the underprivileged (of whom the majority are women), but also for changes in the patriarchal system, which subordinates women in the family, in the educational establishment, in the polity, and in the economy.

French feminists are pressing for passage of an antisexist law that will be the equivalent of an antiracist law enacted in 1975. The Minister for Women's Rights presented a bill to Parliament on March 15, 1983, which would prohibit discrimination based on sex in obtaining jobs, goods, or services, and would punish infractions of such a law. The bill also prohibits sexist messages and images in the mass media which may provoke hate, contempt, violence, or discrimination against women in any aspect of life. Not only can individual women bring cases of sex discrimination to court but women's organizations can do so as well. There has been public debate about the wisdom of passing such a law. An opinion poll revealed that, among workers in advertising, 56 percent of the women favored passage compared with only 25 percent of the men.

Many French women in and outside the work force agree that legislation is necessary but not sufficient in and of itself to ensure equality between the sexes. Women themselves must ensure that the laws are implemented and must be the main agents and supporters of their own liberation at work and in the society. To be sure, there are obstacles to the realization of this strategy, among them the socialization of women to passive and dependent roles and the citizen's perception of the welfare state as the protector of all.

A new approach that is gaining support in France, although still not widely accepted, is that equality with men in a society based on exploitation, competition, and militarism is not a valuable end in itself. Proponents contend that equality should be promoted and can be better promoted in a peaceful society based on cooperation and solidarity, not on competition. To this model, women should be willing to contribute more than men because women pay a higher price for the exploitative model under which we are all still living.

Discussion

It was a pleasure to hear about a country where equal pay for equal work has been the law since 1918. The government of France takes an active role in preserving workers' rights; women's employment rights as mothers and mothers-to-be are protected; there is a substantial health support program for all workers; and the child care system, both public and private, is superior to most.(Nancy Gaenslen)

How did the cooperation between feminists and working women come about? Did the members of women's liberation groups go into factories to seek out workers? In West Germany, they didn't and problems resulted. (Hanna Beate Schöpp-Schilling)

The idea that the class system had to be abolished or markedly changed for women to be liberated originated with the feminists, as did the concept that patriarchy had to be overthrown. These ideas were readily accepted by the leaders of women workers who were already active in trade unions and who never felt that they needed male union leaders to show them how to end sex discrimination. They recognized that they had to act on their own. For example, when a factory was closed by an employer, the women workers did not accept this decision passively. Instead, they took over the factory, operated it, developed new markets, and made it a going concern again. There are many examples where women have done this. (Andrée Michel)

Women workers have had the most challenge, in a way, since many of the industries in the greatest trouble in France in the early 1980s are ones where women workers are concentrated. (Nancy Gaenslen)

10.
Federal Republic of Germany
Hanna Beate Schöpp-Schilling

THE INCREASE IN WOMEN'S REPRESENTATION in the paid labor force probably is the most important labor market development
in most industrialized countries in this century. In the Federal Republic of Germany, however, women's 38 percent share of the work force
in 1980 was only 1 percent higher than their share in 1882 in the German Reich. On the other hand, while women were a minority of the
total labor force in 1980, a majority (52 percent) of women aged 15 to
64 were working and, as in many other Western countries, the number of married women and mothers in paid employment has increased disproportionately. In 1980, 45 percent of all married women
were employed; of these, about half had children under the age of
fifteen.

Three typical patterns can be identified in women's employment
in West Germany today: (1) a one-time short-term interruption of
employment, which is becoming the norm; (2) permanent abandon-
ment of employment at childbirth; and (3) uninterrupted worklives.
The continuous work pattern increasingly applies to wives and mothers. Forecasters predict an increased rate of growth in women's labor
force participation through the 1990s, especially in the employment
of women between 25 and 40 years of age.

Unemployment is higher among West German women than

The author wishes to thank Hedwig Rudolph of the Technical University, Berlin,
for commenting on earlier drafts of this paper. Renate Weitzel's study, "Labor Market
Policies Related to Women and Employment in the Federal Republic of Germany"
(Berlin: International Institute of Management, May 1982) has also been helpful.

among men; this has been so since the early 1970s. And, as in most Western industrialized countries, women workers are concentrated in certain sectors of the labor market, in certain occupations, and at certain levels. In 1980, 71 percent of all female employees in West Germany were in service occupations; 18.5 percent were in manufacturing; 6.9 percent in horticulture, fishery, and animal breeding; and only 1.6 percent in technical occupations.

In this essay I shall discuss recent legal and policy developments affecting the labor market which have been designed with the explicit aim of eliminating discrimination against women and of providing them with opportunities equal to those of men. The role of trade unions, women's organizations, and the feminist movement in creating, monitoring, and implementing laws and policies affecting women in the labor force shall also be analyzed. In order to assess the general importance of these groups, I shall describe each one briefly.

Unions, Women's Groups, and Feminists

Women are still underrepresented in trade unions as well as in the Works Councils, which represent the employees' interests within firms. They are underrepresented in terms of membership, representation on union committees, and in decision-making positions. The German Federation of Trade Unions, an umbrella organization that includes most unions, represents about 36 percent of all employed workers in West Germany, but only 20.7 percent of women workers. Within the federation, problems related to women's employment are handled by special women's committees, which have only advisory status. These women's committees often do important work but in many cases they find it difficult to influence the decision-making process in unions.

The German Women's Council, founded in 1951, is the umbrella organization for women's associations and women's groups in so-called mixed organizations. The council represents the interests of six million German women, ranging from women's committees in trade unions to Catholic women teachers' organizations. It is invited by the government to comment on drafts of proposed legislation, but because of the diversity of its membership, the council finds that its ability to speak out on controversial issues is rather limited.

The two conservative parties and the Social Democratic party have women's groups that deal both with women's issues and with general party questions. In general, these groups identify closely with the goals of their parties. Thus, the conservative parties are concerned with the welfare of the family, the role of the housewife, and the drop in the birthrate, which is now one of the lowest in Europe. The Social Democratic women, in contrast, are more concerned with issues having to do with women and employment. Women in the very small Free Democratic party decided in the 1960s that they would do away with women's groups. They joined with men to form "emancipation groups" which exerted some influence on their party's program and policy actions. The newly created party of the Greens is strongly influenced by feminist ideology. This is clear both from the party program and from the party's current representation in the Federal Parliament where the number of women almost equals the number of men. It was a female member of the Greens who introduced the term "sexism" in the Federal Parliament in 1983. The fact that she earned nothing but laughter and ridicule from the other parties is indicative of the status of feminism in West Germany.

The feminist movement emerged in the late 1960s, during the fight for a liberal abortion law and as a reaction to male chauvinism in the student movement. Its core is the autonomous women's movement, which regards patriarchy as the fundamental form of discrimination and excludes men from all of its activities. In the early 1970s, women in this movement founded women's centers, bookshops, magazines, publishing houses, shelters for battered women, women's studies courses at universities, and the like. For many years, the philosophy of these women's groups was to create a separate women's culture rather than trying to change society by working through existing institutions. With regard to women's employment, some members of the movement were active, on the theoretical level, in demanding wages for housework; others opposed this goal and demanded an improvement in women's employment situation that would allocate 50 percent of all qualified jobs to women. Since the late 1970s, however, partly due to the influence of women's movements in other countries, *Emma* and *Courage*, the two leading feminist magazines, have begun to direct their efforts toward legislative change.[1]

The relationship between women in traditional organizations, in groups within political parties and in the trade unions, on the one hand, and women in the autonomous women's movement, on the

---

1. As of late 1984, *Courage* had ceased publication.

other, has been strained for many years. In fact, the term "feminist" used in the narrow sense of the autonomous women's movement is a bad word in trade union circles and trade unionists dissociate themselves from feminism.

Antidiscrimination Measures

Labor market policies have the potential for establishing equality between women and men in society but they are not without limitations. First, they cannot do much for women as long as their socially ascribed functions as mothers and housewives place them in a marginal position in the work force and as long as other laws and social mechanisms support and reinforce their marginality. Second, sex discrimination is sometimes attributed to the weak supply position of women which, it is said, makes them vulnerable to discrimination. When designing antidiscrimination policies, one has to be careful not to shift the burden of discrimination from one weak social group to another or, for that matter, from one group of women to another. Third, as long as women are in a less favored position than men, policies designed merely to treat women equally with men will not decrease discrimination against women.

Recent research in the United States and in Europe distinguishes among three policy objectives that shape efforts to eliminate discrimination against women in employment. The first objective is the prohibition of unequal treatment under equal conditions. The second is the provision of affirmative action, that is, favoring women under equal conditions; and the third is the provision of equal conditions in the workplace by raising women's qualifications and opportunities for education and by increasing the compatibility between employment and family responsibilities for both women and men.

Up until the mid-1970s, most people in the Federal Republic of Germany believed that a sound legal basis existed for fighting discriminatory practices affecting women workers in Article 3 of the Bonn Basic Law, the constitution, which provides equal rights for men and women; in Paragraph 75 of the Works Council Act, which states that Works Councils have to see to it that no discrimination occurs on the basis of sex; in the Federal Labor Court's 1955 verdict making the category of low-paid "women's wages" illegal according to the principle of equal pay for equal work as based on the constitution; and in ILO regulations and the EEC directives of 1975 and 1976. In practice, however, the legal underpinnings proved to be less sound than they believed.

The prevailing interpretation of the constitution permitted employers to discriminate against women because precedence was given to freedom of contract over the principle of equal rights. The 1955 Federal Labor Court decision had been phrased in such a way that it immediately engendered new job evaluations with their own pay differentials. Jobs were classified as "heavy work" or "light work" and miraculously these classifications turned out to be sex typed. And even though the constitution also provided that all laws in conflict with the principle of equal rights were to be changed by March 1953, the Marriage and Family Law of the German Civil Code was changed only in 1958. A second reform in 1976 finally shifted the power to make decisions about wives' employment away from husbands. Now, the distribution of paid work and unpaid family work between husband and wife is to be based on their "mutual agreement," thereby eliminating legally sanctioned marginal female employment.

In the late 1960s and early 1970s, particularly after the change from a Christian Democratic government to a coalition of the Social Democratic and the Free Democratic parties, a new interpretation of the constitution began to emerge. The principle of freedom of contract began to be subordinated to the principle of equal rights, and a discussion began concerning affirmative action for women on the basis of the constitution. However, the EEC directives of 1975 and 1976 (requiring equal pay for work of equal value, and equal treatment of men and women regarding access to jobs, training, promotion, and working conditions), which were to be incorporated into the laws of the member states by 1976 and 1978 respectively, caused no great stir among politicians, the various women's groups, or the trade unions. All believed that the constitution already contained these regulations.

Then, opinions began to change. Younger German women who observed the equal rights efforts in the United States, the United Kingdom, and the Scandinavian countries were impressed with the new definitions of sex discrimination and the creation of new institutional machinery to combat it. They reassessed the situation in the Federal Republic of Germany and found it wanting.

Women in the Civil Liberties Union (Humanistische Union), following the British model to a certain extent, called for a comprehensive anti−sex discrimination law to affect not only the labor market but education, business, advertising, the media, and the treatment of women in prison. To monitor such a law, they asked for the creation of an independent commission with powers of sanction. Later, the small Free Democratic party adopted this demand and began to draft such a law in its last term as coalition partner in 1981. In contrast to the Free Democratic women, younger women of the Social Democratic party looked to the Swedish model and demanded a new comprehensive labor market policy for women which was to be monitored by an Equality Council in the Federal Chancellor's office as well as in the respective offices of the Prime Ministers of the States (Länder).

Opposition to these demands was strong and came from different ideological camps; consequently, neither of these two political women's groups succeeded in translating their demands into legal reality. But they did manage to educate the public and political representatives on matters of sex discrimination. In the years following, equality offices and women's departments with varying degrees of discretionary power were established at the federal and state levels. So far, none has powers of investigation linked with sanctions.

The anti–sex discrimination legislation which was finally prepared due to pressures from the EEC turned out, after many compromises, to be a reform of the German Labor Law as contained in the Civil Code. This reform, called the EEC Adaptation Act, was passed in August 1980, and it was immediately clear that it satisfied nobody. The government itself decided that a review after two years would be necessary to assess whether its provisions were sufficient and effective.

The most important provisions of this act say that discrimination with regard to sex in hiring, promotion, issuance of directives, or dismissal is illegal as is unequal pay for work of equal or comparable value. In case of conflict, however, it is the employee who has to supply credible evidence that sex discrimination has taken place. Only then must an employer try to demonstrate that the treatment in question had some legitimate basis. In addition, even if the fact of discrimination with regard to hiring has been established, the employer need compensate the employee only for damages resulting from "the breach of trust" (i.e., the trust the applicant had harbored concerning fair treatment). Reimbursement for this type of damage covers only the costs of such items as telephone calls, postage, and travel used in the job application process. There is no other sanction. Other provisions of the law suggest that employers who advertise jobs in the media and within the firm not use sex-specific terms. Retaliatory measures against women who make charges of sex discrimination are discouraged and, finally, employers are encouraged to inform employees about this law.

Political and nonpolitical women's groups, feminist lawyers, and women's groups in the trade unions were unanimous in protesting vigorously against this legislation. Their criticism was based on three arguments. First, the act did not comply with the EEC directive. Second, it did not accord with current legal practice—a criticism advanced by the trade unionists. Third, it did not have any teeth. At a hearing in January 1982 organized by the Federal Ministries of the Interior and of Youth, Family, and Health on the question of whether or not the situation of German women could be improved by comprehensive antidiscrimination legislation, these groups demanded new legislation. A new law, they said, would have to be more explicit in defining direct and indirect discrimination, including discrimination on the basis of marital status and family status; and it would have to require full compensation (awards of jobs, promotions, training, or equivalent financial payments) where discrimination had been shown to exist. They demanded shifting the burden of proof from employees to employers, as well as strong sanctions against employers convicted of discrimination. The feminists also pressed for class-action suits, which are currently not possible under German law.

Despite this criticism, the new government, formed by a coalition of Christian Democrats and Free Democrats in the fall of 1982 and reaffirmed by election the following spring, came to the conclusion that the EEC Adaptation Act was really better than its reputation. Many of the criticisms were insubstantial, it was said, since the existing act could be *interpreted* as covering the provisions the critics demanded. However, the new government rejected full compensation and sanctions. It remains to be seen, therefore, if the EEC will initiate proceedings against the Federal Republic of Germany because the act does not comply with all the commission's regulations.

Given this situation, it is not surprising that only a few employers have been brought to court under the new law. Most of the cases are still pending. Some have been referred to the European Court, asking for clarification on some of the issues that the feminists and the women's groups have been raising. A recent verdict by a German court, which was based on the interpretation of the European Court, required a substantial amount of compensation to be paid by an employer. However, given the German legal situation, this verdict will not necessarily affect future cases. The law itself still needs to be changed.

Job advertisements have become less sex-specific, particularly when placed by employers in the public sector. However, many newspapers still list jobs under "male" and "female" headings. Clerical jobs are still offered mostly to women, while the opposite holds true for technical or professional jobs.

With regard to equal pay, the trade unions have been more active in the last couple of years than previously. They have helped individual women to win a number of cases that resulted in higher pay for women, but the unions claim that the new law was not decisive in these cases. Given the current economic crisis, trade unions may become less ardent in providing assistance to women fighting pay cases. A result in one such case did not set well with them: women's wages were not raised to bring about equal pay; men's wages were lowered instead.

Affirmative Action

Neither the EEC Adaptation Act nor any other piece of German legislation contains a provision for affirmative action as a means of overcoming present inequalities in the labor market. The regulations of the Employment Promotion Act of 1969, which institutionalize the right of individuals to further training and retraining, refer to women entering and reentering the labor force as a special group in need of protection. However, the Employment Promotion Act was not designed to increase equality in the labor market, but was created in a period of economic growth and labor shortage to improve the mobility of workers as well as their adaptation to economic and technological change. Due to the deterioration of the economic situation, its regulations have become increasingly restricted over the years. No specific program has been created to serve women covered by this act, and in all the sex-neutral programs women are underrepresented in terms of their proportion of female employment and unemployment.

Is a mandate for affirmative action implicit in the German constitution? The conservative parties and the Federal Council, which they dominate, decided in 1979 that the constitution does not contain such a mandate and that, in fact, it forbids affirmative action in favor of women. In contrast, women attorneys of the Social Democratic party and women trade unionists claim that the equality article of the constitution, taken together with Article 20, which defines the Federal Republic as a "socially conscious" state, not only allows for affirmative action but charges the government with pursuing it.

In this respect, it is interesting to evaluate the statements made at the 1982 hearing on antidiscrimination legislation mentioned earlier. By this time, the various women's groups were united in their demands for concrete actions though they differed in detail. The women's department of the board of the German Federation of Trade Unions underlined the necessity for affirmative action in the form of preference to women who were as well qualified as men candidates for hiring, promotion, and further training. They advocated goals and timetables, and they asked that such measures be tied to government subsidies and tax deductions. They proposed that the role of the Works Council and of the partners in collective agreements should be strengthened so that they could create and monitor such affirmative action plans. Most of the member organizations of the German Women's Council supported all these demands with one exception: they wanted preference to be given to whichever sex was underrepresented.

The women's groups within the Social Democratic party went several steps further. They demanded quotas for all apprenticeships (i.e., 50 percent to be reserved for girls and 50 percent for boys) and a step-by-step increase up to 40 percent of jobs at all levels and in all areas of employment for the underrepresented sex. Exceptions were only to be permitted if a sufficient number of applicants was lacking. To overcome this obstacle, training measures within firms should ensure that enough applicants would be found in the future. Several bodies were recommended to monitor these measures: an equality commission to be created in firms with more than 150 employees, the Works Councils, and a Federal Equality Commission with comprehensive powers.

Representatives of *Emma* and *Courage*, the feminist magazines, which for the first time participated in a public hearing, demanded that any antidiscrimination legislation and any affirmative action programs should be directed only to women in order to avoid giving further privileges and advantages to men. They asked for fixed quotas for all areas and levels of employment and that the government as an employer should take a leading role in this regard. As mentioned earlier, after the demise of the Social Democratic–Free Democratic government in the fall of 1982, all these proposals came to naught. The successor government took the position that legislated affirmative action may be unconstitutional. Instead, it has tried to encourage firms to take voluntary action on behalf of women and has launched a research program to investigate current activities within firms.

Equal Opportunity

Raising women's level of education is seen as one mechanism for bringing about equality in the workplace. At the same time, researchers and practitioners are beginning to recognize that women with the same educational qualifications as men cannot be assured of receiving equal opportunity in employment. In the Federal Republic of Germany today, the educational qualifications of young women are higher than those of young men, yet despite attaining such high levels of education, these women are found in a limited range of occupations. This is largely due to their traditional socialization, to prejudices on the part of employers, and to the existence of protective laws.

Recent data show that more than 50 percent of all apprenticeships available are in technical areas and that 91 percent of these places are filled by young men. Most of the women working in the industrial sector are unskilled or semiskilled. Motivated by the equal opportunity principle as well as be a predicted shortage of skilled workers in the Federal Republic due to the dramatic drop in the birthrate, both the federal and the state governments initiated a number of pilot projects to train young women for industrial jobs not traditional for their sex. The federal government monitored 22 such projects over a period of five years during which time a total of 1,232 young women were trained; the states supported 8 regional programs under which 8,000 apprenticeships for women were created, predominantly in smaller firms. Criteria for the selection of the apprenticeships were as follows: the work had to be classified as technical; it had to be suitable for women as defined under the protective laws; it had to offer career prospects; the qualification obtained had to be usable for a variety of purposes; and the present representation of women in the occupation had to be between 0 and 5 percent. The financial support given by the federal government covered 75 percent of the extra cost employers might incur in training young women for these jobs. These extra costs might come about because additional toilet facilities would be needed and also because compensatory training for the women might have to be arranged.

An assessment of these programs shows that young women are quite able to handle these jobs. Initial difficulties were overcome by compensatory training. The firms were satisfied with women's performance, and broad media coverage helped to break down some of the public prejudice against women in "men's jobs." On the other hand, the programs did not necessarily create jobs for the women once they had finished their training. When applying for jobs, many of these women encountered the old prejudices and barriers, and this was compounded by a general rise in youth unemployment. In addition, it remains to be seen whether marriage and motherhood, a clear goal for these young women, will impose the usual career impediments.

Policies that seek to relieve the double burden of paid employment and family work for both women and men do exist in the public sector in the form of unpaid parental leave with job guaranteed. In addition, all workers are entitled to a leave of five days per year to care for a sick child. Rather than move further in this direction, both the old and the new government have supported a number of policies that would erect new barriers to the realization of equality between the sexes. One example is extended maternity leave, which entitles an employed mother to an additional four months of paid leave following the period of maternal protection, which is six weeks before birth and eight weeks after. This is a controversial policy because it does not change women's ascribed responsibility for family work. However, at present, 90 percent of eligible women are taking advantage of it. Of these, almost 50 percent return to their jobs immediately after the permissible leave. This suggests not only a great desire on the part of these women to be with their children longer than was previously possible, but also their willingness to stay in the labor market and to combine family and paid work.

A second example is the ongoing discussion about a child-rearing allowance to be paid at the birth of a child to employed mothers who give up employment or to those who do not hold jobs. The present government has promised such payment to all women by 1987. A study by the state government of Rhineland Palatia shows very clearly that such a provision is intended to relieve the labor market and perhaps to raise the birthrate. The effect of this policy would be a circular movement of women in and out of the labor market, cementing once again their marginal position as paid workers, particularly since there are no comprehensive policies in sight for their reintegration into the labor market.

A third example of conservative policy can be seen in the discussion of measures to promote part-time work for women. There is no doubt that a high demand for such work exists among women because many see it as the only means allowing them to combine family work and employment. Yet again, as long as part-time jobs are held predominantly by women, sex-segregated labor markets will continue with all their concurrent inequities.

Reacting to these policies that do nothing to improve women's position in the labor market, feminists and women in trade unions, in women's organizations, in the Social Democratic party, and in the Free Democratic party have focused their attention on the Swedish model. That is, they have been calling for *parental* leave and the shortening of the workday to six hours for *parents* of small children. It remains to be seen to what extent the EEC directive on parental leave will prove helpful in reaching these goals. Women in the trade unions are also trying to introduce their demands for a shortened workday into the general fight for a shortened workweek, which German trade unions see as a strategy for creating new jobs.

To sum up, the Federal Republic of Germany does not have a comprehensive labor market policy designed to protect women from discrimination nor does it have effective individual laws and measures aimed in that direction. What one does find is a rising consciousness among women of all political persuasions about ways of fighting discrimination. Unfortunately—and this may have its roots in German history—these women have not been able to overcome their differences and unite to translate their new knowledge into effective political pressure. Even recent developments—a reduction of financial benefits for extended maternity leave, a rise in fees for public day care, restrictions on the entry of formerly employed homemakers to retraining programs and on their eligibility for employment disability benefits—have not mobilized these women into forming a coalition. Such a coalition, however, is needed if conservative rollbacks are to be counteracted and a comprehensive labor market policy to be developed, one that would bring about true equality between women and men at work.

Discussion

Guest Workers

The presence of guest workers is a major problem for West Germany. When Sweden made the decision to encourage women to enter the labor market in the 1960s, West Germany decided not to encourage German women to work but to rely on migrant workers from Mediterranean countries. It was expected that these workers would be male and single but, in fact, they came with their families. Today, there are some second- and third-generation descendants of migrants in West Germany, some of whom do not speak German and many of whom lack education, even though it is free and available. The government did not have sufficient experience in assimilating such a large group, a problem exacerbated by the traditional fear that Germans have of people different from themselves.

The government of Westphalia recently published a report detailing the kind of jobs the guest workers are filling. It served to counteract the growing xenophobia of German workers because it showed that the migrants are doing the dirty work, the jobs that no German worker is willing to do now. If all the guest workers were to leave the Federal Republic of Germany at once, it would adversely affect not only the labor market but the infrastructure and economy as well. Their children go to day care centers, many of which would close without them; they are taxpayers and the loss of tax revenue would be substantial.

Government policy is currently focused on facilitating the return of guest workers to their homes. Turkish migrants, who are in the majority, do not want to go back to Turkey where there are no jobs. The government of the Federal Republic is now aiming to give families who want to go home an additional bonus to make that possible. (Hanna Beate Schöpp-Schilling)

Male Attitudes

According to a comparative study I did in Israel, the northeastern United States, and the Federal Republic of Germany, the more education men have, the more likely they are to be progressive on the issues of women's roles. The exception was the men of West Germany, who do not seem to have profited from the women's movement. They like their wives to go to work but still hold firmly to the notion that women should put their family duties first and should have less responsible paid jobs than men. These attitudes are so prevalent among educated German men that German women will have to make a concerted effort to educate them. (Judith Buber Agassi)

Patriarchal attitudes and authoritarianism are closely linked and both flourish in West Germany. Another problem is a regressive tax on two-worker families, which serves as a disincentive to German women to work. Still another barrier to women's employment is the organization of the school system. Children come home at 1 p.m. for lunch. (Hanna Beate Schöpp-Schilling)

An American scholar who spent a year working at the German Trade Union office has written an article in a union journal about day-to-day life there. He concludes, "The thing that surprised me was the sexism on the staff, including the academic staff." They are ready to accept broad pronouncements of policy against sex discrimination, but, in everyday life, they harass their secretaries. (Alice Hanson Cook)

11.
Sweden

Ylva Ericsson

THERE ARE TWO COMPLETELY different yet equally true ways of describing the situation of women in the Swedish labor market; one is negative, the other positive.

The positive picture shows women entering employment in large numbers during the 1960s and 1970s. At the beginning of the 1960s, only 40 percent of women were gainfully employed; today, 80 percent of women between the ages of 20 and 64 are in the labor force, a very high figure by international standards. A mere 10 percentage point difference between men's and women's work participation rates is probably unique in the Western world. Perhaps the most surprising fact is that women with young children have the highest participation rate. The labor force includes 81 percent of all women with children under the age of 7 and no less than 87 percent of women with children between 7 and 16 years of age. Despite a severe economic crisis and a higher than usual unemployment rate, Swedish women have done comparatively well in holding their ground in the work force.

In fact, the labor force participation rate of women is increasing while that of men is declining. On the other hand, the proportion of unemployed women is somewhat higher than that of men, which means that instead of just "going back to the kitchen," women are hanging on and fighting for their jobs even in times of adversity. In addition, there is the very encouraging fact that the gap between women's and men's wages is narrowing. Women in manufacturing now earn 90 percent of men's hourly wages; in the labor force as a whole, women's average hourly wage is 81 percent of men's.

Another feature of the positive picture is that men are beginning to share the responsibility for children and home care. The Swedish program of parental insurance introduced in 1975 entitles fathers as well as mothers to paid leaves of absence to care for their children at home. A parent is entitled to a fully paid leave of up to nine months after a child is born; the leave can be divided between a mother and father. In this realm, this legislation is gradually bringing about equality in Swedish life, since about 22 percent of new fathers are taking some portion of the parental leave to which they are entitled.

Why have such large numbers of women entered employment in Sweden? Why has Sweden made relatively good progress toward equality between the sexes? The following are probably the most important factors.

First, rapid expansion of the public sector has increased the number of job opportunities, making employment available to large groups of new entrants. The number of persons employed in the public sector has almost doubled since 1970. The Social Democratic party, which has ruled in Sweden since 1932, except from 1976 through 1982, has always utilized the public sector to give citizens security throughout the life cycle. Transport, residential services, social welfare, care of the elderly and of children are just a few examples of public services that were expanded to eliminate obstacles to gainful employment and which, at the same time, provided job opportunities for hundreds of thousands of women.

A second important factor is Sweden's prosperity, which created a positive climate for new reforms, even expensive ones. Industry's need for more workers made it easier to gain acceptance for measures aimed at eliminating obstacles to the employment of women.

Third, a system of taxation was introduced which abolished the tradition that the man was the principal provider and the woman guaranteed a livelihood through marriage. Legislation was passed in 1970 establishing separate taxation of husband and wife; each gainfully employed person is regarded as a separate individual with his or her own income. In addition, the "housewife deduction" was gradually reduced making it worthwhile for a family to have two sources of income. On the other hand, a fairly steep scale of progressive taxation served to encourage part-time employment and to discourage overtime work.

Fourth, a powerful trade union movement came to play an important role in the promotion of equality between the sexes. For example, the Swedish Trade Union Confederation has been very active in the matter of child care services and was instrumental in bringing about an ambitious program of expansion of facilities. A large proportion of Swedish workers are members of trade unions: between 80 and 90 percent of women are organized, about the same proportion as men. For some years now, committees and special equal opportunity officers have existed at all levels to monitor the status of women at workplaces all over the country as the result of special agreements within large sectors of the labor market.

A fifth factor has been the development of strong women's movements within the political parties. Not only have they put pressure on the parties to further equality between the sexes, but these women also have the additional advantage of access to parliamentary channels. As a result, reforms favoring sex equality have been successfully introduced in the Riksdag (parliament). Abortions are a case in point. For several decades, the women's movements in all political parties, except for the most conservative, campaigned for free abortions, but were opposed by powerful lobbies. Legislation was finally passed in 1974 by the Riksdag entitling women to decide for themselves whether and when they wish to bear children.

The sixth and last positive factor is the relatively high representation of women in decision-making bodies. Women now occupy one-third of the seats in the parliament, in county councils, and in municipal councils, though, of course, there are regional variations. There are a number of big cities where women constitute half of all policymakers, while in other regions they make up fewer than 10 percent.

So much for the positive image. Now I would like to turn to the problems. Sweden still has a long way to go before there is real equality between women and men. The positive developments I have described have not resulted in women acquiring parity of status with men in the Swedish labor market; women's position is still a great deal weaker than that of men.

Nearly half of all gainfully employed women work part time. Since they are still primarily responsible for their homes and children, it is difficult for them to be completely self-supporting and this puts them at a permanent disadvantage in the work force. Working hours are unevenly distributed between the sexes, with men working an average of about ten hours more per week than women.

What is more, Swedish women are employed in a limited number of occupations, most of which have low status. Accordingly, their labor market is narrower than men's and they are at a disadvantage when competing with men for available jobs. Of course in Sweden, as in other countries, there are historical reasons for the segregated labor market. With the coming of the Industrial Revolution, men entered the range of new jobs that had been created while women, in the main, stayed home and cared for their children. It was only where one person's wages were insufficient for family support that women went out to work. When women began to enter employment in earnest, they became nurses, service workers, office workers. Today, the man's world of work in Sweden comprises about three hundred occupations while the woman's world consists of about thirty. It is exceptional for members of either sex to penetrate the opposite "world." Since women are clustered in a narrow band of jobs, they are more vulnerable than men to processes of change and adjustment in the labor market.

The labor market is also characterized by vertical segregation Men constitute an overwhelming majority of qualified engineers and economists. There are few women executives; management of private business is very much a male preserve. Only about 10 percent of company directors are women, and women constitute only 1 percent of managing directors and senior executives, the real decision makers. The lack of equality between the sexes is evident in the small numbers of women who occupy positions of power. This makes it difficult to gain acceptance for social changes that benefit women.

Things are better, but by no means satisfactory, in the public sector, where decision makers are democratically elected. As mentioned earlier, women constitute about one-third of the membership in municipal policy-making bodies. But this is not enough because it means that women are in the minority wherever the most important decisions are made—decisions, for example, concerning long-range planning and the economy.

Another problem is that women still bear the primary responsibility for children and the home. Now that most families have two earners instead of one, women have relieved men of a large proportion of economic responsibility, but men have fallen short of expectations in the extent to which they are relieving women of their family responsibility. Women spend an average of about thirty-five hours per week working in the home, while men average between seven and eight hours. About three-quarters of new fathers do not take a single day of the leave to which they are entitled under the parental insurance program.

These are the most conspicuous problems in Sweden in terms of equality between the sexes. How are they to be dealt with? What is the Swedish government doing to strengthen the position of women in the labor market?

The main political issue is the entitlement of both women and men to work. Equal entitlement is a concept that must be, and will be, included in Sweden's planning for social development and employment. Great changes are now pending that will naturally influence the public assessment of women's entitlement to work. The traditional sexual stereotypes are a memory in Sweden, but a living memory, and it is not difficult to evoke prejudice. Arguments that women are taking jobs away from men and that women ought to return to their homes and children do not always fall on deaf ears.

What can we foresee for the future? Industry is unlikely to need more workers, even if output rises, because technical progress will result in production becoming increasingly automated. In the private sector, rapid computerization is likely to reduce the demand for workers. The public sector will be expanded but at a slower rate than in the 1960s and 1970s. The reason the public sector needs additional personnel is that there are many needs yet to be filled through work that cannot be done by robots. These are jobs where human care and attention are needed.

All in all, however, total working hours are likely to diminish in the future, in a continuing decline. Yet, a 13 percent drop in working hours since 1965 has been accompanied by the addition of more than half a million employed people who, inferentially, shared the available jobs. As a matter of fact, if everybody gainfully employed today were to work the same amount of time, Sweden would have a workweek of just under thirty hours.

During the current decade, the number of persons seeking employment will continue to increase by at least 200,000, out of a population of 8.3 million. At the same time, many women who are employed part time want to increase their working hours. In other words, there will be more and more people capable of sharing the jobs that need doing. Society will therefore have to be organized in such a way that leisure, employment, and money are fairly distributed. This is no easy matter but it presents a fascinating challenge.

Finally, let me present a number of goals, which, if realized, could have crucial bearing on sexual equality in the workplace. The first goal is the abolition of sexual segregation in the labor market. The computer society is upon us; new occupational groups will emerge and there will be a growing need for skilled labor. It is in the best interests of employees, employers, and society itself to broaden the labor market for women to include new sectors. Women constitute the largest talent reserve in Sweden. Occupational integration will make better use of available talent and, at the same time, improve mobility in the labor market. Perhaps most important, it will influence attitudes toward males and females in this generation and in the future.

A study group has been appointed by the government to recommend ways to improve the situation of women workers and to broaden women's employment opportunities. In addition, a campaign to recruit women into industry has been launched. This yearlong campaign is part of a long-term strategy At the regional level, experience from the campaign is to be analyzed in relation to the current employment situation and forecasts. At the governmental level, similar coordination between data collectors and forecasters is being effected through the study group. The campaign will include a concerted effort to ascertain why more girls are not pursuing technical studies. (The proportion of female students who prepare for technical careers was 7 percent of the total in 1971 and 18 percent in 1982.) Teachers, counselors, and girls in the lower schools will be interviewed to try to figure out how to encourage more women to apply to Sweden's four technical colleges.

The second important issue for the future concerns the role of the public sector. Expansion of the public sector must continue in order to enhance people's security and to ensure the entitlement of women to remuneration for the care that they provide. There are still important needs that should be filled under public auspices: child care is insufficiently developed; care of the elderly and the sick is not what it ought to be; institutional and noninstitutional medical services require a great deal more personnel.

A third important question for the future concerns working hours. Several reductions in hours of work took place during the 1960s and 1970s. In addition, workers won longer holidays, extended parental and educational leaves, partial retirement pensions, and the right to carry on trade union business during paid working hours. Economic growth was such that employees could receive full compensation for shorter working hours. There was also enough money available to finance better pay and provide more public sector jobs.

The situation is different today when we are being forced to make different kinds of decisions such as whether to accept shorter working hours in place of raises in pay. Are men prepared to work fewer hours for the benefit of their children and in order to equalize working hours within the family? Shorter working hours have an important bearing on sexual equality. A six-hour working day was proposed in Sweden throughout the 1970s, above all by women. This demand is a logical consequence of the transition from one to two family providers. A close and serious discussion of an equitable labor policy in this regard must be seen as important as discussions of equitable wage policy or equitable income distribution policy. Advocates of equality between the sexes must demand working hour reductions to equalize the hours worked by women and men. This can be achieved by expanding parental insurance, introducing sex-quota stipulations, expanding part-time employment opportunities for men, and reducing general working hours. The government has appointed a special advisory committee to compile documentation on which to base recommendations for future reductions of working hours.

A serious examination and discussion of the role of men is a fourth goal. The emancipation of women will remain conditional so long as the traditional role of men continues to be obstinately defended. Changes in one group invariably affect the other group as well. Increasing economic activity on the part of women necessitates a new view of man, and the high divorce rate in Sweden highlights the issue of men's and women's roles and their relationship with their children. It will not be possible in the future for questions of equality between the sexes to be seen as "women's issues."

Legislation on parental insurance was a means of trying to induce Swedish men to find a new role by accepting their share of responsibility for the care and upbringing of their children. A recent survey report, "Swedish Men," showed among other things that while men feel that fathers should take time off to look after their children, for some reason they do not do so themselves. We have dubbed these believers who do not act the "in principle men."

Nevertheless, there are signs of the emergence of a new man— younger and on more nearly equal terms with women—who accepts his responsibility for his children and is not afraid to acknowledge his weaknesses and feelings. Signs that men are changing can be seen in the extent to which men take parental leave. During the first six months of a child's life, few men do. Perhaps we should not lament that because mothers are nursing their babies during this time and getting their strength back. During the following six months, however, a fourth of the new fathers do take leave. At this point, the number of fathers taking leave is of greater interest than the length of their leaves. It is the fact that things are starting to happen that is encouraging.

To accelerate the development of this new man and to eliminate barriers in his path, the Equal Opportunities Minister has appointed a discussion group with members representing the social partners: management and labor. Needless to say, the group will have a male chair. We are convinced that men themselves have everything to gain from greater equality between the sexes. Men have a higher suicide rate than women do and are more often involved in violence and accidents. They have a higher incidence of heart attacks and other stress related diseases associated with the welfare society. The most extreme and dramatic manifestation of sexual inequality—wife-battering— affects not only the victim but also the assailant. We are seeking to understand and prevent such violence against women.

In addition, the government has appointed an advisory committee on equal opportunities research, a field much neglected in Sweden. This advisory committee is to coordinate and monitor research in the field of equal opportunity, initiate research, and transmit findings to the people who can make practical use of them.

Let me conclude with a few words about the Equal Opportunities Act, which became law in Sweden in July 1980. It aims to promote equal rights in work, working conditions, and opportunities for self-fulfillment in employment. Employment in both the public and the private sectors is covered by the act, which is targeted at employers. A government-appointed Equal Opportunities Ombudsman is responsible for compliance. The act has two main parts: one part contains rules dealing with the prohibition of discrimination on grounds of sex; the other deals with active measures to promote equality. The social partners were none too keen about this legislation when it was introduced, but they subsequently revised their opinion. Both employers and employees now see the act as a useful tool for combating discrimination against women and improving their status at work. This law is now accepted as a necessary part of the efforts to promote equality between the sexes in Sweden.

Discussion

Equality

The ideology of equality is strong in Sweden as it is in Italy and as it is beginning to be in France. Sweden is perhaps the most advanced country in the world in terms of the changes it has brought about in family law, in education, and in social services. But those changes seem to have had the least effect within the labor market. The male leaders of the unions may not recognize it, but the fact is that Sweden's equal opportunity approach does very little to change the fundamental balance of power between the sexes. It creates the possibility of further change but it does not guarantee it. (Ronnie Steinberg)

12.
Switzerland
Ilda Simona

ON THE LONG AND DIFFICULT ROAD toward equal rights for women in Switzerland, two recent events stand out as landmarks: in 1971 women were given equal political rights in federal affairs, and ten years later the principle of equal rights for women and men was included in the Swiss constitution. The first event occurred when Swiss male citizens finally accepted a modification in the federal constitution granting women the right to vote in federal elections and to be elected themselves, a right that had been granted to women in most European countries after World War II. The second event was the amendment of Article 4 of the Swiss constitution which had read "All Swiss are equal before the law" and was altered to include three important phrases: "Men and women have equal rights. The law provides equality, in particular in the area of the family, of education, and of work. Men and women have a right to equal pay for work of equal value." These changes were urgently needed. In 1979, eight years after women had been granted suffrage, the Swiss government assessed the situation of women in Switzerland in the following terms: "Men and women in Switzerland are not yet equal before the Law. Neither are they equal in daily life."[1]

Only a few years have passed since the adoption of the constitutional principle of equal rights which has raised many hopes. It is too early to establish its full impact on the condition of women. Changes in daily life need time; they cannot be changed suddenly. This is particularly true with respect to the condition of women, because evolution in this field touches the basis of our social structures.

---

1. Message du conseil fédéral sur l'initiative populaire pour l'égalité des droits, 1979.

In this paper, I summarize the condition of women in Switzerland in the three areas specifically mentioned in the new article of the constitution and in which the law has to provide equality: family, education, and workplace.

The current status of the wife in the Swiss family can be deduced from the following provisions of Swiss family law:

> The husband is the head of the family. He chooses the common residence. He provides for the maintenance of the family, mainly through a lucrative activity.
>
> The wife leads the household. She takes care of the children and of the housekeeping. She can represent the household only in terms of the needs of the housekeeping. The husband is entitled to withdraw such right from her.
>
> The wife can have a profession only with the consent of the husband. If she decides to work outside the home against his will, she must demonstrate before the court that her work is required in the interest of the family.
>
> The wife carries the name of the husband and acquires his nationality.

The preeminence of the husband is also evident in the rules regulating the administration of a wife's property and the family property.

In its statement on the revision of this law, the Swiss government confirmed what a great many Swiss women feel, namely, that the legal inferiority of the married woman interferes with her personal dignity. In the sense of depriving an individual of dignity as a human being, the family law is in violation of the spirit of the Swiss constitution and the traditions of Switzerland. As the statement put it, "The legal provisions now in force are no longer compatible with the principle of equal rights, which directs that the spouses must be put on the same level in every respect."[2]

The revision of the civil law is part of a widespread legislative movement all across Europe. In Switzerland, a commission of experts has been charged with the task of developing revision. According to its proposals, the husband will no longer be the "head of the family"; the husband and wife will both contribute to the maintenance of the family according to their ability; the spouse who takes care of the home and children and who has no personal income will regularly receive from the other spouse an amount of money to manage freely; both spouses shall represent the family; the residence shall be chosen

---

2. Message, p. 13.

by joint decision. As to employment, the spouses will have to consider one another's interests and the interests of the family as a whole. Unless the spouses choose some other arrangement, both spouses shall share the family assets.

The new provisions would place marriage on a relation of a partnership, leading to cooperation based on equal rights and obligations. No longer would different rights be attributed to the spouses. Housekeeping, education, and care of the children would be considered essential contributions to the welfare of the family. It is to be hoped that this revision will be adopted by the Parliament.

Considerable progress has been made in Switzerland in the area of education during the last ten years. More and more girls are continuing their education after compulsory school and more and more young women are pursuing higher education although their numbers are far below their proportion of the population. At the university level, the number of female students is low; in the academic year 1979–80, they constituted only 30 percent of university students despite the fact that Switzerland was the first country in the world to make university education available to women.[3]

In the area of vocational training, the differences between the sexes are even more pronounced. Among those completing apprenticeships, young men far outnumber young women. The largest disparities are in occupations regulated by the Vocational Training Act of 1979 and in trades requiring comparatively long apprenticeships. Although the provisions of the Vocational Training Act specifically apply without discrimination to both sexes, young women are concentrated in one single job category—commercial employees—and in a small number of other trades.[4]

Why are girls choosing (or being guided into) a narrower range of occupations than boys? One of the major reasons is that even today less importance is attached to the vocational choice and training of a daughter than of a son. Girls receive less encouragement than boys from parents, teachers, counselors, and public opinion to pursue difficult and time-consuming training, and they lack role models in jobs requiring such sustained preparation.

According to the Swiss Trade Union Congress, no less than 45

---

3. "La femme et la vie professionnelle," Rapport de l'Association suisse de politique sociale, 1970, p. 13.

4. *Vie economique*, September 1982, p. 684.

percent of women compared with 15 percent of men have had no vocational training. At the end of compulsory education, women tend to leave school and go to work. In the workplace, their lack of specific training means that they lose any chance for further education.[5] However, the deep-seated social belief that training and education are more important for males than females may be eroding slowly as demonstrated by a slow but steady increase in the number and proportion of women in vocational training and at the university.

Women make up about one-third of the labor force in Switzerland. The proportion of women in the population who are gainfully employed varies by marital status, age, number of children, nationality, and region.[6] More than half the women workers are in service occupations where they constitute 47 percent of the workers. About 30 percent of the women of working age in the German- and French-speaking regions of Switzerland are in the labor force; in the Italian-speaking canton of Tessin, the labor force participation rate of women is lower—25 percent. Only 30 percent of married women are in the labor force, representing 42 percent of women workers. More than four-fifths of women workers are Swiss; the remainder are foreigners.

The majority of women workers are in jobs that require little education or training, have comparatively low pay, and present little or no possibility for promotion. Women's jobs are less secure than men's, especially in times of economic recession. An additional problem is that employers use every pretext to avoid paying women and men the same wages for work of equal value.[7]

On the average, the wages of women in the private sector, where the principle of freedom of bargaining to determine wages is applied, are about 25 to 30 percent lower than men's wages, even where the work performed and the skills required are the same. Women's wages react more rapidly and sharply than men's to fluctuations in the market and to regional economic changes. These differences become more important with age, because women generally have less seniority and fewer years of service than men. Even among workers who hold college degrees, the difference between men's and women's wages is of the order of 25 percent. This situation confirms how justi-

---

5. Message, p. 11.
6. "La situation de la femme en Suisse, le partie, société et économie." Commission fédéral pour les questions feminines, November 1979, p. 57.
7. *Revue syndicale*, Congrès des femmes USS, March/April 1983, no. 3/4, p. 60.

fied and urgent it was to include in the constitution a special paragraph saying that "men and women have a right to equal pay for a work of equal value" and guaranteeing that this right can be invoked before the court.

In Switzerland, collective agreements vary considerably with regard to wages and salaries. Certain agreements do not contain any provision regarding wages, which are fixed solely by individual arrangements between employees and employers. The new paragraph in the constitution will have no effect on such agreements. Other agreements, however, give plant committees the right to fix wages. In such cases, plant committees have to apply the principle of equal pay. Some collective agreements have set different minimum wages for men and women. Such discriminatory clauses are no longer valid and must be eliminated. In still other collective agreements, wages are fixed according to job classifications. Men and women are classified in different jobs with men invariably in the better paid classifications. One of these classifications is based simply on the difference between "light work" (women's, as a rule) and "heavy work" (typically men's jobs).

Increasingly trade unions are negotiating with employers to include the principle of equal pay in collective agreements. An example is a contract recently signed by the Federation of Textile, Chemical, and Paper Workers giving women employed in these industries a monthly wage increase of 30 Swiss Francs over and above other raises normally given. These special rates were to continue until equal pay would be achieved in 1984.

Women are strongly underrepresented in public life in spite of certain progress during the last ten years. There is not one woman in the Swiss Federal Council and very few women have been elected to the governments of the Swiss cantons.[8] In the Swiss Parliament, at the opening of the legislature in November 1979, women represented about 10 percent of the deputies. In the Lower House (*Conseil National*) there are 22 women out of 200 representatives; in the Senate (*Conseil des États*) there are 3 women out of 46 representatives. In the Swiss cantons the Geneva government is an exception, with women making up 22 percent of the members. Very few women are to be found in high jobs of federal and cantonal administrations. In 1979,

---

8. This situation was changed when Mrs. E. Kopp of the Swiss Liberal party (FDP) was elected in October 1984. She is the first woman ever to serve in the Federal Council.

there were only 24 women (1 percent) out of 2,147 civil servants in high positions in the federal administration.

Women constitute about one-fifth of the membership of the political parties and of the trade unions in Switzerland, and are seldom leaders in either of these groups. In the last few years, however, the trade unions have taken steps to increase the participation of women in their activities at all levels. There is now a woman president of the Public Service Workers Union and a woman vice president of the Swiss Trade Union Congress. New structures have been created in several unions—the Swiss Metalworkers' Union now has a Women's Department and a Women's Committee, and the union as a whole has adopted a policy of working for the implementation of equal rights for women. Unfortunately, these trade union efforts take place in a period of economic recession which makes progress more difficult.

The debate on equal rights for women in Switzerland has been waged for decades. The amendments to the constitution of 1971 and 1981 have given us the legal groundwork. Much of the credit for pushing through these amendments is due to the women's associations, the trade unions, and especially to the Swiss Federal Commission for Women's Issues. But there seem to be three major obstacles to progress.

The first obstacle is the deeply rooted traditional belief in Switzerland that women and men have different roles. The woman is to be wife, mother, and housekeeper; the man is to be provider and head of the family. The second obstacle to the achievement of equality is the existence of two distinct labor markets: one for men, one for women. The better remunerated jobs carrying prestige and responsibility are the province of men, while the routine jobs requiring a low level of skills are reserved for women. The third obstacle is the widespread resistance to the implementation of the principle of equal pay.

These obstacles are deeply interrelated and strongly influence the labor market policy for women. Along with the new legal provisions of the new article of the constitution, a change of attitude at all levels of Swiss society, including public authorities, is essential to achieve a labor market policy fairer to women and to accelerate an evolution ensuring equal status to men and women in Switzerland.

Discussion

Women's Suffrage

An important factor in understanding the status of Swiss women is that Switzerland has not been through a war. In other countries, war has brought new opportunities to women. They have had a chance to show that they could do what had been thought to be "men's work." Another factor has been the relative prosperity Switzerland has enjoyed. I believe that these two explanations go a long way toward helping us understand why women in Switzerland were not motivated to fight for the vote until relatively recently. (Marion Janjic)

I concur to some extent, but don't forget that it was men who had to grant emancipation. In fact, they had to vote twice on this issue and there had to be a majority to bring about constitutional change. At one point, the Supreme Court ruled that Article 4 ("All Swiss are equal before the law") did not mean that women could vote in federal elections. So the Swiss men had to vote twice. And it was not easy. One problem is that Swiss men do not, by custom, discuss political matters with their wives. The women's associations were influential in putting on enough pressure. (Ilda Simona)

Not every single group was helpful. There was, for example, an organization called Women's Association against Women's Right to Vote. (Marion Janjic)

Guest Workers

In Switzerland, as in other countries, guest workers were imported to do the kinds of jobs that native citizens did not like to do. I doubt that they account for the low labor force participation rate of Swiss women, since it has always been the official attitude in Switzerland that single women may work but married women with small children should stay home. It is all right for mothers of grown children to work—if there is financial need. That official posture has been taken by representatives of the Swiss government in many international meetings, at Mexico City for example, and at ILO conferences. (Ilda Simona)

13.
Italy
Bianca Beccalli

THE DECADE 1973 to 1983 saw dramatic changes in the relationship between women and work in Italy with the reversal of the long-term decline in women's labor force participation. This change was connected with diverse and dramatic changes in the society and culture, which affected other crucial aspects of women's lives such as childbearing, their social and cultural participation, and their relation to politics. Indeed, a women's movement of unprecedented strength and radicalism swept through Italian society in the 1970s, spreading across class lines and involving middle-class as well as working women.

Despite these changes and the existence of the women's movement, labor market policies affecting women have been extremely deficient during the last decade. Although the increased numbers of women workers always have been placed in the least prestigious jobs and have remained stuck in them, this more or less obvious discrimination has not been attacked by any active policies on the part of the state, the unions, or the women's movement. This is all the more surprising considering that, until the 1960s, legislation concerning women's work and trade union policies toward women were relatively better in Italy than in other countries.[1]

Why were there such poor policies, despite a number of favorable circumstances? The main concern of this paper is to describe and attempt to explain this paradox. First, I review the basic structural

---

1. For a more extended analysis of the policies of the state, the women's movement, and the unions in particular, see my chapter "Women and Trade Unions in Italy" in *Women and Trade Unions in Eleven Industrialized Countries,* eds. Alice H. Cook et al. (Philadelphia: Temple University Press, 1984).

data, showing the main changes and continuities in women's work and condition. Next, I describe the political background: the policies that the state and trade unions developed towards women's work from World War II until the mid 1970s, and the breakthrough of the "new feminism," which could not deal with issues of work at the outset. I then analyze the Equal Employment Opportunities Law, pointing to some of its internal flaws and the overall failure in its implementation. Both the flaws in the law and the lack of implementation are associated with the weakness of the social pressures behind the law and with a number of specific obstacles which the unions, the women's movement, and the state will need to overcome if they are to develop active labor market policies on women's behalf. These obstacles are described along with the debate that they have stimulated. The paper concludes by looking at this ongoing debate, which for the first time is bringing feminists, unionists, and policymakers together to confront the problems of women and work.

Structural Changes and Continuities

There has been a reversal of the long decline in Italian women's participation in the work force, a decline that was one of the special characteristics of Italy in comparison with the other industrialized countries. The decline had already begun in the last decades of the nineteenth century as women's participation sloped down from quite high levels. In 1881, an estimated 43 percent of all workers were women; at the beginning of the twentieth century, 32 percent of all women were active in the labor market. They made up 35 percent of the industrial work force and 40 percent of the agricultural work force (still the most important sector of employment). The decline continued through the decades until women's participation rate reached its lowest point in 1972: 21.3 percent compared with 55.4 percent among men. Although the absolute levels of women's employment were doubtless higher than the official statistics suggest because of the substantial number of unreported women family workers, the declining trend in participation was clear.

The trend began a reversal in 1973. Of the 1.5 million people newly employed between 1972 and 1980, 253,000 were men and 1,247,000 women. In 1981, women made up two-thirds of the "unemployed" (those officially registered as looking for jobs); and women's participation in the labor market grew to 26.5 percent, compared with 54.7 among men. The change mainly affected women between 25 and 35 years of age, that is the female age group that had typically abandoned the labor market in Italy more than in other industrialized countries. The percentage of married women in the female work force also rose, from 50 percent in 1971 to 65 percent in 1981.

The changes in women's participation in the labor market in these years were paralleled by remarkable changes in women's education and in demographic patterns. In a period during which access to higher education was dramatically increasing for everyone, the sex composition of the student body changed very quickly; women now constitute almost 50 percent of high school and university students. The fertility rate during the same period declined from 68 percent per thousand women age 15 to 44 in 1970 to 48 in 1980, a change that is more strongly marked in the industrial North and the urban areas of Italy than elsewhere.

Despite the economic crisis, the new trend of greater female labor market participation is likely to continue. The crisis can (and has) hit women in particular: other things being equal, employers prefer to lay off women, who are not as well protected as men by unions and by the state. But, in fact, other things are not equal and the trend toward increasing women's labor market participation is connected with forces affecting both the demand and the supply sides of the labor market, including the growth of the service sector and changes in the social and cultural condition of women.

Nevertheless, both within and beyond the sphere of work, there have been remarkable continuities in the Italian situation. For example, job segregation by sex is not changing. In fact, a recent study of the long-term evolution of sex segregation in manual and nonmanual occupations found a slight increase in segregation.[2] Moreover, the division of labor in the household remains substantially unequal. Although changes in the home are difficult to assess, a striking image of the present situation was presented in a recent survey of families in Milan, the major city in the most modern area of the country: Women in the sample spent an average of 45 hours a week in work "for the family"; 72 percent reported receiving no help from their partners;

---

2. P. Barile and L. Zanuso, "La segregazione occupazionale in Italia" (Franco Angeli, 1984).

and only 9 percent said their partners helped them more than 4 hours a week.[3]

Insofar as women's work is concerned, if we look at the tradition after World War II and until the late 1970s, state legislation has been fairly progressive; the unions have been well disposed, in that not only did they not discriminate against women, but they also backed policies directly or indirectly favorable to women; and the women's movement was strong, very "political," with a remarkable influence on the labor movement. One might ask how things could be better in relation to women and work.

This question leads to a second, and opposite, observation. As far as explicit and specific policies on behalf of women in the sphere of work are concerned, neither the state, the unions, nor the women's groups developed any active labor market policies. This is even more remarkable with respect to the last decade when there was less action (bargaining, legislation, implementation of legislation) than in the past, despite, paradoxically, the impressive structural and political changes in women's condition during the 1970s.

Political Background:
State, Union, and Feminist Policies

After World War II, trade unions developed relatively "open" and progressive policies toward women workers. The openness was mainly a result of the general orientation of Italian trade unions rather than of a specific concern for women. In fact, "class unions," as Italian trade unions define themselves (as compared with "business unions" or "association unions"), are oriented towards the defense of class interests, wider than those of their members; concern themselves with the weaker sectors of the work force, not just their own constituencies; and press for progressive legislation and for including social issues in collective bargaining out of a responsibility for the overall development of society beyond strictly limited economic issues. Women workers were bound to benefit from this broad orientation of Italian political, class unionism: they are in the most disadvantaged areas of the work force, and their problems as workers are largely influenced

---

3. L. Zanuso, "Il lavoro delle donne," in "La qualità della vita a Milano," ed. G. Martinotti, Bilanci Sociali di Area, Municipality of Milano, 1983.

by social conditions outside the workplace. Indeed women workers did benefit from trade union policies, even from those policies not addressed specifically to them.

The relative openness of trade unions toward women is also evident in their pattern of organization. In Italy, as elsewhere, unions are predominantly male-led organizations, but unlike other countries, in Italy women were never historically barred from any union, and in the 1980s their rates of unionization are almost as high as those of men. Only the data on women's representation in leadership positions reveal clearly their inferior status in the organization, and even here, apart from a remarkable series of historical exceptions of women as top union leaders, the figures show fewer sharp differences with men than in the other industrialized countries.

To speak of women in unions and of union policies for women does not mean to speak only of a small sector of the population of working women. On the contrary, because of the strength of the unions and the structure of industrial relations, trade union policies affect the whole population of working women in Italy. In the last fifteen years trade unions in Italy have been very strong, and rates of unionization have been among the highest in the industrialized countries.[4] But besides this fact, the very structure of Italian industrial relations does not allow for "nonunion sectors" because the results of collective bargaining are automatically extended to all workers, including nonunion members. Hence the influence of trade union policies reaches all strata of working women.

The progressive policies of trade unions and, in general, of the whole labor movement toward women workers had an impact on the policies of the state, which also had a relatively good record, in the areas of equality and protection of women workers in the early postwar period.

The two themes of protection and equality for women workers were developed in tandem for several years after World War II. Both in collective bargaining and in legislation, the two were pursued as parallel goals without any perception of a contradiction between them, in contrast with the debate at the turn of the century around the dilemma of protection versus equality which had divided both the women's movement and the labor movement.

Protective policies achieved their major success in the maternity

---

4. Cook et al., eds., *Women and Trade Unions*.

law, first passed in 1950 and improved in later years. The law was the result of a powerful two-year campaign of the left wing parties (especially Communist women) and the trade unions (especially the mostly female clothing and textile union led by the most famous postwar woman trade unionist, Teresa Noce). The law provided for compulsory paid maternity leave from work for five months around childbirth, at 80 percent salary; made it illegal to fire a woman during her pregnancy and until her baby was one year old; compiled a list of jobs prohibited to pregnant women and to those who had just given birth; provided for breaks for breastfeeding during working hours in the first year of the child's life; and permitted unpaid leaves in the case of a child's illness during the first three years of life. As the law was judged at the time—and as it seems in retrospect from a comparative analysis—it was one of the most favorable maternity laws for working mothers in the Western countries.[5] This was a striking achievement in a poor, relatively underdeveloped country as Italy was in the early 1950s. To have a law, however, does not mean that it is implemented; Italy has had a tradition of progressive legislation and of poor implementation.

The policies oriented toward equality were less clear than the protective policies. Equality is sanctioned in the Italian constitution, but in an ambiguously worded article (no. 37): "The woman worker has the same rights and, for equal work, the same remuneration due to the man. Working conditions *should permit the fulfillment of her essential family function, and assure the mother and her child a special, adequate protection*" (emphasis added). The ambiguity in this statement reflected not only a compromise between the Catholic and conservative forces on one side and the lay and left-wing parties on the other, but also ambivalence within the labor movement itself. Trade unions broadly speaking were in favor of equality between the sexes. The Charter of Working Women, approved in 1947 by the first trade union congress after World War II, affirmed the unions' commitment to women's right to work and to equal treatment. But the conception that unions had of the division of labor between the sexes in the family was not so different from the conservative view: women were to take care of family work, and men were to be the main breadwinners. Therefore, women's right to work, which was acknowledged in princi-

---

5. Recently, women were granted the right to take maternity leave without loss of credit towards retirement.

ple, was also seen as subordinate to men's right to work whenever a choice had to be made. This is clearly shown, for instance, by the policies of the CGIL (Confederazione Generale Italiana del Lavoro) with regard to the problems of postwar redundancy. The choice they made was to defend the heads of families on the ground that they were the main breadwinners. Women, who had entered the work force in great numbers during the war years, were laid off in preference to men with union approval, just as in other Western countries. However, in Italy this did not happen through the operation of a seniority system, which had never been introduced in Italian industrial relations, but with deliberate consideration of the "different" role of women.

Ambiguities aside, a long march toward equality between women and men workers did take place from the 1950s through the 1970s, and trade unions were the major force behind it. Until the early 1960s there was an explicit policy of equal treatment; from the late 1960s onwards, the relative improvements in the treatment of women workers were the unintended outcome of broader egalitarian union policies.

Equal pay was a main target of trade union action. Although the Italian government had ratified the 1954 ILO recommendations on equal pay in 1956, the impact of this action was nil. The equal treatment that the Italian constitution had sanctioned in principle was not implemented, even in its most elementary and formal aspects, such as equal pay for "equal" work. The judicial interpretation of the ambiguous constitutional norm legitimated employers' use of sex differentials: in the few cases that came to trial, "equal work" was interpreted as work with the "same productivity." Collective bargaining reflected this practice as well, by officially classifying women and men workers in separate sets of categories.

In 1960 and 1961, when equal pay was eventually achieved through collective bargaining, after years of mass campaigns and industrial action, it was considered a landmark in trade union policies for women workers as well as the solution to the "problem" of women workers, insofar as trade unions were concerned. The consequences of the collective agreements were indeed remarkable: the differential between men's and women's wages was reduced by about 15 percent in the early 1960s. However, the structural root of inequality in the workplace beyond equal pay—occupational segregation—was not even discussed until the late 1970s. After the implementation of the equal pay agreements, trade unions directed very little attention to the problems of women workers. They considered that the remaining problems were common to all workers and not specific to women. Hence, soon after the equal pay agreements the unions dissolved the women's commissions, the organizations that had been established after World War II to deal specifically with women workers' problems.

Despite this lack of specific interest in the problems of women workers, Italian unions favored women indirectly in their wage and job classification policies between the late 1960s and late 1970s. In fact, the powerful push of trade union militancy that began in 1968 was associated with an egalitarian orientation in trade union policies; flat-rate, across-the-board increases as opposed to percentage increases in base wages; simplification of the job classification ladder based on skill differentials; and flat-rate indexing agreements to protect against inflation (*scala mobile*). By favoring low-paid workers rather than the more advantaged segments of the working class, these policies favored women workers. For example, in manufacturing the average hourly earnings of women, which had been 70 percent of those of men in 1969, were 85 percent of the male average in 1981, one of the lowest differentials in the industrialized countries. In the words of the Italian labor economist Paolo Santi, with a nod to Molière: "Italian unions have followed a feminist policy 'sans le savoir'" (without knowing it).[6]

Feminism developed in the 1970s in Italy. While it did involve women workers and trade unionists, it did not address issues of women and work. The movement was more powerful and different from previous women's mobilizations in Italy. It actually looked with mistrust on the older women's struggles, especially those oriented toward equality and emancipation. The new feminist movement was oriented toward a radical critique of the "public" male world: it questioned its ruling principles based on competition and hierarchy; and demanded the right to be "different," not to be integrated on equal footing into the male world. The emphasis was on the "personal" realm—on personal politics, on issues of identity. The first political issues raised by the new feminist movement were not in the sphere of women's work, but in the reproductive sphere where women's differ-

---

6. Paolo Santi, "Le retribuzioni femminili in Italia: tra discriminzione ed egualitarismo," unpublished paper, May 1984.

ence is rooted. In fact, reproductive issues—for instance, the abortion campaign of 1976–77—marked the peak of political mobilization.

As in other industrialized countries the movement started as a middle-class mobilization. Women students, teachers, educated housewives, former participants in the 1968 students' movement and in the subsequent general political mobilization were the actors in the first stage of feminism. In contrast with other industrialized countries, however, the movement in Italy diffused across class lines, involving women workers and especially trade unionists. In the trade unions, the movement gained surprising mass support even while maintaining some of its original orientation: it was very critical of "male" trade unionism; called attention to women's "difference"; and developed an autonomous, almost entirely separatist, organization parallel to the official trade union structure. The movement had remarkable success, gaining legitimacy inside the trade union organization itself—possibly a unique development among industrialized countries.

Paradoxically, although the movement had the mass support of women workers and activists, it did not focus on issues of women in the workplace. Instead, it used the workplace and the union as a forum for discussing the broad issues of gender roles, women's health and sexuality, and women's identity. The movement claimed that the traditional dilemmas caused by policies toward women workers, such as protection versus equality, were false: traditional protective policies were wrong but policies of equality were not appealing either; women's specificity, women's difference, had to be proclaimed and placed at the center of trade union policy toward women workers. However, women's difference had to be the pivot of a policy of general change in the male-shaped world of work and not be used to justify traditional protective policies.

The claim of a "third alternative" beyond protection or equality was the message of feminism in Italian trade unions. But the message was stated as a matter of principle and did not become the foundation for specific policies on women and work. Further, the dismissal of the traditional alternative solutions, protection versus equality, was not at all easy, as demonstrated by the problems raised by equal employment opportunity legislation after 1977.

At the end of 1977 an equal opportunities law was passed, making it illegal to discriminate on the basis of sex in all areas of work

—training, hiring, treatment on the job, promotion, firing, pension benefits.[7] The law came out of the blue. The trade unions had not pushed for it as they had for the maternity law and the equal pay agreements. The idea of an action against sex discrimination in the workplace had never emerged in trade union circles, and for a while after the legislation was passed the unions seemed unaware of it. The women's movement also had not pressed for passage of the law; only some time after it was passed did the question arise as to whether its provisions were favorable or unfavorable to women. The women's movement did not develop a real interest in the problems of discrimination and equal opportunities until the 1980s. The overall absence of social pressure and interest probably explains not only the weaknesses and flaws of the sex discrimination law but also the very poor implementation of the law.

Some parts of the law which abolished previous legally sanctioned differences of treatment between the sexes were simply and automatically implemented. This was the case, for instance, in the cancellation of the compulsory retirement age limit for women, which had been five years earlier than that of men. However, in one of the few aspects of the law that provided a form of positive discrimination for women, they were given the option of retiring earlier. In addition, the state-controlled lists of the unemployed, which previously had separated men and women, were unified. The unification of these lists brought about considerable changes in women's employment in the late 1970s. Since employers who wanted to hire unemployed workers were compelled by law to hire their unskilled workers from the public lists of the unemployed, hiring blindly without individual selection, after the establishment of unified unemployed lists in 1977 they had to hire women whenever they were next in order on the rolls. Women were in fact overrepresented on such lists and hence were hired in great numbers, even for jobs that had previously not been open to them. For instance, 10,000 women were hired for the automobile assembly lines at Fiat for the first time. Fiat had never hired women for such jobs.[8] But the impact of the change was limited

---

7. For a good analysis of the law and its shortcomings, against the background of a historical reconstruction of labor legislation, see M. V. Ballestrero, "Dalla tutela alla parità," *Il Mulino* (1980).

8. Bianca Beccalli and Rita Invernizzi, "Women in Non-traditional Jobs: The Italian Case," paper presented at the conference on the Empowerment of Women, Gröningen, Sweden, 1984.

by definition to unskilled labor and areas of expanding demand, and it was limited in practice by the inefficiency of the public hiring system and the many ways of getting around it.[9]

Other parts of the law abolished other previously legal differential treatment but in more complicated ways. Protective norms for women workers were cancelled, with two exceptions: the prohibition on nightwork remains, but collective bargaining can remove it; and the prohibition on heavy and unhealthy jobs was repealed, but collective bargaining can reintroduce it. Therefore, as part of a general change in labor law and industrial relations, the sex discrimination law assigns a crucial role in implementation to trade unions and to collective bargaining.[10] The law required the unions to develop a clear understanding of the law and to supply resources for its implementation, both of which proved difficult, and very little happened.

Only an individual employee is entitled to file a complaint; the law does not allow for class action. The individual employee has the burden of proving discrimination and the standards for proof are not clear, except where employers have violated unemployment list priorities. In the first judgments handed down under the law, the employees not only had to prove discrimination but also the employer's intent to discriminate. The sanctions in the law are extremely limited: a small fine against an employer who has violated the law; no back pay to an employee who has proved discrimination; no compensatory action other than prohibition of the particular action that was found to be discriminatory.

In general the law does not provide for positive (affirmative) action on behalf of women, and, according to some interpretations, such action is proscribed by its literal use of the concept of equal treatment, an interpretation that can lead to problems of reverse discrimination. In fact, it is ironic that, within the context of very poor implementation of the law, some of the few complaints brought before the courts charge reverse discrimination. For example, in March 1984, a judge in Liguria found a local municipality guilty of reverse discrimination for having provided an EEC-funded professional training course for women only.

In the years immediately following the approval of the law, because of very low consciousness of the difficulties of bringing about

---

9. P. Ichino, "Il collocamento impossibile" (Franco Angeli, 1983).
10. L. Hoesch, "La legge di parità: un bilancio," *Lavoro* 80 (1983).

the division of labor between the sexes, especially among the public authorities, no social or cultural policies were developed to support the law. The provisions related to discrimination at the workplace produced one of the lowest rates of litigation on record: forty cases in six years. In addition, some of the law's minor but significant provisions, such as parental leave for fathers, were not only unimplemented but were virtually unknown to the public. It was not until the end of 1983, six years after the passage of the law, that a National Commission for Equal Opportunities was established.

Perspectives on the Future

Why was it so difficult for the women's movement, the unions, and the state to develop labor market policies for women in Italy? Broadly, the answer can be drawn from the historical sketch presented earlier. But specifically it is possible to show how the existence of equal opportunities legislation gives more visiblity to the problems and contradictions in the orientation and the policies of the women's movement, the unions, and the state.

The women's movement, in the form which the new feminism took in Italy in the 1970s, had obvious difficulties in developing labor market policies for women; some of the difficulties can be seen as transient or nation-specific; others are probably constant and common to many countries. The contradictions of equality, the dilemmas between "equality" and "difference," are in the background of all women's movements. These problems are likely to arise more frequently in regard to work than reproduction. For quite a while Italian feminists preferred to deal with reproductive issues and evaded the problem of work. When they finally confronted the problems of women in the workplace, they had to immediately face the question whether it is necessary for women to adopt the same model of work and career that men have historically developed. The question was all the more difficult to answer because of two specific developments. On the one hand, the equal opportunities law gave women access only to the lowest occupational positions, including those from which women had been previously excluded, in some cases by reason of protective norms. Was it worthwhile, for the sake of equality, to encourage women to take unhealthy and risky jobs, night shifts, and the like? Was it worthwhile to push for implementing the equal opportunities legislation if it meant losing protective norms? On the other hand, since the law did not make provision for positive action, the women's movement could have picked up that flaw and pushed for creating new positive policies. However, the movement was conditioned by its specific historical inheritance: the egalitarian ideology it had inherited from the political mobilization of the late 1960s and early 1970s and which it had helped to reinvigorate was difficult to square with the notions of advancement and career that are inherent in positive action policies.

The trade unions, for their part, were dedicated to equality in general but not to specific policies to promote disadvantaged groups. The logic of political "class" unionism, which allowed for policies that benefited the lowest strata of the working class and thereby benefited women, was the same logic that had always kept unions from developing specific active labor market policies. It was the logic of class unionism to invest union resources to protect the wages of *all* workers from inflation; to change the *overall* pattern of industrial investment from the industrialized North to the backward South; and to defend *all* workers against unemployment. Specific action for target groups of workers was beyond the logic of class unionism.[11] The tradition of general defense versus specific promotion has deep-rooted historical origins connected with the weakness of unions in Italy from their beginnings until the 1960s, but it has endured beyond the historical circumstances which engendered it. It is fed by the continuing preoccupation of Italian unions not to lose central control, fragment class action in the distribution of small benefits, or antagonize some sectors of the working population while trying to promote others; and it is fed by the matching unresponsiveness of the state to policies of promotion that would require public action.

The state is in fact a very unreliable partner. First of all, there is no tradition of action against discrimination in Italy, due partly to the fact that the legal system and public policies never had to face such clear-cut problems of discrimination as countries with ethnic and racial minorities. Hence, the state does not have the legal and institutional background against which action against sex discrimination could take place. Further, insofar as the judiciary is concerned, the

---

11. Very little collective bargaining took place on the basis of the new legislation, as shown by an analysis of collective agreements in the Milan area: F. Borgogelli, "Legislazione e contratazione collective," unpublished research report, Milan, March 1983. For a general analysis of labor market policies, see I. Regalia, "Le politiche del lavoro" in *Le politiche del welfare state in Italia*, ed. U. Ascoli (Franco Angeli, 1983).

role of litigation has never been as significant as collective bargaining in Italian industrial relations; and insofar as the governmental machinery is concerned, the Italian bureaucracy is both inefficient and corrupt.

At the end of the 1970s, it seemed as if all these difficulties had produced a real stalemate. The case for positive action for women workers seemed lost, having missed the favorable moment in which trade union strength, a rising women's movement, and institutional reform could have happily interacted. Contrary to these expectations, remarkable changes have been taking place since 1983, and new perspectives are being defined.

A debate has developed in the women's movement around issues of women and work and of women and power, breaking the silence that accompanied the movement's decline at the end of the 1970s. The renewal of participation after this intermission and the shifting of interests from reproduction to issues of women's work and public life seemed to mark the second stage of the women's movement, involving both the "radical" feminists and the feminists in the trade unions.[12] The latter group is playing a distinct role in this second stage, having left behind their own first stage of advancing demands based on general principles, the feminist unionists have started tackling issues of women in the workplace, and confronting the union leadership with specific claims to be put on the bargaining agenda. The unions respond, even if reluctantly, to this pressure. They themselves have been forced to make a number of changes by external circumstances such as the economic crisis, governmental "deregulation" of the labor market, and rapid changes in the labor force. The unions are being pushed to develop new active labor market policies instead of relying on their traditional policies of general defense of all workers. Although this could easily result in dropping women's issues from their agenda, at the moment the new pressure of the feminist unionists is having some results, for instance, Equal Opportunities Centers for women workers.

Although compared with the other possible agents of labor policies for women the state is the least likely to undergo fast and profound changes, some institutional changes are taking place. The establishment of an Equal Opportunities Commission has been

---

12. A document by a group of radical feminists was a significant beginning of this debate: "Piu donne che uomini," Sottosopra, December 1982. For a discussion of these developments, see Bianca Beccalli, "Classe, sesso e potere," *Quaderni Piacentini*, 1983.

followed with interest by the women's movement in general and by the feminist unionists in particular.

This is not a "happy ending." The changes described are the outcome of complex structural changes and of political processes. Although they are remarkable changes, they do not cancel all the difficulties. Some of the difficulties and resources for change are common to industrialized countries; some are specific to Italy. The international comparison will help both the intellectual understanding and the development of policies.

Discussion

Child Care

Italy is more progressive than the United States with regard to child care. The commune (local authority) has good care available, virtually free, not so much for infants but certainly for children over three. There is another child care institution in Italy: the nonna (grandmother). It is much more common to have a family member take care of the children in Italy than it is elsewhere. This frees up the young mother to enter the labor market. (Carol Bohmer)

I am impressed with the Italian approach to maternity leave; I contrast that with the American trend toward treating maternity as a disability. One way to look at it is to ask ourselves if we are trying to support homemakers or to encourage women to see themselves as workers with a lifelong commitment to work that will make them independent. (Barbara Bergmann)

Labor Education

An Italian experiment in labor education came about because of pressure from the Metalworkers Union. An agreement made possible up to 150 hours of released time for study per worker, either to complete the equivalent of a high school education, to take special courses, or to begin college-level study. In Milan alone, in an eight-year period, no fewer than 19,000 workers were able to take advantage of this educational opportunity.

I initiated a series of courses on women's issues. I designed them originally to focus on labor history and collective bargaining but I found that the women wanted to start by exploring much more personal issues, such as sexuality, divorce, and the meaning of work in their lives. Later, they were able to move to more general themes, but the focus in Italy is always more personal than is the case with the labor education courses in the United States. (Bianca Beccalli)

14.
The United States of America

Barbara Bergmann

OUR ASSESSMENT OF THE CURRENT American scene should be a positive one: there has indeed been progress. One of the most significant recent developments in the United States has been the emergence of a gender gap in voting patterns. Women are voting differently from men for the first time in American history. By so doing, they are demonstrating a rising consciousness of unfairness in the system.

There has been progress for women in the United States job market, but not as much as anticipated by many feminists. Where entry into professional jobs has been mediated by affirmative action taken by universities, there has been considerable progress: there are increasing numbers of women students of medicine, law, and business—and they are getting jobs after graduation. What has been slow has been the desegregation of many other occupations; the same pattern of "women's jobs" and "men's jobs" keeps repeating itself. I teach a course on the economics of sex roles and ask students to do field research at their own places of work. They report finding sex segregation in many situations. For example, at a shop where jeans are sold, only male workers are stationed in the back, near the manager; and in the fast food restaurants, women are not allowed to cook. Yet, in both cases, male and female workers have the same qualifications.

The United States has the legal foundation for equality on the job: Title VII of the Civil Rights Act of 1964 outlaws discrimination against women and minority groups in hiring, job assignment, promotion, and pay. For the first few years after passage of this legislation, the provision against sex discrimination was rarely invoked, but it is now recognized as the law of the land and is unlikely to be repealed. What is needed is stricter enforcement. The gap between the median annual earnings of women and men full-time workers has shown no change since the passage of the Civil Rights Act. At that time, the female median was 60 percent of the male median, and it remains so today.

Why so little progress? During the Reagan administration, government policies fostering the deregulation of business, restricting the use of affirmative action regulations, and decreasing funding for innovative training programs have not been in the best interests of women. However, there was not in previous administrations an assiduous effort to improve the situation of American working women through aggressive labor market policy either. Ironically, the especially negative effect of the policies of the Reagan administration appear to have contributed to the raising of women's consciousness.

One positive aspect of the United States laws against sex discrimination is that they provide for serious penalties. Employers found guilty of sex discrimination may have to pay large sums of money in back pay awards to employees. Private firms serving as federal government contractors that are found in violation of affirmative action regulations can become ineligible to receive future federal contracts and can be deprived of current contracts. These are potentially powerful sanctions, but unfortunately the penalties are not automatically applied. Charges of violations of the Civil Rights Act or of the affirmative action regulations usually involve legal suits which have proven to be extremely expensive and time consuming. I have served a number of times as an expert witness in sex discrimination cases. Not once have I been called into court before the case was eight years old. Typically, it went on for three years longer before a judgment was reached. The suit brought by women at Cornell University has been in federal court since October 1980.[1]

Even successful cases do not guarantee a change in the underlying attitudes that caused the problem in the first place. Sometimes money damages are assessed and paid without any change in policies. I recall a case where a woman was awarded a large pension settlement because she had missed out on a promotion, but the question of

---

1. Preliminary approval to a settlement agreement between the Cornell Eleven plaintiffs and Cornell University was granted by Judge Howard G. Munson of the Northern District of New York, U.S. Federal Court on September 26, 1984.

changing the employer's promotion procedure was never addressed. Plaintiffs and their attorneys bring a lawsuit for money damages to compensate for losses due to discrimination, not for an enforceable promise that the employer will not break the law again. There is no system for monitoring progress within a firm after a lawsuit has been won.

Lawsuits charging discrimination seldom can deal with bias in hiring. When a woman is turned down for a job for which she has applied, she does not have the resources, the support, or even the knowledge necessary to bring a complaint even if she believes she is a victim of discrimination. Only people inside an organization can get together as a group, file a joint complaint, hire an attorney, and proceed with a grievance. Nevertheless, the ability to file class actions places American women at an advantage over women in many other countries who are permitted only to file individual complaints.

How can American women speed progress? First of all, the women's movement must get behind the drive for affirmative action. Up to now, affirmative action has been seen mainly in a racial context. Black organizations have been in favor of it, as have some federal judges. Women's groups, in contrast, have been less vocal on the issue, especially on the importance of numerical goals and timetables for hiring underrepresented population groups. It is a mistake to accept the argument that goals and timetables are necessary because past discrimination has rendered minorities and women less competent than white males. Rather, goals and timetables are necessary to provide a numerical standard to use to measure changes in the composition and status of a work force. Despite some disadvantages, goals and timetables are indispensable tools for monitoring personnel practices.

We also need comparable worth pay adjustments to supplement affirmative action. The press for equal pay for work of comparable value—to get employers to realign wages—was born of discouragement at the slow progress under the Civil Rights Act. In a sense, it represents a turning away from activism dedicated to occupational desegregation toward support for higher pay in traditional women's occupations. However, there is no reason why the push to encourage women to enter nontraditional occupations should not go forward full force at the same time.

How practical is comparable worth? Its best chance of success is in the public sector. It has been pushed by unions of public employees and by state legislatures, which can bring it about by fiat. A state will not go out of business if its payroll is increased by 25 percent. If we establish the principle of equal pay for work of comparable value in the public sector, which is large in the United States, this will affect supply and demand in the private sphere. More women would receive better wages in the public sector and this, in turn, would tend to raise women's salaries in private employment.

It would be best if women's wages could be brought up to men's and then go on from there. Second best would be to bring men's wages down to where women's wages are or to have some compromise between these two options. Worst would be maintaining the status quo—continuing to have inequality. I have done a study of the costs of certain options. For instance, if earnings of women were brought up to men's level, it would increase payrolls by 25 percent. Another possibility is to take money that would have been allocated for all increases in a given year and give most of it to women. An amount of money sufficient to finance a 7 percent across-the-board increase would, if given entirely to women, finance a 27 percent increase in women's pay. The reason is that women are about 43 percent of the work force and their wages are 60 percent of men's. Thus, we could wipe out a great deal of the wage gap in one year. There are ways and means of closing the gap, but men have to be willing either to stand still or take a very low relative increase.

We need to reorder our priorities. American women have been wasting a great deal of time in the campaign for an Equal Rights Amendment to the federal consitution. While it might have a symbolic effect, it is hard to see that it would do much concrete good. By and large, what will be most affected by passage of the ERA will be trivia: for example, the fact that a deceased solider's brother, under present law, has a better chance of getting his medals than his sister does. I am in favor of the ERA, but I think we have expended too much energy on it.

The women's movement also goes off track by concentrating on doing things for housewives, such as providing them with pensions at public expense. Cuvillier makes the point that providing a pension for a housewife is insuring that there will always be domestic service available to men.[2] We need to concentrate on helping working women.

---

2. "The Housewife: An Unjustified Financial Burden on the Community," *Journal of Social Policy* 8, no. 1 (1979): 1–26.

The issue of sharing housework is a vital one. We need to make this a public issue, to stimulate discussion and debate through the media. We should be advocating a change to the "hotel style of living" where the building we live in provides facilities for child care, laundry, cafeteria, cleaning service. However, we should not wait for the government—in the United States or in the Soviet Union—to achieve this type of living arrangement. We should organize it ourselves. It would be helpful if a foundation were to set up a model hotel living unit for urban working families. Such a model just might catch on.

Time-use studies might help to get the issue of sharing housework into public forums. Research suggests that the problem is continuing in the younger generation in that boys today do less housework than girls. We have to put pressure on the men to do half the work at home.

In general, the women's movement has done a terrible job in recruiting male allies, although there are many men who are potential supporters. Ways have to be devised to enlist them in women's cause.

Enormous changes are coming in American society. The breakup of the union shop and the demise of smokestack industries mean that there are a lot more men working for the minimum wage—men in their thirties and forties. Some men are being forced into the situation many women have always been in. An additional important change is the introduction of office automation, which is going forward at a furious pace. Skilled clerical work, as we know it now, may be virtually obsolete within ten years.

Dealing with unemployment is going to require certain changes in the structure of work in the United States. We need a drop in standard hours—a shortening of the workday. This has not happened since World War II. Why? A drop in the workweek would reduce unemployment and would help in providing more time for the sharing of housework. One reason employers want long hours is that fringe benefits have increased. The major benefit—health insurance—is computed on a per head basis. An employer who pays for health insurance wants to get as many hours as possible out of an employee. If health insurance were not linked to employment, it would be easier to bring about a drop in hours. In addition, part-time workers in the United States do not get fringe benefits as a rule. Thus, many women and men who may want to work part time cannot do so because of the loss of benefits.

The American feminist legislative agenda should include (1) health insurance as a government function with no link to employment, (2) no employer tax deductions for fringe benefits, (3) similar wages and fringe benefits for part- and full-time workers, (4) more funding for enforcement of antidiscrimination laws, (5) government-provided child care, (6) high child-support awards and better enforcement of payment, and (7) lower standard hours of work. Each of these reforms can benefit women workers; they present a challenge and an opportunity.

It is clear that there is a lot of work to be done.

Discussion

Comparable Worth

One public sector union in Connecticut is investigating the introduction of equal pay for work of comparable value. How can it gain public understanding of this move if, for instance, the pay for nurse's aide is upgraded to $8 an hour? (Deborah King)

Deborah King should not expect the Connecticut union to act all alone. How can one small union in one of the smallest states attempt to make so drastic a change all by itself? Their move toward comparable worth is path breaking. This is a cutting-edge issue because it violates all the norms of the American free market system. (Ronnie Steinberg)

Women Union Members

The role of women's groups within the trade union movement in the United States has been interesting. I have two developments in mind. The first is the Coalition of Labor Union Women (CLUW), which is an organization of women members of many different trade unions. It developed independently of the AFL-CIO, the male-dominated federation, and has remained separate from it. The second landmark was the foundation of 925, the organization of women clerical workers. A fair amount of effort is being expended in the United States now to organize clerical workers, either into their own unions like 925, or into mainstream unions like the Service Employees International. (Brigid O'Farrell)

I believe CLUW is unique in the world. In Germany, Austria, Switzerland, and other countries, individual unions have women's departments, women's committees, perhaps even women representatives on the executive councils; and there are conferences on women's issues and activities for women. In France and in several unions in Great Britain, unions have special staff members assigned to women's concerns. To be sure, there are still unions that do not have any of these in place yet. (Ilda Simona)

Many American unions favor offering "cafeteria style" benefits to workers, letting individual workers choose what benefits they need at various stages in their lives. I believe this helps women. (Edna Berger Marks) Unions in the United States have always supported both national health insurance and a shorter working day. (Jackie Kienzle) I concede that some unions have done progressive things, but I hold to the necessity for a new alliance between trade unions and women workers. I believe that the unions must place a higher priority on reforms that will help women. (Barbara Bergmann)

Availability of Data
In the United States, researchers have less access to labor market data than in the past. Under the current administration, many ongoing projects that used to result in useful statistics have been cut off. We do not know, for example, what kind of jobs are now available for what kind of people. We lack information on ages, on women's employment, on poverty. It is all very well to call for studies and analyses but without the data, we cannot do them. (Olivia Mitchell)

Afterword

Alice Hanson Cook

FIRST AND CHIEFLY I want only to say "thank you" for all that you have contributed to what I have done, for, in a sense, the participants in this event in all their individuality and diversity embody my fifth career.

I began as a social worker. I was a labor educator and organizer. I was a foreign service officer. And I was a professor. In my retirement, I began something that is hard to designate—a combination of self-employed researcher and activist on questions of women's employment.

I am happy to have had these last eleven years of "retirement" from academe because they have given me a rare opportunity to work in a completely unregimented atmosphere. Nobody has said, Do this! Do that! You must. . . There's a meeting. . . . or Watch out! Well, of course, some people have said, "Watch out!" But I have not had to watch out. Altogether, I cannot recommend the state of retirement too highly and the real freedom that it brings: the freedom to work on what one chooses; the freedom to say "no" (a freedom I have found hard to exercise); and chiefly, the freedom to say "I'll be glad to do that," even when no payment was in the offing. The rewards in every case have been liberating and exhilarating.

In this "thank-you" moment, I want to mention three of my nearest and dearest friends, each of whom has contributed immeasurably to me and to making this conference possible: Jennie Farley, its organizer and my stalwart and indefatigable companion in the struggle for women's equality at Cornell University; Rose Goldsen, my intellectual mentor; and Fran Herman, friend and fellow traveler in many places in the world. Without them my life would not have been nearly so complete. In addition, I would like to pay tribute to Barbara Wertheimer who was my intimate friend for thirty years, from the days in which we were both engaged in labor education until her last working weeks when she contributed the chapter on women and trade unions to my most recent book. My tribute goes first to her courage and then to her generosity. She was the person who started me on my fifth career. She drew the attention of the Ford Foundation to my availability in the fall of 1972 to start off on worldwide travels to look at the development of social policy for working mothers in nine countries. Thus I never had to experience the trauma of retirement.

At my retirement party in 1972, I already knew that I was off on a long trip to Europe and perhaps further; I knew that I wanted to look at programs in communist and noncommunist countries; I had some friends and many contacts. With that preparation I left for a year and a half. Thus, I never had to face the loss of classes I wouldn't be meeting, of committees on which I would no longer serve, or how I now could make a place for myself outside the university that had absorbed almost my whole life. All that was left behind. I started on something totally new and fresh. It proved to be a very demanding, strenuous, improvised, and rewarding eighteen months.

I came back radicalized as a feminist. I found that, no matter what the economic system, working women were suffering from the same difficulties in the East and in the West. In many of the papers in this collection, their problems have been outlined afresh: the difficulties of subordination in the home and workplace; job segregation; the double burden; the consequences of part-time work; the need for child care; few opportunities for skill training either on or off the job; the inadequate representation of women and their concerns within the trade unions; the imperfect realization of equal pay for equal work; and the dawning recognition that the solution lies with equal pay for work of equal value, that is, with "comparable worth" as we Americans call the issue. Yet, one of the happiest notes sounded in these reports in that change in the sense of progress, while it has slowed in many countries, chiefly in Great Britain and the United States under reactionary political leadership, has nevertheless continued. When I look back to 1972 I can testify that we have come a long way. The women's world of 1983 is different from the world into which I plunged in 1972. But we still have a long way to go.

Nowhere is child care adequate to meet the need for it. Paternity leave, while more and more recognized as a desirable contribution to infant care and care of sick children is largely unused, even where it has been made available. Women's needs for job training have been forgotten in the face of worldwide unemployment; indeed in most countries, women's unemployment rates and even numbers exceed those of men. Women's job opportunities are severely limited by the constraints of job segregation, and women's work continues to be paid substantially less than men's even when their contributions to the employer are virtually equal. Sexual harassment on the job as well as on the street testifies to the expression of the worst aspects of patriarchy in the male-female relationship on and off the job. Protective legislation continues to be applied only to women, with resulting restrictive effects on their opportunities for work, while men, free of these protective restrictions, continue to be exposed to killing stress and lethal toxic exposures.

Progress takes place piecemeal for the most part and sometimes even contradictorally by creating new problems and inequities to balance those it has solved. Only in one or two countries in Scandinavia have national movements espoused thoroughgoing policies of equity that apply both to the labor market and to social and family welfare. And even there, the heavy hand of traditional patriarchy slows progress toward the ultimate goal.

While I shall not live to see the realization of the goals we have set, the joy and the rewards I have experienced from this tribute encourage me to say, "Let's go on! Women's equality deserves our every effort."

What I want most to think about is how we can make our studies in law, government, history, public policy, economics, sociology, psychology, and labor relations truly interdisciplinary. We must find the way to bridge the disciplines so as to bring many different viewpoints to bear on the problems of working women throughout the world.

In my retirement I have been able to know the pleasure of activism and to respond to its compulsion. What I hope now is that we can put scholarship in the service of activism, increasing its scope, its power, and its possibilities.

APPENDIX A
Books and Articles by Alice Hanson Cook

1985   *A Casebook on Comparable Worth in the Public Sector.* Hawaii: Industrial Relations Center, University of Hawaii.

"Equality in the Workplace: The Role of Trade Unions in Market Economics." In *Women and Structural Transformation: The Crisis of Work and Family Life,* edited by Lourdes Beneria and Catharine R. Stimpson, New Brunswick, N.J.: Rutgers University Press.

1984   "Comparable Worth: Recent Developments in Selected States." In *Comparable Worth,* edited by Helen Remick. Philadelphia: Temple University Press.

"Women and Work in Industrial Societies." In *Urbanism and Urbanization,* edited by Noel Iverson. The Netherlands: E. J. Brill.

Women and Trade Unions in Eleven Industrialized Countries, edited with Val R. Lorwin and Arlene Kaplan Daniels. Philadelphia: Temple University Press.

1983   *Comparable Worth: The Problem and States' Approaches to Wage Equity.* Hawaii: Industrial Relations Center, University of Hawaii-Manoa.

1982   "Comparable Worth, Background and Current Issues." Industrial Relations Center Reports. Honolulu: University of Hawaii.

1980   "Labor Education in America: Marriage of Convenience?" In *Trade Unionism in the United States. A Symposium in Honor of Jack Barbash,* edited by James L. Stern and Barbara D. Dennis. Madison: Industrial Relations Institute, University of Wisconsin.

"The Most Difficult Revolution: Women and Trade Unions." *Equal Opportunities International* 1, number 2.

"Labor Education and Women Workers: An International Comparison" (with Roberta Till-Retz). In *Labor Education for Women Workers,* edited by Barbara M. Wertheimer. Philadelphia: Temple University Press.

"The Representation of Women and Their Interests in Industrial Relations Institutions: Women in Trade Unions." In *Women and Industrial Relations,* edited by Dorothea Gaudart. Geneva: International Institute for Labour Studies, ILO.

Working Women in Japan: Discrimination, Resistance, and Reform (with Hiroko Hayashi). Cornell International Industrial and Labor Relations Report Number 10. Ithaca: New York State School of Industrial and Labor Relations, Cornell University.

"Collective Bargaining As a Strategy for Achieving Equal Opportunity and Equal Pay: Sweden and Germany." In *Equal Employment Policy for Women,* edited by Ronnie S. Ratner. Philadelphia: Temple University Press.

"Vocational Training, the Labor Market and the Unions." In *Equal Employment Policy for Women,* edited by Ronnie S. Ratner. Philadelphia: Temple University Press.

1979   *Equal Employment Opportunity, the Merit System and Collective Bargaining in Public Employment in the State of Hawaii.* Honolulu: Industrial Relations Center, University of Hawaii, and the State Department of Personnel.

"Working Women: European Experience and American Need." In *American Women Workers in a Full Employment Economy,* edited by Ann Foote Cahn. New York: Praeger. (Originally appeared as a report to the Joint Economic Committee of Congress, Washington, D.C., GPO, 1977.)

1978   *The Working Mother: A Survey of Problems and Programs in Nine Countries.* Revised edition. Ithaca: New York State School of Industrial and Labor Relations, Cornell University.

1977   "Mothers Working." *Cornell Alumni News.*

1976   Contributor, *Women in Blue Collar Jobs*. New York: Ford
                Foundation.

1975   "Maternity Benefits." International Society for Labor Law
                and Social Legislation, United States National Committee,
                Bulletin 8:3, October.

                "Equal Pay—Where Is It?" *Industrial Relations*, May.

                "Mothers at Work Abroad." *Industrial and Labor Relations
                Report*, Winter.

1972   "Sex Discrimination at Universities: An Ombudsman's
                View." *AAUP Bulletin*, September.

1971   *Public Employee Labor Relations in Japan: Three Aspects* (with
                Solomon B. Levine and Tadashi Mitsufuji). Ann Arbor: In-
                stitute of Labor and Industrial Relations, University of
                Michigan and Wayne State University.

1970   "Public Employee Bargaining in New York City" (with Lois
                Gray). *Industrial Relations*, May.

1969   "Labor Relations in the Public Service, a Unique Branch of
                Labor Relations Practice: The Japanese Case in Local Gov-
                ernment." In *The Changing Patterns of Industrial Relations in
                Asian Countries*. Proceedings of the Japan Institute of Labor,
                Asian Regional Conference. Tokyo: Japan Institute of La-
                bor.

                "Labor and Politics." *Issues in Industrial Society* 1, number 2.

                "Political Action and Trade Unions: A Case Study of the
                Coal Miners in Japan." *Monumenta Nipponica* 22, numbers
                1/2.

                "Labor and Politics." *ILR Research*, October.

1968   "The Status of Working Women." *American Labor Review*
                (Tokyo), January.

                "Women and American Trade Unions." *Annals of the Ameri-
                can Academy of Political and Social Science*, January.

                "The ILO and Japanese Politics, II: Gain or Loss for La-
                bor." *Industrial and Labor Relations Review*, April.

1967   "The International Posture of the American Labor Move-
              ment: The Relevance of American Experience to World
              Labor Problems." In *The Labor Movement, a Re-examination:
              A Conference in Honor of David J. Saposs*. Madison: University
              of Wisconsin Industrial Relations Research Institute and
              the State Historical Society of Wisconsin.

1966   *Introduction to Japanese Trade Unionism*. Ithaca: New York
              State School of Industrial and Labor Relations, Cornell
              University.

              "Labor Relations in New York City." *Industrial Relations*,
              May.

              "Organization among Local Government Employees in the
              U.S." *American Labor Review* (Tokyo), August.

              "Adaptations of Union Structure for Municipal Collective
              Bargaining," *Proceedings of the Industrial Relations Research
              Association*, Spring.

              "Union Structure in Municipal Collective Bargaining."
              Monthly Labor Review, June.

1965   "The International Labor Organization and Japanese Poli-
              tics." *Industrial and Labor Relations Review*, October.

1964   *Union Democracy: Practice and Ideal*. Ithaca: New York State
              School of Industrial and Labor Relations, Cornell Univer-
              sity.

1962   "Dual Government in Unions." *Industrial and Labor Relations
              Review*, April.

1958   *Labor Education Outside the Unions* (with Agnes Douty).
              Ithaca: New York State School of Industrial and Labor Re-
              lations, Cornell University.

1955   *Labor's Role in Community Affairs*. Ithaca: New York State
              School of Industrial and Labor Relations, Cornell Univer-
              sity.

1954   *Adult Education in Citizenship in Postwar Germany*. Fund for
              Adult Education.

Conference Participants

Lynne S. Abel, Associate Dean, College of Arts and Sciences, Goldwin Smith Hall, Cornell University

Judith Buber Agassi, Research Fellow, Department of Sociology, Lund University, Sweden

Josephine A. V. Allen, Assistant Professor, Department of Human Service Studies, N-136-C Van Rensselaer Hall, Cornell University

Judith E. Aronson, Director of Admissions, Graduate School, 108 Sage Graduate Center, Cornell University

Robert L. Aronson, Professor Emeritus, Industrial and Labor Relations, 158 Ives Hall, Cornell University

Samuel B. Bacharach, Professor, Industrial and Labor Relations, 300 ILR Research Building, Cornell University

Holly M. Bailey, Managing Editor, ILR Press, Cornell University

Rivka Bar-Yosef, Professor, Sociology, Hebrew National University, Jerusalem, Israel

Bianca Beccalli, Universita degli studi di Milano, Cattedra de sociologia della Lavoro e del'Industria, Milan, Italy

Frances Benson, Director, ILR Press, Cornell University

Barbara Bergmann, Professor, Economics, University of Maryland, College Park, Maryland

Naomi Black, Professor, Political Science, York University, 4700 Keele Street, Downsview, Ontario M3J 1P3, Canada

Laura Blankertz, 39 Rabbit Run, Rose Valley, Pennsylvania

Carol Bohmer, Visiting Assistant Professor of Sociology and Law, Uris Hall, Cornell University

Esther S. Bondareff, 5608 Broad Branch Road, Washington, D.C.

Jean Bowering, Professor, Nutrition, Syracuse University, Syracuse, New York

Karen W. Brazell, Professor, Japanese Literature, 378 Rockefeller Hall, Cornell University

Vernon Briggs, Professor, Industrial and Labor Relations, 393 Ives Hall, Cornell University

George W. Brooks, Professor Emeritus, Industrial and Labor Relations, 302 ILR Extension, Cornell University

Joan Jacobs Brumberg, Assistant Professor, Women's Studies and Human Development/Family Studies, G-105 Van Rensselaer Hall, Cornell University

Susan Buck-Morss, Associate Professor of Government, B-46 McGraw Hall, Cornell University

Olivera Burić, Professor Emeritus, Institute of Social Policy, Belgrade, Yugoslavia

Gwen J. Bymers, Professor Emeritus, Consumer Economics and Housing, 409 Linn Street, Ithaca, New York

M. Gardner Clark, Professor Emeritus, Industrial and Labor Relations, 266 Ives Hall, Cornell University

Avis H. Cohen, Research Associate, Veterinary Physiology, W 115 Seeley G. Mudd Building, Cornell University

Jeanne Marie Col, Professor, Public Administration, Sangamon State University, Springfield, Illinois

Charlotte Williams Conable, 381 N Street SW, Washington, D.C.

Alice Hanson Cook, Professor Emerita, Industrial and Labor Relations, 111 ILR Extension, Cornell University

Constance E. Cook, Attorney at Law, 209 Coy Glen Road, Ithaca, New York

Charles Craypo, Professor, Industrial and Labor Relations, 110 ILR Extension, Cornell University

William E. Cross, Jr., Associate Professor, Africana Studies, Africana Studies and Research Center, Cornell University

Donald E. Cullen, Professor, Industrial and Labor Relations, 201 ILR Research Building, Cornell University

Mary T. Cullen, Senior Editor, Industrial and Labor Relations Report, 194 Ives Hall, Cornell University

Philip R. Dankert, Collection Development Librarian, M.P. Catherwood Library, Cornell University

Brett deBary, Associate Professor, Japanese Literature, and Chair, Asian Studies, 370 Rockefeller Hall, Cornell University

Donna Dempster, Human Development and Family Studies, NG-14 Van Rensselaer Hall, Cornell University

Edward C. Devereux, Professor Emeritus, Human Development and Family Studies, Cornell University

Edwina Devereux, 142 Hawthorne Place, Ithaca, New York

Deborah Dietrich, Senior Research Analyst, Office of the Speaker, New York State Assembly, 221 DuBois Road, Ithaca, New York

Shirley K. Egan, Associate University Counsel, 449 Day Hall, Cornell University

Joän Roos Egner, Associate Provost and Professor, Education, 304 Day Hall, Cornell University

Ronald G. Ehrenberg, Professor, Industrial and Labor Relations, 256 Ives Hall, Cornell University

Zillah Eisenstein, Professor, Politics, Ithaca College, Ithaca, New York

Sarah Elbert, Professor, History, State University of New York, Binghamton, New York

Caryl G. Emerson, Assistant Professor, Russian Literature, 260 Goldwin Smith, Cornell University

Ylva Ericsson, Political Adviser to the Minister on Equality between Women and Men, Ministry of Labor, Stockholm, Sweden

Jennie Farley, Associate Professor, Industrial and Labor Relations, 112 ILR Extension, Cornell University

Frances W. Fejer, Federal Women's Program Adviser, North Atlantic Region, U.S. Department of Agriculture Research Service, 222A U.S. Plant Soil and Nutrition Laboratory, Cornell University

Harold Feldman, Professor Emeritus, Human Development and Family Studies, Cornell University

Margaret Feldman, Professor Emeritus, Psychology, 105 Cascadilla Park, Ithaca, New York

Shelley Feldman, Visiting Fellow, Department of Rural Sociology, Warren Hall, Cornell University

Bernard Flaherty, Labor Relations Specialist, School of Industrial and Labor Relations, 120 ILR Conference Center, Cornell University

J. Anthony Gaenslen, Attorney at Law, 108 W. Buffalo Street, Ithaca, New York

Nancy T. Gaenslen, Lecturer, Department of Modern Languages and Linguistics, 403 Morrill Hall, Cornell University

Jennifer Gerner, Associate Professor, Consumer Economics and Housing, 137 Van Rensselaer Hall, Cornell University

Kay W. Gilcher, Director, Career Services, Industrial and Labor Relations, 198 Ives Hall, Cornell University

Michael Evan Gold, Associate Professor, Industrial and Labor Relations, 293 Ives Hall, Cornell University

Carla Golden, Assistant Professor, Psychology, Ithaca College, Ithaca, New York

Rose K. Goldsen, Professor, Sociology, 330 Uris Hall, Cornell University

Joan Goodin, 3701 Harrison Street NW, Washington, D.C.

Anne Gosline, Maine State Employees Association, 65 State Street, Augusta, Maine

Joan Graff, Legal Aid Society, 693 Mission Street, 2nd Floor, San Francisco, California

Lois S. Gray, Associate Dean, Industrial and Labor Relations, Division of Extension and Public Service, 213 ILR Extension, Cornell University

Joan Greenspan, Associate National Executive Secretary, American Guild of Musical Artists, 1841 Broadway, New York, New York

Eleanor M. Hadley, Adjunct Professor, Economics, George Washington University, Washington, D.C.

Lois Haignere, Center for Women in Government, 302 Draper Hall, SUNY/Albany, 1400 Washington Avenue, Albany, New York

Shirley F. Harper, Director, Catherwood Library, School of Industrial and Labor Relations, Cornell University

Joycelyn R. Hart, Assistant Dean, Graduate School, 206 Sage Graduate Center, Cornell University

Anne L. Heald, Associate Program Officer, German Marshall Fund of the United States, 11 DuPont Circle NW, Washington, D.C.

Rita Heller, "The Women of Summer" Film Project, 14 Marcotte Lane, Tenafly, New Jersey

Francine A. Herman, Associate Professor, Hotel Administration, 537 Statler Hall, Cornell University

Ann M. Herson, Registrar, Off-Campus Credit Programs, School of Industrial and Labor Relations, Cornell University

Anne Hoffman, Legal Department, District 1, Communication Workers of America, 80 Pine Street, 37th Floor, New York, New York

Laura H. Holmberg, Wiggins, Holmberg, Galbraith & Holmberg, 308 N. Tioga Street, Ithaca, New York

Elizabeth Gilmore Holt, Bay Point Road, Georgetown, Maine

Florence Howe, Professor, English, Feminist Press, Box 334, Old Westbury, New York

Robert M. Hutchens, Associate Professor, Industrial and Labor Relations, 263 Ives Hall, Cornell University

Marion Janjic, Women's Department, 7-158, International Labour Office, Geneva, Switzerland

Helen Johnson, Administrative Aide, Women's Studies Program, 332 Uris Hall, Cornell University

Pam McAllister Johnson, Publisher, *The Ithaca Journal*, 123 West State Street, Ithaca, New York

Mary Fainsod Katzenstein, Associate Professor, Government, Uris Hall, Cornell University

Debra R. Kaufman, Department of Sociology and Anthropology, Northeastern University, 360 Huntington Avenue, Boston, Massachusetts

Jackie Kienzle, Assistant Education Director, AFL-CIO, 815 16th Street NW, Washington, D.C.

Chung N. Kim, Catalogue Librarian, Industrial and Labor Relations, Cornell University

Deborah King, 10 Scofield Place, Westport, Connecticut

Betsy Knapp, Indian Oven Farm, R.D. 1, Fayetteville, New York

Joyce Kornbluh, Institute of Labor and Industrial Relations, University of Michigan, Hutchins Hall, Ann Arbor, Michigan

Joseph Kossmann, Graduate Student, Industrial and Labor Relations, Cornell University

Haralyn D. Kuckes, President, Ithaca Teachers Association, 508 North Aurora Street, Ithaca, New York

Miroljub Labus, Fulbright Scholar, Department of Economics, 492 Uris Hall, Cornell University

Linda A. Lafferty, Federal Services Impasses Panel, 500 C Street SW, Washington, D.C.

Lee C. Lee, Associate Professor, Human Development and Family Studies, G-52 Van Rensselaer Hall, Cornell University

Antje Lemke, Professor Emeritus, Library Science, Cobblestone House, North Manlius Street, Fayetteville, New York

Risa Lieberwitz, Assistant Professor, Industrial and Labor Relations, Cornell University

David B. Lipsky, Professor, Industrial and Labor Relations, 293 Ives Hall, Cornell University

Judith Long, Associate Professor, Sociology, Syracuse University, Syracuse, New York

Sandra Lyons, Displaced Homemakers Committee of Tompkins County, 309 Mitchell Street, Ithaca, New York

Emma MacLennan, Research Officer, Low Pay Unit, 9 Poland Street, London WIV 3DG, England

Sally McConnell-Ginet, Associate Professor, Linguistics, 332 Uris Hall, Cornell University

J. Tucker McHugh, Counselor and Psychometrician, Career Center, 203 Barnes Hall, Cornell University

Jean McPheeters, Organizer, Cornell UAW, Bailor Road, Brooktondale, New York

Susan T. Mackenzie, 845 West End Avenue, Apt. 16A, New York, New York

Edna Berger Marks, 350 W. 57th Street, New York, New York

Dale Rogers Marshall, Professor, Political Science, University of California, Davis, California

Beverly Martin, Director, Affirmative Action, Ithaca City School District, Lake Street, Ithaca, New York

Nancy S. Meltzer, Assistant Dean, College of Human Ecology, N-111 C Van Rensselaer Hall, Cornell University

Andrée Michel, Research Director, Centre National de la Recherche Scientifique, 82, Rue Cardinet, 75017 Paris, France

Frank B. Miller, Professor, Industrial and Labor Relations, 101 Ives Hall, Cornell University

Jeanne Milstein, Permanent Commission on the Status of Women, State of Connecticut, 188 Euclid Avenue, Albany, New York

Barbara Mink, News Director, WHCU, 212 The Commons East, Ithaca, New York

Olivia Mitchell, Assistant Professor, Industrial and Labor Relations, 167 Ives Hall, Cornell University

Phyllis Moen, Assistant Professor, Human Development and Family Studies, G-60-B Van Rensselaer Hall, Cornell University

James O. Morris, Professor, Industrial and Labor Relations, 165 Ives Hall, Cornell University

Catherine Murray-Rust, Chair, Provost's Advisory Committee on the Status of Women, 104 Olin Library, Cornell University

Laura Mustiko, Class of 1986, College of Agriculture and Life Sciences, Cornell University

Anne H. Nelson, Codirector, Institute on Women and Work, 15 East 26th Street, New York, New York

Maurice Neufeld, Professor Emeritus, Industrial and Labor Relations, 264 Ives Hall, Cornell University

Benjamin Nichols, Professor, Electrical Engineering, 402 Phillips Hall, Cornell University

Ethel B. Nichols, Tompkins County Board of Representatives, 109 Llenroc Court, Ithaca, New York

James Nickum, Visiting Associate Professor, Asian Studies, 387 Rockefeller Hall, Cornell University

Mary Beth Norton, Professor, History, 325 McGraw Hall, Cornell University

Brigid O'Farrell, Research Associate, Center for Research on Women, Wellesley College/Harvard Trade Union Program, Wellesley, Massachusetts

Joan L. Ormondroyd, Librarian and Coordinator, Reference Instruction, Uris Library, Cornell University

Hanna Papanek, Senior Research Associate, Center for Asian Development Studies, Boston University, Boston, Massachusetts

Nancy Parkhurst, Class of 1985, Arts and Sciences, Cornell University

Eve W. Paul, 500 East 77th Street, New York, New York

Jean G. Pearson, Administrative Supervisor, Cornell Institute for Social and Economic Research, 392 Uris Hall, Cornell University

Sandra Pollack, Associate Professor, Humanities, Tompkins Cortland Community College, 170 North Street, Dryden, New York

Rhoda R. Possen, Assistant Director, Admissions, College of Arts and Sciences, Cornell University

Margaret Rawson, Foxes Spy, 7924 Rocky Springs Road, Frederick, Maryland

Paula Rayman, Director, New England Unemployment Project, Department of Sociology, Brandeis University, Waltham, Massachusetts

Julie Reddy, Graduate Student, Industrial and Labor Relations, Cornell University

Charles M. Rehmus, Dean, New York State School of Industrial and Labor Relations, 187 Ives Hall, Cornell University

Robert F. Risley, Professor, Industrial and Labor Relations, 393 Ives Hall, Cornell University

Ann Roscoe, Executive Staff Assistant, Study Abroad Programs, Center for International Studies, Uris Hall, Cornell University

Beth Rubin, Assistant Professor, Sociology, Uris Hall, Cornell University

Janet Salaff, Associate Professor, Sociology, University of Toronto, Toronto M5S 1A1, Ontario, Canada

Nicholas Salvatore, Assistant Professor, Industrial and Labor Relations, 268 Ives Hall, Cornell University

Vicki A Saporta, Director of Organizing, International Brotherhood of Teamsters, 926 Lido Lane, Foster City, California

Karen Sauvigne, Working Women's Institute, 593 Park Avenue, New York, New York

Dolores Barracano Schmidt, Assistant Vice Chancellor for Affirmative Action, State University of New York, 99 Washington Avenue, Albany, New York

Mary Ellen Schoonmaker, 163 President Street, Brooklyn, New York

Hanna Beate Schöpp-Schilling, Aspen Institute Berlin, Inselstrasse 10, 1000 Berlin 38, Federal Republic of Germany

Hilda Scott, 79 Martin Street, Cambridge, Massachusetts

Vivienne B. Shue, Professor, Government, B-6 McGraw Hall, Cornell University

Rachel J. Siegel, Member, Executive Board, Cornell University Women's Studies Program, 108 West Buffalo Street, Ithaca, New York

Ilda Simona, Head, Department for Women Workers, Youth, Vocational Training, Non-Manual Workers, and Foreign Workers, International Metalworkers' Federation, Route des Acacias 54 bis, Case postale 563, CH-1227 Geneva, Switzerland

Robert S. Smith, Professor, Industrial and Labor Relations, 259 Ives Hall, Cornell University

Janet Smith Kintner, Assistant Director, Learning Skills Center, 375 Olin Hall, Cornell University

Jozetta H. Srb, Research Associate, Industrial and Labor Relations, 209 ILR Research Building, Cornell University

Ronnie Steinberg, Research Associate, Center for Women in Government, 302 Draper Hall, SUNY/Abany, 1400 Washington Avenue, Albany, New York

Robert N. Stern, Associate Professor, Industrial and Labor Relations, 387 Ives Hall, Cornell University

Judith A. Stewart, Acting Assistant Professor, Industrial and Labor Relations, 390 Ives Hall, Cornell University

Patricia Carry Stewart, Vice President, Edna McConnell Clark Foundation, 250 Park Avenue, New York, New York

Richard Strassberg, Director, Labor/Management Documentation Center, 144 Ives Hall, Cornell University

Rachelle Taqqu, 145 Cascadilla Park, Ithaca, New York

Sidney G. Tarrow, Professor, Government, 102 McGraw Hall, Cornell University

Karen Thompson, 223 Eddy Street, Ithaca, New York

Roberta Till-Retz, Program Director, Labor Center, University of Iowa, Oakdale, Iowa

Pamela Tolbert, Assistant Professor, Industrial and Labor Relations, Ives Hall, Cornell University

Martha Tolpin, Professor and Chair, Department of History, Bentley College, Waltham, Massachusetts

Ethel L. Vatter, Professor Emerita, Consumer Economics and Housing, 117B Van Rensselaer Hall, Cornell University

William J. Wasmuth, Professor, Industrial and Labor Relations, 101 ILR Extension, Cornell University

Linda R. Waugh, Associate Professor, Linguistics, Department of Modern Languages and Linguistics, 315 Morrill Hall, Cornell University

Kathleen Weslock, GTE, Northlake, Illinois

Antoinette M. Wilkinson, Senior Lecturer, Communication Arts, 13 Roberts Hall, Cornell University

Lawrence K. Williams, Professor, Industrial and Labor Relations, 367 Ives Hall, Cornell University

Marilyn E. Williams, Secretary of the College of Arts and Sciences, 159 Goldwin Smith Hall, Cornell University

Margery Wolf, Center for Research on Women, Stanford University, 526 Campus Drive, Stanford, California

Keiko Yamanaka, Department of Sociology, 369 Uris Hall, Cornell University

Index

Abortion, 24, 56, 140, 162
Adopted children, leave for, 10
Affirmative action, 2, 118, 127, 131, 164, 171
Agassi, Judith Buber, 11, 79, 80, 136–37
Agriculture, women in, 30, 34–36, 57, 78–79, 81, 85
Akamatsu, Rioko, 65
Alcoholism, 30, 32
All China Women's Federation, 41, 44, 46
Arab society, 74
Asian women, 84, 110
Attitudes toward women's work, 17, 39, 48, 76, 85, 112, 136–37, 143, 149, 173
Australia, wage differential in, 6
Austria, xvii, 56, 176; wage differential in, 6

Bangladesh, xiii, 12, 84–86, 88–89
Baranskaia, Natalia, 14
Bar-Yosef, Rivka, vii, xiii, 68–78, 79–80
Beccalli, Bianca, vii, xiv, 154–69
Beijing Women's Federation, 45–46
Benefits, 39, 175, 176; cafeteria-style, 176
Bergmann, Barbara, vii, xiv, 79, 109–10, 168, 170-76
Biological differences, between the sexes, 20–21, 30, 33–34, 39, 59, 68, 112
Birth control, 56
Birthrate, 13, 14, 15, 24, 56, 133, 156
Black women, 110
Bohmer, Carol, 168
Bonn Basic Law, 127
Brezhnev, Leonid, 14
Burić, Olivera, vii, xii, 49–56

Canada, wage differential in, 6
Carribean women, 110
Charter of Working Women, 159
Childbirth, 31, 80
Child care, xv, 8, 28, 30, 40, 44, 46–47, 52, 55, 65–66, 72, 76, 99–100, 108, 111, 123, 134, 139, 168, 174, 178
China, People's Republic of, xii, 30, 33–48

Christian Democratic government, 128, 130
Civil Liberties Union, 128
Civil Rights Act of 1964, Title VII of, 170, 171, 172
Class action law suits, 130, 164, 172
Coalition of Labor Union Women (CLUW), 175–76
Cohen, Avis, 11
Communal facilities, 30
Communist party, 66, 158–59
Comparable worth, xiv, xv, 117, 129, 150, 172–73, 175, 178
Constitutions: France, 116; Germany, 7, 127–28; Israel, 69; Italy, 159; Japan, 59–60; Switzerland, 147–49; United States, 173
Cook, Alice Hanson, vii, viii, ix, xi, xv, xvii–xix, 63–64, 65, 66–67, 137, 177–79, 180–83
Courage, 126, 132
Cultural Revolution, 41, 43–44, 45
Czechoslovakia, 29

Dalsimer, Marlyn, 45
Daughters, as earners, 47
Defense Service Act, 70
deBary, Brett, 63, 65–66
Denmark, 65, 113
Department of Employment (UK), 105
Deregulation of employment: in England, 91, 101–6; in Italy, 167; in United States, 171
Developing world, women in the, 1, 2, 9, 81–89
Devereux, Edward, 31, 64
Distribution of female labor force, 18–21
Divorce rate, 14, 24, 32, 175
"Double day," 23, 39, 48, 66, 178
Dual labor markets. *See* Job segregation
Dual legal system, in Israel, 72

Earnings differential. *See* Pay gap
Education, 21, 38–39, 48, 50–51, 75, 82, 83–84, 88–89, 113, 133, 149, 156,

Education (*continued*)
170; extension, 88; labor, 168–69;
technical, 20–21. *See also* Training
Egypt, xiii, 81–84
Elderly, support for, 48, 80, 139, 143
Electronics, 89, 114
Emerson, Caryl, 30, 31
Emigration, 48, 55–56, 83, 136
Emma, 126, 132
Employment Act of 1980 (UK), 104
Employment Equality Act (Japan), 62
Employment of Women Law (Israel), 70
Employment Protection Act (UK), 97, 104
Employment Protection Consolidation Act (UK), 97
Employment Security Act (Japan), 59
Employment Severance Compensation Law (Israel), 71
Engineers, women as, 7
Equal Employment Opportunities Law: Israel, 69; Italy, 155, 162–63, 164–65
Equal Opportunities Act (Sweden), 145
Equal Opportunities Centers, 168
Equal Opportunities Commission: England, 7, 96, 102–3, 106; Italy, 167–68
Equal Pay Act, 95, 109
Equal pay for equal work, xii, 6, 35, 49, 129, 131, 150, 151, 160, 170, 178
Equal Rights Amendment, 65, 173
Equality, between sexes, 9, 29, 31, 77–78, 91, 123, 127, 142, 144, 158, 159, 160, 162, 165, 179
Ericsson, Ylva, viii, xiv, 138–45
European Communities Act, 105–6
European Court, 106, 130–31
European Economic Community (EEC), 2, 3, 5, 7, 113, 116, 127–28, 129, 130, 135, 164; Adaptation Act, 129–31

Fair Wages Resolution (FWR), 106–7
Family, balance between work and, 25–28; impact of women's work on, 23–25; responsibilities, 3, 8, 21, 23, 53; in totalitarian society, 30–31
Family responsibility system, 42–43
Family status production, 82, 86–87
Farley, Jennie, viii, xi–xv, 177
Federal Equality Commission (Germany), 132
Federal Republic of Germany. *See* Germany, West
Federation of Textile, Chemical, and Paper Workers, 151
Feldman, Margaret, 89
Feldman, Shelley, 11–12, 88–89

Feminism, 48, 66–67, 82, 108, 111, 117–18, 119, 121, 123, 125–27, 136–37, 140, 155, 157, 161, 162, 165, 170, 173, 178; radical, 26, 167
Fiat, 163
Finland, 4
Five Guarantees, 48
Five-year plans, 16, 27
Flexible work schedules, 18, 22–23
Floating wage, 45
Fonda, Nickie, viii, xiii, 90–109
Ford Foundation, xix, 178
France, xiii, 6, 7, 112–23, 146, 176
Free Democratic party, 126, 128, 129, 130, 132, 135

Gaenslen, Nancy, 123
Gender gap, in voting patterns, 170
German Federation of Trade Unions, 125, 132, 137
German Women's Council, 125, 132
Germany, West (FRG), xiii–xiv, xvii, 7, 63, 123, 124–37, 176
Ghana, 89
Goals and timetables, 172
Goldsen, Rose, 177
Government Official Act (Japan), 60
Gray, Lois S., viii, xvii–xix
Great Britain, xiii, 90–111, 176, 178
Great Leap Forward, 34, 44
Greens party, 126
Guangdong, 42
Guest workers, 136, 153

Hayashi, Hiroko, ix, xii, 57–63, 65
Health insurance, 174–76
Health, in the workplace, 22, 120–21, 164, 165, 179
Heavy work, in Germany, 128; in Switzerland, 151; in Italy, 164
Hebrew language, 69
Herman, Fran, 177
Hiring, discrimination in, 51–52, 58–59, 129, 163, 170–71, 172
Histadrut, 71–72
Home care, xv, 8, 11, 23, 53, 141, 174; male participation in, 11, 25, 37, 40
Housework. *See* Home care
Housing, 31, 38, 55
Howe, Geoffrey, 104

ILO Conventions, 9, 61–62, 105; No. 100, 2, 5, 7, 62; No. 111, 2; no. 156, 8
India, xiii, 81, 84
Indonesia, 64–65, 85
Industrial Revolution, 141

Infant care, 37, 178
"In principle" men, 144
Interdependence, of rich and poor countries, 11–12
Interdisciplinary studies, need for, 53, 179
International Labour Office (ILO), xi, 1–12, 127, 153
International Women's Decade, 49–50, 61
International Women's Year, xii, 49, 52
Israel, xiii, 68–80, 136
Italy, xiv, 146, 154–69

Janjic, Marion, ix, xi, 1–11, 80, 153
Japan, xii, xviii, 33, 57–67, 86
Japanese Labor Standards Act, 58, 59–60
Jenkin, Patrick, 90
Job evaluation, 7, 36
Job segregation, xv, 4, 18–21, 34, 44–45, 50, 75, 78–79, 94, 123, 135, 140–41, 142, 152, 156, 160–61, 170, 172, 179
Job sharing, 51
Journalists, women, as advocates, 66–67, 126

Kibbutz, 74, 76, 78
Kienzle, Jackie, 176
King, Deborah, 175
Knesset, 69
Korea, 64–65, 89

Labor force participation, by women, 2, 13, 15–18, 49, 50, 57, 74–75, 82, 84–85, 91–93, 101–2, 114, 124–25, 138, 150, 154–55
Labor party, 70
Labus, Miroljub, 54–55
Lapidus, Gail W., ix, xii, 13–28, 30
Lee, Lee C., 46–47
Lenin, 23
Light work, in Germany, 128; in Switzerland, 151
Literacy rates, 81
Low-income countries, 81–89

MacLennan, Emma, ix, 90–111
Management, women in, 20, 55, 103, 114, 141
Manufacturing, women in, 4, 51, 125, 161
Mao Zedong, 33, 34
Marks, Edna Berger, 176
Marriage and Family Law, German Civil Code, 128
Marxism, 15–16, 29

Maternity leave, 8, 26, 27–28, 40, 44, 46, 52–53, 119, 120, 134, 159, 168. *See also* Parental leave
Maternity protection, xv, 9, 10, 71, 72, 97–98, 104, 134, 158–59
Media image of women, 121
Men, role of, 144, 174. *See also* Home care
Menstruation, 37, 65
Metalworkers Union: in Italy 168–69; in Switzerland, 152
Michel, Andrée, ix, xiii, 32, 112–23
Military service, 70, 73
Minimum wage, 98, 110
Ministry for Women's Rights (France), 118, 122
Mitchell, Olivia, 176
Moslems, xiii, 13, 72, 77

National Agency for Job Seekers (ANPE), 119
National Commission for Equal Opportunities (Italy), 165, 167–68
National Insurance Act, 71–72
National Insurance Fund, 99
National Union of Public Employees, 99
National Women's Federation Congress, 45
Nelson, Anne, 48, 65, 66
Netherlands, wage differential in, 6
New Law on Working Relations, 52–53
Nightwork, 9, 62, 164
925, 175
Nisonoff, Laurie, 45
Nissan case, 66–67
Noce, Teresa, 159
North-South shift of industry, 11, 166
Norway, 7, 10
Nursing mothers, 37, 159

O'Farrell, Brigid, 175
Oil crisis, 2
Organization for Economic Cooperation and Development (OECD), 2, 3, 6, 92

Papanek, Hanna, x, xiii, 30, 64–65, 81–88
Parental leave, xiv, xv, 8, 120, 135, 139, 144–45, 165, 178
Part-time work, xv, 18, 22–23, 27, 46, 51, 58, 65, 75, 79, 98–99, 109–10, 116, 135, 139, 140, 175, 178
Party Congress, 14, 27
Pay gap, between women's earnings and men's, xii, xiv, xv, 3, 5–8, 21, 35–36, 38–39, 52, 62, 76, 92, 94, 102, 115, 138, 150–51, 161, 171, 173, 178–79

People's Republic of China. *See* China, People's Republic of
Pollak, Sandra, 31
Power, women and, 87, 9l, 141, 167
Privatization, 106–7
Professions, women in the, 19–20, 48, 87, 94, 131, 170
Promotion, 58, 79, 80, 117, 130, 150, 170–71, 172
Pronatalism, 26, 80
Protection, of employment, in England, 91–100
Protective labor legislation, 9–1121–23, 179
Protectionism 9–11, 64–65, 70–71, 158–59, 164–66
Public sector, role of, 143, 172–73
Public Service Workers Union, 152
Purdah, 85

Quotas, based on sex, xviii, 21, 119, 132

Reagan, Ronald, 171
Re-entry into labor force, 5, 65, 131
Retirement, 31, 40, 58–59, 61, 66–67, 71–72, 75, 163; credit toward, for childrearing, 121
Rome, Treaty of, 5, 116
Roudy Law, 117, 118, 120
Roudy, Yvette, xiii, 117
Rowbotham, Sheila, 111
Royal College of Nursing, 109
Rural-urban differences, 38, 40–42, 74
Russia. *See* Soviet Union

Salaff, Janet, 47, 89
Santi, Paolo, 161
Schöpp-Schilling, Hanna Beate, x, xiii–xiv, 123, 124–37
Scott, Hilda, 28–29, 32
Segregation, occupational, by sex. *See* Job segregation
Self-management system, 53–55
Service Employees International, 175
Sex Discrimination Act (UK), 96–97
Sex discrimination cases, 66–67, 131, 164–65, 170–72
Sexual harassment, 137, 179
Shortened workday, 23, 80, 143, 144, 175, 176
Simona, Ilda, x, xiv, 147–52, 153, 176
Singapore, 89
Social Democratic party: in Germany, 125–26, 128, 131–32, 135; in Sweden, 139
Social feminist orientation, in USSR, 26
Soviet Union, xii, 13–32

Sri Lanka, 9
Statistics, on work force, unreliability of, 88; availability of, 176
Steinberg, Ronnie, 146, 175
Suffrage, women's, 147, 153
Sumitomo Cement Company, 60–61
Suzuki, Setsuko, 60
Sweden, xiv, 5, 6, 8, 10, 129, 135, 136, 138–46
Swedish Trade Union Confederation, 139
Swiss Federal Commission for Women's Issues, xiv, 152
Swiss Trade Union Congress, 149–50, 152
Switzerland, xi, xiv, 147–53, 176

Target workers, 77
Tax, as disincentive to women's work, 137; as incentive, 139; deductions to employers, 175
Technology, impact of new, 2, 4, 11
Textile industry, 2, 50, 89, 114
Thatcher, Margaret, 104
Till-Retz, Roberta, 109–110
Time-use in families, 8, 25, 39–40, 141, 156–57, 174
Trade Union Act (Japan), 59
Trades Union Congress, 95, 98
Training, 5, 58, 99–100, 107, 113, 117, 130, 133–34, 142–43, 149, 150, 178–79; centers, 118–19
Training Opportunities Scheme (TOPS), 100
Tristan, Flora, 112
Turkey, 136
Two-person career, 64

Unemployment, 3, 35, 43, 102, 103, 107, 108, 115, 124–25, 138, 163, 166, 174, 178–79
Unions, 7, 14, 41–42, 50, 56, 61, 64, 66–67, 71, 80, 94–95, 99, 108–9, 110–11, 118, 119, 121, 125, 130–31, 139–40, 146, 151, 152, 157, 158, 162–63, 166, 174, 175–76, 178
United Kingdom, 6, 7, 128. *See also* Great Britain
United Nations, 49–50, 65
United States of America, 6, 20, 89, 136, 168, 170–76, 178
Urban-rural differences. *See* Rural-urban differences

Venezuela, 12
Versailles, Treaty of, 116
Vocational Training Act, 149

Wages Councils, 104 5
Weitzel, Renate, 124
Well-baby clinics, 52
Wertheimer, Barbara, 177–78
Wife, role of, 86, 148
Wife battering, 145
Wolf, Margery, x, xii, 33–46, 47–48
Women's Equal Rights Act (Israel), 69
Women's Liberation Movement, *See*
  Feminism
Workers' Councils, 55

Working Women's Welfare Act (Japan),
  60
Works Councils, 125, 127, 132
World War I, 116
World War II, xiv, xvii, 16, 49, 63, 121,
  147, 153, 155, 157, 158, 159, 161, 174

Youth Training Scheme, 107
Yugoslavia, xii, 49–56, 81

Zionist settlement, 69–70